SEAN O'CASEY

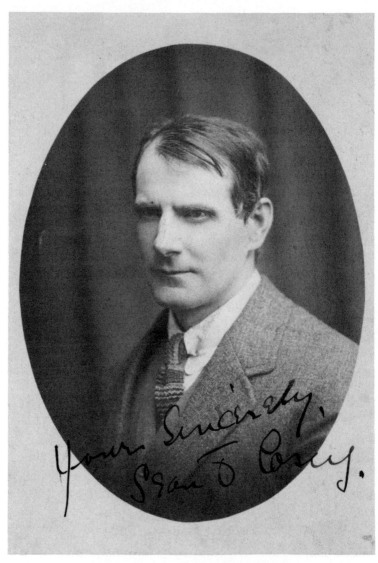

Sean O'Casey, dramatist, aged 44.

SEAN O'CASEY _{1880 - 1964}

The Man I Knew

by

GABRIEL FALLON

LITTLE, BROWN AND COMPANY · BOSTON · TORONTO

To Colin and to Rose without whose gentle
encouragement and ever present help this book
could not have been completed

Contents

Illustrations

Preface

SEAN O'CASEY, last of thirteen children, eight of whom had already died in infancy, was born to Michael and Susan Casey on the 30th March, 1880, at 85 Upper Dorset Street, Dublin, just a short walk from the house in Lower Dorset Street in which the dramatist Richard Brinsley Sheridan was born. The site of O'Casey's birthplace is now occupied by a branch of the Hibernian Bank.

Michael Casey, who came from Limerick, was the product of a mixed marriage. When his Roman Catholic father died at an early age Michael's Protestant mother reared the boy in her own faith. On coming to Dublin Michael Casey met and fell in love with Susan Archer, a Protestant girl from County Wicklow. He married Susan in 1863. At that time Michael was working as a commercial clerk. He continued in this employment until his strong Protestant convictions led him to seek employment with the Irish Church Missions, an organisation at that time pledged to the conversion of Irish Roman Catholics. Michael Casey died suddenly as the result of a spinal injury at the age of forty-nine when his youngest son was six years old.

Poverty and tenement life became the lot of Susan Casey and her five surviving children. To make matters worse her little Johnny contracted a chronic and painful eye-disease which called for medical treatment involving drops and bandages as well as a total avoidance of strong light. Schooling as we know it was out of the question but his beloved mother taught him his letters; and the praeternatural inquisitiveness of the half-blind boy led to his mastery of the art of reading at an early age.

In his autobiographical volumes he has given us dramatically heightened descriptions of his life in the tenements and of his early employments, various, arduous and ill-paid. Despite many vicissitudes the year 1905 found him teaching the Irish language which he had taught himself to read and write with considerable competence. Readers of *Feathers from the Green Crow*, a collection of his writings from 1905 to 1925, can sense the depth of his enthusiasm for things Irish as well as the fanatical fervour of his militant nationalism. In or around 1911 or 1912 he met his first hero, James Larkin, the labour leader, and served as one of the lieutenants grouped around that man through the terrible lock-out of 1913. Becoming secretary of the Citizen Army, a well-trained militant body which, though pledged to the cause of labour, fought gallantly in the rebellion of 1916, Sean published, as his first major piece of writing, a short history of that organisation.

The urge to write was always with him. In 1919 he sent his first play *The Frost in the Flower* to the Abbey Theatre. It was rejected, but not without encouragement. He sent others; but these, too, were returned to him. Finally a play called *The Shadow of a Gunman* was accepted and presented for three nights only on the 12th April 1923, its author then being forty-three years of age. It was an immediate success. By this time he had endured much hardship, illness, unemployment, hunger, constant eye trouble, as well as the death of his mother to whom he was passionately attached. *The Gunman* was frequently presented at the Abbey Theatre in response to popular demand and it was obvious that Sean O'Casey's course was set fair to be a notable Irish dramatist; provided, of course, that he could deliver the goods. It was at this point in his story that I made my entrance, to be acknowledged in the space of a few short months as his 'first friend in literature and the drama'.

I have often been asked how it was that such a close friendship as that which so quickly bound us together could happen to such seemingly disparate persons, the forty-three year old ex-labourer and the twenty-five year old actor-cum-civil servant. I have often been asked, too, how such a friendship could fall apart as ours did. The only answer I can think of which will meet the truth and both questions is that given by Montaigne in his essay *De L'Amitié* concerning a friendship which had a happier outcome than ours.

> Parce que c'etait moi; parce que c'etait lui.

Yes, indeed, it was 'because it was I, because it was he' that we came together and, after good times and bad, parted.

Anatole France, clinging to his text that the good critic is he who relates the adventures of his soul amongst masterpieces, once opened a lecture by saying something like this: 'Gentlemen, I intend to speak of myself *à propos* Shakespeare, Corneille, Racine, etc., etc.' If this book has a purpose that purpose might be expressed as follows: Gentle Reader, I propose to speak of myself *à propos* Sean O'Casey, his many works and (I regret to say) his sometimes pomps. I would much prefer to speak of myself *à propos* an old friend, the kindly hospitable man I walked the streets of Dublin with long, long ago, but my commitment compels me honestly to record impressions of that near-stranger who emerges by and large and in the long run from an Irish exile's prolonged engagement to English literature. Will all concerned then please note that this book is nothing more than it professes to be, and kindly read on from here.

G.F.

My sincere thanks are due to Dr. A. C. Edwards of the University of Kansas for his permission to use material some of which has already appeared in that University's quarterly 'Modern Drama' of which he is the distinguished Editor.

SEAN O'CASEY

One

WARM it was that evening, warm with the lingering sun of a lingering summer as I stood outside Cahill's the Chemists at that point where the meandering North Circular Road is bisected by the wide straight line of Dorset Street.

Dorset Street . . . why the man I was on my way to see was born here, on the second last day of March 1880, in No. 85, not two hundred yards from the birthplace of Richard Brinsley Sheridan. Sheridan's house bears a plaque commemorating the nativity of a great Irish dramatist, but this other man's birthplace has long since been demolished. In its stead there stands a bank.

I took his letter from my pocket. 'It's a straight walk up Portland Row and N.C. Road', it read; 'cross over Dorset Street and continue up the N.C.R. passing Cahill's Chemist shop on the left-hand side as you cross.' So far so good. 'The house (422, on the corner of a lane) has a small sycamore growing in the front garden, and is about fifty steps from Cahill's the Chemists.'

Well, fifty steps, and here was a house at the corner of a lane. But was that a sycamore? There it stood in this front garden, thin, shrivelled, soot-laden, sparrow-haunted, a true child of the tenements; its sickly branches, in which no nightingale would ever sing, catching the last rays of the setting sun with all the frisson of a Chopin nocturne.

I looked at the letter again. 'Dear Gaby' it said, 'Come up tomorrow, Wednesday, say, about 7.30 up to 8 o'c.' Well, it was now 7.45 p.m. on Wednesday, 3rd September 1924. I looked up at the house, a three-story tenement with basement and attic. A *respectable* tenement, its hall door closed; landlord's orders, he said. Broken stone flags leading to two steps leading over more broken stone flags to two steps leading to the heavy hall door.

On the left, the front drawing-room, its two tall windows over-looking the wizened grass plot of the railed-in front garden where stood the spindly sycamore.

So it was here in this front drawing-room that he received his first royalties on *The Shadow of a Gunman*; it was here he wrote his ill-fated *Kathleen Listens In*. It was to this room he returned after the Abbey Theatre's curtain had fallen in silence on that symbolistic farce in which he had lacerated every one of the far too many political parties in the infant Free State. It was here he sat down at his second-hand typewriter and swore an oath that the like would never happen again; and then, still shrinking with the shame of the few half-hearted handclaps, bent over the machine and fingered out the opening line of his next play:

On a little bye-road, out beyant Finglas, he was found.

What had he said? 'One knock for the first floor, two for the second, three for the third: and if you want the attic you'll have to shout.' One knock; and here he was—it was obvious he had been expecting me—in slippers, slacks, a brown pull-over, and an aura of hospitality. Carefully closing the hall-door he bowed me into the room.

Its most remarkable feature was its fireplace and the fire it held. I felt the heat of it as soon as I entered the room. There was a stretcher-bed to the left of the door, its head towards the near window; a washstand beside the bed-head. Rough book-shelves lined with second-hand books stood between the windows. There was a small table under the far window and on it the well-worn typewriter; beside it a plain chair. Each side of the fireplace there were shelved cupboards. On the right-hand wall going in, more book-shelves. In the centre of the room stood a round mahogany table; on it stood an oil lamp, books and papers. To the right of the fireplace there was an easy chair; and, facing the fireplace, a small settee.

'Did you have your tea, Gaby?' Again one is conscious of the quietly insistent, almost regal, note of hospitality. A throwback to the high halls and the groaning tables of royal Kincora. Yes, I have had my tea, thanks. He takes my light overcoat and folding it with care lays it across the end of his bed. He offers me a choice of the easy chair or the settee. I take the easy chair. Gradually, I become acclimatised to the fire. He asks me about rehearsals of *Nannie's Night Out* now in progress.

2

We talk and talk and talk and I am conscious of the enveloping personality of this man, the labourer who had just then laid down the shovel and the hod never to take them up again. Outside those windows he was merely another Abbey dramatist, but to me he was a dramatist with a difference. We talked on and on till the fire sank low and he promptly built it up again.

> Not till the fire is dying in the grate
> Look we for any kinship in the stars.

Years after he was to write on the frontispiece of his first significant published work *The Story of the Citizen Army*: 'To Gaby Fallon, first friend in Literature and the Drama, in remembrance of many important hours sitting couched in front of the Big Fire in 422 North Circular Road.'

What had attracted me towards this man? Why did I so firmly believe him to be a dramatist with a difference; indeed, a dramatist of genius, despite contemporary opinion? What hoops of steel helped to bind a twenty-six-year-old civil servant, and part-time Abbey Theatre actor, to an ex-labourer Abbey Theatre dramatist, eighteen years his senior?

On a mild spring day in 1923 the telephone in the Transport Section of the Statistical Office in Dublin Castle rang just before noon. The senior clerical officer, holding the receiver in his hand, looked in my direction.

'Eh, you . . .' he said, with undisguised contempt, 'the Abbey Theatre!' I went to his desk and took the receiver from him. 'Hello!' I could hear the persuasively apologetic tones of Arthur (Boss) Shields, the Abbey's stage manager. 'A new play . . . rehearsal at one-fifteen . . . can you make it?' I said 'Yes', left the receiver down and returned to my desk.

A new play; this was unusual, for we were just at the end of the season and there hadn't been the slightest hint of anything like this on the theatrical grape-vine. I wondered if Will was in it. Will was William Shields, a brother of Arthur Shields. Like myself he was a civil servant by day, two blocks away from me in another office of the youthful Department of Industry and Commerce. By night he was Barry Fitzgerald of the Abbey Theatre. Dare I phone him? No, I couldn't risk that.

A voice broke in on my cogitation. 'Hand me over that record of ton-miles!' I handed them over. A new play? Possibly another by the prolific George Shiels. Hardly likely though; weren't we

3

to finish the season with his *Paul Twyning*. Well, I'd know soon enough. Suddenly I was conscious of the senior clerical officer standing at my elbow. 'Look, Fallon' he said, 'how long will it take you to get these "operation statistics" finished?' 'Oh...' I said, in my most off-hand professional manner, 'I think I should have them for you about ... let me see ... three o'clock this afternoon.' 'Well, see to it that you have!' And he greeted my accommodating smile with the dirtiest of dirty looks. Actors, no less, posing as civil servants! You couldn't fool a senior clerical officer.

One o'clock came at last. I sprinted down the rickety stairs and into the Castle Yard. A tram from South Great George's Street rattled and swayed me to O'Connell Bridge. It was seven minutes after one as I raced past Mooney's clock on Eden Quay. Sixty seconds later I was pushing open the stage door of the Abbey Theatre.

To 'part-timers' like Barry Fitzgerald and myself the lunch-time rehearsal had become a familiar chore. The six professional players retained by the Abbey began rehearsal at 11 a.m. the stage-manager 'reading-in' the parts to be played by the 'part timers'. When we arrived at 1.15 p.m. we rehearsed for half-an-hour, and generally managed to snatch a sandwich and a cup of coffee before returning to our office desks at 2 p.m. Leaving our office at 4.30 (subsequently 5 p.m.) we rushed to the Theatre and rehearsed for an hour and a half. At 6.30 p.m. we managed to fit in the main meal of the day and an hour later most of us were to be seen in our dressing-rooms putting on 'make-up' for the night's performance.

The labour and the sacrifices involved in this strenuous routine were a measure of our intense love of the theatre in general and of the Abbey Theatre in particular. As a reward for our services—which in those days included a Saturday matinee as well as nightly performances—we were given the munificent sum of thirty—subsequently raised to fifty—shillings a week irrespective of the size of the part played. The professional 'whole-timers' were paid £4 a week, the theatre's manager, who was also an actor, receiving £6 7s. It was as much as the then unsubsidised Abbey Theatre could afford.

I pushed open the stage door which was always left ajar at this time of day and descended the six steps which immediately led through a second door to the open stage. At the far centre F. J. McCormick (in private life Peter Judge) one of the Abbey's

4

greatest professionals was sitting on an unfurnished iron bedstead reading from a script. On this side of the stage sat Arthur Shields, script in hand, at a small table upon which was a well-used typewriter. Lennox Robinson, also armed with script, sat in the front row of the stalls.

As I reached stage level my ear caught some of the richest Dublin dialogue I had ever heard, at least on the stage of the Abbey Theatre. It was spoken by F. J. McCormick with that proud consciousness of origin that marks the true-born Dubliner, every nuance charged with an intensity of meaning. Lennox, who was producing this play, called for a five-minute break, and I approached McCormick. 'It's terrific' he said, 'isn't it?' 'It is' I replied, 'but what is it?' 'It's a new play by a chap called O'Casey, a Dublin labourer.' Shields interrupted at this point by telling me to go to the Green Room and collect a script.

On the Call Board outside the Green Room hung a cast list for a play entitled *The Shadow of a Gunman* by S. Casey. Surely this wasn't the Casey, also a Dubliner, who had written two plays for the Abbey, *The Suburban Groove* and *The Man who Missed the Tide,* and who subsequently became editor of London's *The Times.* No it couldn't be, since this chap is a labourer. I collected my script. The part was Mr. Gallogher, one of the residents of a tenement adjoining a tenement at Kiljoy Square in a room of which the play was set. I rushed through a rehearsal for positions and movements, and returned to the office.

That night I had a chat with my friend Johnny Perrin, the Theatre's genial Secretary. Yes, it was true that this Casey chap was a labourer 'wears a cap, trench-coat, and hob-nailed boots, no less'. The play had been submitted in manuscript and Lady Gregory had had it typed. It had been called *On the Run* but the Directors did not consider this to be a good title so they changed it to *The Shadow of a Gunman,* the last four words of the first act. I asked Perrin how it was that we were putting on this play for three nights only instead of the customary week. He said that Lady Gregory had told him that they were only putting it on in order 'to let the poor fellow see how bad it was'.

Now there can be no doubt about the fact that the directors believed that the script had merit and that its author had promise. Otherwise they wouldn't have bothered about it in the first place. And they can be forgiven, I think, for being rather nonplussed about a script depicting a way of life which was completely foreign to them. With Dubliners like F. J. McCormick, Arthur

5

Shields and myself it was a different story. We knew that this script had life because we were familiar with the life it had. F. J. McCormick and I used to vie with each other in depicting Dublin 'character' as we saw and heard it in various parts of the city. We felt that this play would be an uproarious success at least with Dublin audiences. And we were perfectly right.

On Thursday, 12th April 1923, *The Shadow of a Gunman* was presented at the Abbey Theatre before the customary small (about forty per cent) audience. There was nothing in the critics' remarks about the play to suggest that a genius had arrived or, indeed, that a presentation out of the ordinary was on foot at the Abbey. Nevertheless, the news had gone round. On Friday night the theatre was filled to three-fourths of its capacity. The Saturday matinee was noticeably larger than usual and that night the story was 'standing room only'.

In those days the Abbey Theatre season opened in August, with an eye to Horse Show Week and visitors, and closed in or around April. When we opened in August 1923, it was, naturally, with *The Shadow of a Gunman*; and this time for a week instead of three days. There were many presentations of it after that; indeed, so many, that it ranks with *Juno and the Paycock* and *The Plough and the Stars* as one of the most 'revived' plays in the repertoire of the Abbey Theatre. In actual fact the first place is held by *Juno and the Paycock* (1924) with 340 performances. Then comes *The Plough and the Stars* (1926) with 321 performances. Lady Gregory's *The Rising of the Moon* (1907) follows with 316 performances. Lennox Robinson's *The Whiteheaded Boy* (1916) holds fourth place with 284 performances; and then comes *The Shadow of a Gunman* (1923) with a total of 264 performances.

One evening during the summer season of 1923 I finished my preparations for appearing as Mr. Gallogher and on hearing the cry 'Overture, Beginners'—which in the tones used by our stage manager, Arthur Shields, always suggested to me the voice of a muezzin crying from his tower—I left my dressing-room and made for the stage. To do this I had to pass along a corridor which divided those flimsy match-wood constructions called dressing-rooms and walk down fourteen wooden steps flanked on the right by the Green Room and on the left by the Scene Dock. It was this portion of the theatre which proved to be so inflammable in the disastrous fire of 1951.

There was plenty of time. I might have sat for ten minutes in the Green Room and then made the stage and my entrance without undue haste. However, I wasn't built that way. I have known players who could suddenly break off an argument or lay down a hand of bridge or poker to rush down the further five steps which led from the Green Room to the Scene Dock and thence across the Scene Dock's concrete floor through its high doors to the wooden stage. My temperament was such—though I often wished it otherwise—that I had to soak myself in the atmosphere of the play before appearing in it.

This evening, just before I turned through the high doors with Old Gallogher's heavy half-laced boots clip-clopping on the concrete, I could hear the Abbey's tiny orchestra with Dr. John Larchet's unmistakable piano touch flowing through Mendelssohn's overture *Son and Stranger*. Above the music I heard F. J. McCormick's voice saying: 'Certainly. And why not? You'll be alright there, Sean?' As I clumped on to the side of the stage I saw a figure standing in the wings. The door of the box-set was open and F. J. was in the act of settling himself comfortably into his tenement bed. I closed the door of the box-set and as I did so the man standing in the wings said: 'Are you sure I won't be in the way here?' I said to him, rather curtly, I'm afraid, 'Not at all!'

'Sean' F.J. had called him. So this must be the author of *The Gunman*—Sean O'Casey. I hadn't seen him on the opening night. No doubt he had taken the customary 'curtain call' but by that time—for Gallogher appears only in Act 1—I was probably half-way out of my stage clothes or half-way into my street ones. I had heard that F.J. and the new playwright were great friends and that they were seeing much of each other. Yes, this must be O'Casey. Well, at first sight, I didn't care much for the fellow. I thought his tones in asking if he would be in the way much too obsequious. Dammit, hadn't he written the play; hadn't he every right to be there? Just before the orchestra finished with Mendelssohn I put this point to him. He replied rather softly but very persuasively: 'The stage is really the actor's place. Only *he* has the right to be here.' Then the first gong went. Thirty seconds from now the curtain would rise. May Craig in the role of Mrs. Grigson arrived preparing to shrill her: 'Are yeh awake Mister Shields—Mr. Shields are yeh awake?' The play barriered further conversation between us.

There has been much miswriting about the sartorial habits of

7

Sean O'Casey. A book, published in America, and purporting to be a history of the Abbey Theatre, tells its readers that O'Casey 'being a typical peasant' always kept his cap on, that no Irish countryman would even consider taking off his cap in a house! The same book also assures its readers that William Butler Yeats attended the first night of *The Gunman* 'as usual in full evening dress'. This piece of misinformation—which the late James Agate would have described as *poppycock*—gives its writer a wonderful opportunity of bringing forth a poet and peasant contrast for he goes on to say that though Yeats spoke to O'Casey he maintained his aristocratic role, and since O'Casey was not a poet, Yeats greeted him with bored enthusiasm. A fine piece of imaginative hindsight but far from the truth.

A somewhat more scholarly work also published in America taking its cue from this earlier volume repeats the ridiculous statement that Yeats always attended the theatre 'regally attired in formal evening clothes'. Indeed, the writer in this instance goes one better and says that Yeats did so 'in the company of the social elite'. Again we are given the contrast between the 'patrician poet' and the dramatist in his 'democratic cap, which he seldom removed, and his familiar turtle-neck sweater' the whole being described as 'a plebian uniform that he has proudly continued to wear through the years'.

When the curtain fell on the first act of *The Gunman* I remained at the side of the stage to continue my conversation with its author. A fine figure of a man he appeared to be; it was obvious that his body was inured to hard physical work. He wore a cap and a trench-coat beneath which I caught a glimpse of a pair of rough serge trousers and heavy boots of a type that in Dublin—and elsewhere, for all I know—used to be called 'Bluchers'. It was possible to see at the revers opening of the trench-coat that he was wearing a woollen pull-over and a shirt with a collar and tie.

The trench-coat, buff in colour, a three-quarter length belted garment made of rough waterproofed cloth, first became fashionable in the Flanders mud of 1914–18. It took on an added and unsuspected significance when it became what might be described as the battle-dress of the I.R.A. in both our island wars. It is true, of course, that many a peace-loving citizen—myself included—affected a trench-coat, only to find oneself the object of suspicion from more than the forces of the British Crown. Whatever today's audiences may be like the significance

8

of Captain Boyle's line in *Juno and the Paycock* was never lost on those who first saw the play. After his reference to the 'terrible tatheraraa' at the front door and Joxer's refusal to stick his head out of the window 'an' mebbe get a bullet in the kisser' Boyle looks out cautiously and says: 'It's a fella in a Thrench coat'; early audiences always felt the intended *frisson*.

Well here was the author in a trench-coat and above it a cap. As I was to discover later the cap was worn because its peak, slightly drawn down, provided a shade which prevented light from penetrating to eyes already inflamed with a long-standing disease of the cornea. But Sean O'Casey did not *always* wear a cap. As a resident in St. John's Wood, London, he wore a wide-brimmed Stetson which may be plainly seen in a very fine photograph taken of himself and Augustus John at that time. As for his alleged 'peasant' habit of wearing his cap in the house, he never did so in my presence in 422 North Circular Road, Dublin, nor again in his bungalow at Chalfont St. Giles.

So much for the famous cap. Now for the collar and tie. When Joxer Daly in the first act of *Juno* is finally compelled to come in through the window from the roof of the return room (on to which the impending wrath of Mrs. Boyle as well as the con-nivance of the Captain had driven him) he says to Boyle with unconcealed sarcasm that Joxer out on the roof with the win' blown' through him was nothin' to you 'an' your friend with the collar an' tie!' But that fact didn't prevent the author of the play from wearing both these articles of male adornment. Indeed, the tie in particular caused a certain amount of sensation in fashion-able quarters on his arrival in London in 1926. It was a knitted tie barred in two colours, yellow and black. (That these colours were also the colours of a famous soccer team in the parish—St. Laurence O'Toole R.C.; St. Barnabas C. of I.—in which the dramatist lived for so long is, as Hollywood would say, merely coincidental. 'Strandville' was the name of the soccer team; they were popularly known as 'The Wasps'.) When the two great O'Casey plays took London by storm and photographs of the dramatist began to appear all over the place someone got the bright idea of starting a fashion in 'Sean O'Casey ties'. Had our own industrial house been in full Sean Lemass order at the time we might have been able to meet the demand. As it was we could only chuckle quietly at the turn things had taken and wish the author and the wearers well.

'Turtle-neck sweaters' only came into O'Casey's life as a

dramatist after his arrival in London. I have no doubt that he wears them primarily—as I wear mine—for ease and comfort. That he should refuse to change them for formal occasions arises as much from an inherent cussedness even more than from any desire to shock the bourgeoisie. On one occasion he discussed the wearing of formal evening dress with me and he visibly wilted at the idea of anyone encasing himself in a shirt 'like a bloody steel breastplate that you can hear creakin' at every step'. That one might do it as a sacrifice to the occasion, or not to incommode one's neighbour, did not weigh with him one whit. He had attended a number of formal occasions in London without making any concession to custom, and as he said to me 'the result was that I was the most distinguished looking man in the place'. Well, as an old Irishwoman once said to me: 'Every cripple has his own way of walkin'.'

But there may be another reason for a man's addiction to turtle-neck sweaters. After all, Yeats in his early days was known by his cape and his black flowing bow. And literary Dublin of the 'twenties sincerely believed that the writer and the artist should be distinguished by an originality if not by a sweet disorder in dress. Most writers in that flowering time affected broad-brimmed Stetsons. Actors, not to be outdone, wore coloured shirts and bows—I myself had a tidy collection of them. These marked us off from the common herd and indicated that we walked with art if not with God. Lennox Robinson's magenta shirts, Brinsley MacNamara's broad-brimmed black hats, Austin Clarke's blackthorns, Sean O'Casey's London-donned sweaters, what are they but pennants signifying the artist's isolation? What a pity that no one even in those brave old days thought of emulating poor Gerard de Nerval and trailing round a lobster at the end of a string. On second thoughts, this might have translated him from the status of the artist to that of 'the character'. Of these, at that time, even Dublin had more than her share.

Outside the theatre it was raining heavily. 'Doc' Larchet's orchestra was nearing the middle of his version of Schubert's *Unfinished Symphony*. In a corner of the Scene Dock O'Casey and I continued our conversation. Here I had a better opportunity of studying the sharp profile, the red-rimmed peering eyes and the quietly persuasive tones of the voice with its marked notation of the Dublin accent. It was a desperate night, and had I far to go when I left the theatre? To the North Strand, Leinster Avenue, did he know it? Every stone of it, for hadn't the O'Toole's Pipers' Band a club-room there and wasn't he at one time a member. The first gong went for the second act. Look, I said, why not wait in the Green Room until I change, or do you want to see the second act from the wings? No, he could see that another time; he would wait for me in the Green Room.

That was the first of many waitings in the Green Room. If he wasn't waiting for me there he would be waiting for me at the coffee bar alcove in the vestibule which led to the stalls. We had much to talk about—there was life and literature but, above all, there was the theatre. Sometimes, when I met him after an early finish in a first-act part, we would walk round to O'Connell Street for coffee in the Broadway Soda Fountain Parlour, an Abbey Theatre equivalent of London's Cafe Royal, frequented by players and playwrights who did not wish to spend all their spare time in pubs. You might meet Lennox Robinson there having a meal between rehearsals, or my friend John Lyle Donaghy, the young Trinity poet with the beautiful speaking voice; or Arthur Shields or Barry Fitzgerald, who helped me on a memorable occasion to entertain Lady Gregory to tea at one of its narrow tables. Indeed, it was here in the thirties I was introduced by Percy Hutchinson whose play *To What Red Hell* was running in London's West End, to a young man who assured me that he had a full-blooded Chinese grandmother. Fact or fiction, he looked as if he had. His name was Orson Welles.

I think I am right in saying that at this particular stage in our acquaintance Sean may have been more interested in me than I in him. He struck me as being something of a 'bird alone'. Of course, there was much of this quality in my own make-up. Actors and actresses, though basically generous creatures, can be notoriously selfish in some ways. I was bursting with ideas about the theatre at this time. I had theories about acting, about production, about *décor*, about lighting, and I had them to spare. Sean was a good listener. It must have been with these occasions in mind that he was prompted in *Inishfallen, Fare Thee Well* to make a passing reference to that 'Gaby Fallon, who had a very fine understanding of acting, stage and production'. I was interested, too, in literature, but I was not less interested in life, particularly that rich pulsating throb of it that pushed its way through the varicose quarters of Dublin. These things we had in common.

I knew nothing about this man's background at that time, and

I cared less. I had heard it said that he had been 'in the movement' and had left it, that he had always been a cantankerous individual, and, indeed, there were those who pointedly said that he was disreputable company even for an Abbey actor. I didn't give a damn; I was taking this man as I found him and I found him to be a good listener. To me he was anything but cantankerous. We never thought, at this stage, of discussing 'the movement'. I talked and he listened and that was all that mattered.

Two

☙

'SATIRE' wrote Swift, 'is a sort of glass wherein beholders do generally discover everybody's face but their own.' In the second week of September 1923, I noticed the cast of a new play on the Call Board. Was I in it? I was. That all-important point settled I saw that it was entitled *Kathleen Listens In* and that its 'author was Sean O'Casey.

Ah, yes, I remember him speaking about this effort, but to tell the truth, I had paid scant attention to him. At this stage it was the man I was interested in rather than the dramatist. It was true that he had written *The Gunman*, a striking out-of-the-rut contribution to the Abbey's repertoire but hardly an earth-shaking play.

The cast list on the Call Board revealed little or nothing about the nature of the new venture. I recalled that he had said something to me about its being a 'political phantasy'; I think the conversation had its origin in the spelling of the second word. Well, the title *Kathleen Listens In* more or less explained itself since in the cast list 'Kathleen' was described as the daughter of one Michael O'Houlihan. Kathleen was Ireland, then—Kathleen the daughter of Houlihan, in short, Kathleen Ni Houlihan. As for 'Listens In' 1923 fell within the exciting period of crystal sets, cats' whiskers, and headphones. It was the era of 2LO.

Apart from the O'Houlihan family the cast consisted of such pointed types as The Free Stater, The Republican, The Business Man, The Farmer, A Labourer, The Man with the Big Drum, etc. I was down to play The Man in the Kilts. Opening rehearsals revealed little of the script's content. Lennox Robinson, who directed, contented himself with giving us positions and movements. Gradually it dawned upon some of us that we were taking part in a piece of blistering satire directed at everything and almost everyone in the infant State. My own part was intended to lampoon the Gaelic League and its enthusiasm for the revival of the Irish language.

Not all the players saw it this way. Most of them were enjoying the novelty of the script which was liberally interspersed with snatches of satirical song. In a sense this was Brecht before Brecht of whose existence neither the author nor the Abbey Theatre had then the slightest idea. The author attended rehearsals at Robinson's request and sang the songs for us as he would like them to be sung; but try as we might we couldn't hope to reproduce the sting with which the author himself invested his lines. Few of the cast ventured an opinion as to how the audience would receive this work. A couple of them considered that, to use a Dublin expression, 'it was a great bit o' gas' and felt it likely that the audience would take it that way. But some of us thought otherwise.

Kathleen Listens In was presented at the Abbey Theatre on the evening of 1st October 1923. Since it was in one act, lasting approximately twenty-five minutes, Shaw's *The Man of Destiny* and Lady Gregory's *The Rising of the Moon* were presented with it. There was a large audience; the popularity of *The Gunman* had seen to that. Throughout the performance of *Kathleen* there was much sectional laughter. Hardly more than ten per cent of the audience laughed together. The effect on the stage was slightly unnerving. In a flash it became clear what was happening. You laughed when my party fell under O'Casey's lash; I laughed when your party caught it. Both of us tried to laugh when the other fellow's party was made to squirm. And then slowly but surely all the laughing died away. When the curtain came down there were a few dispirited hand-claps obviously intended for the players. During the week things were a little better; the laughter was more general: but it was obvious that *Kathleen Listens In* was not likely to appear amongst the Abbey Theatre's revivals. It never did.

Yet the critics were not, on the whole, ill-disposed towards the play. The critic of *The Evening Telegraph* held that 'all expectations as to the wittiness of the play and its aptness and interest were more than fulfilled; but it was a play to slightly puzzle a first-night audience . . . The play is hilarious throughout in its irony . . . *Kathleen Listens In* was most appreciatively received.' This latter statement was far from being true. The author himself in *Inishfallen, Fare Thee Well* tells us that the audience received the play in dead silence, that they all got up from their seats and silently left the theatre. Later in the week the critic of *The Evening Telegraph* saw the play a second time. He voted it a success '—though the first night it seemed to show the fault of being above the heads of its audience. As soon as the latter had realised its type, however, and as the week went on, they expressed their approval warmly . . . '

The critic of *The Evening Herald* declared that the work was not a play at all, but a quip, a whimsicality, 'a safety valve for some funny opinions he (Mr. O'Casey) holds on present day Ireland'. This critic held that the new work would neither add to nor detract from the reputation the author had gained with *The Gunman*. He thought that the dramatist while having a good sense of 'the essentials of stage atmosphere' had very little dramatic technique and that his work was inclined to be of 'the jester, ephemeral type rather than that of real comedy or tragedy'. Charitably enough the critic suggested that this might be due to the fact that 'Mr. O'Casey has not yet found himself and just cannot quite decide upon which is the better way of saying that which he has got to say.'

In George Russell's weekly *The Irish Statesman* the play was reviewed by Susan L. Mitchell (S.L.M.) herself a satirist of no mean order. She it was who had described the George Moore trilogy *Hail and Farewell* as those books in which George Moore elected to invent the story of his life, a description which some not very original cynics are now beginning to apply to Mr. O'Casey's autobiographical volumes. Miss Mitchell wrote: 'The new play at the Abbey Theatre, *Kathleen Listens In*, calls itself a Phantasy, and is not, we imagine, taking itself very seriously as a play; but it invites serious consideration as an allegory, or perhaps we might say a rough and tumble morality play.' 'Casey is not Shaw', she concluded, 'but he has a lively mind and no bitterness, and though a guffaw so near tragedy as we are just now may offend the taste of some, others will find it salutary.' The tragedy to which Miss Mitchell refers was the tragedy of the aftermath of civil war and naturally there were some people who considered that a guffaw was not in order, even though Mr. Robert Hogan in the December 1961 issue of the University of Kansas journal, *Modern Drama*, finds it 'hard to see how a perceptive Irishman in the 1920's would not have been fairly tickled and delighted by its (the play's) liveliness, its songs, and its wit.' The indisputable gaiety of this scholarly remark, made

15

from within the security of a transatlantic campus and a time-lag of over a quarter of a century, can only be equated with the fabled question: 'But apart from the death of your husband, Mrs. Lincoln, what did you think of the play?'

Mr. Hogan's meticulously documented article is entitled *O'Casey's Dramatic Apprenticeship* and therefore the reader is surprised to find no mention whatever of *The Cooing of Doves* despite the arduous researches of a sabbatical year, several reported conversations with the playwright, and the fact that there is an important reference to the play in Mr. O'Casey's *Inishfallen, Fare Thee Well*, which work Mr. Hogan gives evidence of having consulted. This play was submitted to the Abbey Theatre along with *Kathleen Listens In*. It was not accepted much to the disappointment of its author who considered it to be 'definitely better as a play than the first'. It was 'full of wild discussions and rows in a public house' and was later used 'to form the second act of a later play'. Mr. O'Casey did not mention this play till much later in our acquaintance and then he did not make it clear that he had submitted it along with *Kathleen*. It came into our conversation following an injunction to me never to destroy anything I had written because one never knew 'how handy it may come in later on'. Then followed the reference to *The Cooing of Doves* which the Abbey had rejected. Since he didn't say when, I was inclined to accept it as being among the pre-*Gunman* rejections.

When the curtain fell on the first night of *Kathleen Listens In* and I had removed my fairly elaborate 'make-up' (in a full beard and wearing kilts and a beret I looked rather like Hall Caine turned Scotsman) I went down to the Green Room expecting to find the author. But there was no Sean O'Casey. He told me afterwards that he left the theatre, his cheeks burning with the shame of the play's reception, in no mood to meet anyone. He drives this home in a passage in *Inishfallen, Fare Thee Well* in which he reflects that he was the one and only playwright to have had a play received in silence by an Abbey audience; 'the only one to be deprived of even a single timid hand-clasp'. Like all artists he was super-sensitive, and this super-sensitivity caused him to magnify this blow to his pride. But his pride would survive bigger blows than this. Cap well down and hands in pockets he walked home that night to 422. Once inside he swore an oath that he would write a play which would be such that the

Abbey would not be big enough to hold the audiences that would want to see it. He kept that oath.

He had been telling me for some time about a play he had mapped out, a play which would deal with the tragedy of a crippled I.R.A. man, one Johnny Boyle. He mentioned this play many times and always it was the tragedy of Johnny. I cannot recall that he once spoke about Juno or Joxer or the Captain; always Johnny. I do not know how much of this play he had completed by the time that the first night of *Kathleen* sent him, dismal but determined, home to his room in '422'. But I remember him telling me about the oath which he took as he removed his cap. And I understood him to say that the first line of the new play which had hitherto evaded him came to him now without difficulty and that he had tapped it out on his typewriter:

> On a little bye-road, out beyant Finglas, he was found.

Surely this is the most intriguing, the most interest-catching opening line in the history of modern drama.

'They were sisters' wrote William Butler Yeats: 'one all simplicity, her mind shaped by folk song and folk story; the other sophisticated, lyrical and subtle.'

As a secondary schoolboy spending a hard-won sixpence in the back stalls of the Abbey Theatre I had seen them both—those incomparable actresses Sara Allgood and Maire O'Neill. Little did I think then that I would play on the same stage with Sara. In 1920 after a prolonged stay in Australia Sara Allgood returned to Dublin and the Abbey Theatre. Her good friend Lady Gregory gave her a warm sympathetic welcome, for tragedy had struck her favourite actress; her husband and only child had been carried off in the terrible epidemic of influenza which had followed the '14-'18 war. She had had many good offers to stay on in Australia but she was anxious to escape bitter memories and a season of work in the theatre she loved best seemed to provide a harbour of refuge at this stage of her career.

I had just joined the company, a step which is a story in itself, and one of my first assignments was to play with Sara in Synge's *Riders to the Sea*. The part of Mauyra in this play, the old mother who loses her sons to the sea, was one of her greatest roles. Sara had a remarkable voice, deep-toned, rich, and vibrant. It was a voice which possessed the rare quality of retaining its smoothness throughout the entire gamut of expression. Come to think of it,

17

I have never heard her *shriek*. Like her sister Maire O'Neill she had been trained by that master of fine speech, Frank J. Fay (one of the two brothers who helped in the foundation of the Abbey Theatre) to whose 'beautiful speaking' Yeats had dedicated his play *The King's Threshold*.

I had joined the Abbey Theatre, believe it or not, with the hope of becoming a writer of sorts, but the art of the actor intrigued me so much that I decided that a stick of Leichner's grease-paint was for the present at all events every bit as mighty as the pen or typewriter. However, I was still something of a child taking notes amongst my fellow-players and amongst other things I jotted down my impressions of that first appearance with Sara Allgood in Synge's one-act tragedy. Here they are for what they are worth:

> The women are keening softly. Cathleen and Nora kneel at the table; the men kneel by the door. A rich deep throbbing voice wells up from an abyss of sorrow. The drip, drip, drip, through the tense silence, of the water in which they had drenched the sail cloth. 'They're all gone now . . . ' Something that clutches the heart inside you and freezes the marrow of your bones as you kneel there in a white bawneen on a stage that is a stage no longer. The voice rises, billows, falls and rises again.
> '. . . and there is nothing more the sea can do to me . . .'
> You hear behind you the deep anger of Atlantic rollers menacing their way through the scene dock. You hear the voice of Nora whispering: 'She's quiet now and easy; but the day Michael was drowned you could hear her crying out from this to the spring well.' The tension holds, the spell is still unbroken. Then slowly lifting like a ninth great wave the voice rises to its final cadence and the stage is drowned beneath a deluge of falling waters. 'They're all together this time, and the end is come . . . May the Almighty God have mercy on Bartley's soul . . . and may He have mercy on my soul, Nora, and on the souls of everyone . . . left living in the world.' A long time after that you hear the voice of the stage-manager shouting 'Clear stage, please!' Somebody kicks you and tells you to get up.

Yes, Sara Allgood's acting was like that. When she returned to the Abbey she appeared in a number of her famous roles, comic as well as tragic. But tragedy was her *forte*: and although she played a very fine Aunt Ellen in Lennox Robinson's great comedy *The Whiteheaded Boy* she lacked the subtlety and the sparkle and the lightning wit of her sister, Maire O'Neill.

Sean O'Casey and I still met each other for chats over cups of coffee and for long talking walks, or if you like walking talks, through the streets of Dublin. He still spoke of the work he had in hand, the tragedy he was writing about a young man called Johnny Boyle. There was not a great deal to be gleaned from what he said and I didn't burden him with questions. Then on a morning in the middle of February 1924, Lennox Robinson pinned up the cast of a new O'Casey play on the Call Board, with Michael J. Dolan, the Abbey's manager, named as its producer. On account of the difficulty of getting the professionals and the 'part-timers' together it was decided to hold a reading of the play in the Green Room at 5 p.m. I discovered that my part in the play was that of a young man called Bentham. I thought this a strange piece of casting for hitherto I had specialised in old men's parts and had made quite a name for myself in the playing of them. Of course, the manager, Michael Dolan, had specialised in them too, and this, hinted Barry Fitzgerald, was the reason for the change-over. 'You will have to learn to be not so good in old men's parts' said Barry, 'at least not as good as our manager.' This was but one of the exigencies of the theatrical life I had to learn. Later on I was compelled to learn others.

We could make nothing of the reading of *Juno and the Paycock* as it was called. It seemed to be a strange baffling mixture of comedy and tragedy; and none of us could say, with any certainty, whether or not it would stand up on the stage. Sara Allgood had some difficulty in reading her script—several times she referred to 'Joxer Daly' as '*Boxer* Daly' and had to be corrected for it. Barry Fitzgerald mumbled his way through the part of Captain Boyle and gave not the slightest indication that it was likely to be funny. F. J. McCormick applied his well-known Dublin technique to the part of Joxer yet nothing much worthwhile seemed to be emerging from it. All were agreed that the title of the play was not a good one and that the dialogue written for the part of Jerry Devine, which was to be played by that manly forthright actor P. J. Carolan, was possibly the most stilted ever written in the history of the Abbey Theatre. There was a general feeling that the play lacked form, that it was much too 'bitty', that the mixture of tragedy and comedy 'would not go' and that the author of *The Gunman* might well have overshot his mark.

Discussing it that night with Barry Fitzgerald we both agreed that there were good things in it and that we should withhold our judgment until we had seen the play in action. I wondered if the fact that the play was being produced by Dolan and not by Robinson, who had produced both *The Gunman* and *Kathleen*, indicated the state of the latter's feeling about the play. It was difficult to say. But good things or not Barry agreed that at this stage it would be impossible to forecast a result with any degree of accuracy. The play might go; or it might not. Of course, if it didn't it would be too bad for Sean O'Casey. We both thought that the play lacked form; that is 'form' as we had noted it in the plays of Abbey dramatists. We thought the author had much to learn about 'construction'; again we were taking our ideas about 'construction' from the plays of Abbey dramatists. I reminded him that it was generally held that actors' opinions concerning plays were notoriously faulty ones. He replied that actors' opinions about anything in the world were notoriously faulty and remarking that we had to sign an attendance book in the office of the Minister for Industry and Commerce in the morning at 9.30 a.m. said: 'Thank the Lord, Gaby, that you and I have our feet upon solid ground!'

I didn't see much of Sean O'Casey during the rehearsals of *Juno and the Paycock*. The Abbey's work of weekly repertory went on and I was kept fairly busy. In the week preceding the dress rehearsal of *Juno* Lady Gregory came to town. If she attended rehearsals I didn't see her. My part of Bentham was almost wholly rehearsed at the 1 o'clock luncheon break; the old difficulty of getting the professionals and the 'part-timers' together saw to that. I have no doubt that the Old Lady, as we called her, spent some time in the company of her beloved actress, 'Sally' Allgood, but whatever views she may have expressed about the play I had no means of finding out. Not, indeed, that I was particularly interested. The play would go on and that was that.

The dress-rehearsal was planned for Sunday March 2nd at 11.30 a.m. That would give everyone ample time for Mass, or Church, or a long sleep. But there was a difficulty. For some time past an Abbey party had been planned to take place on the night of Saturday March 1st, after the final curtain. Now an Abbey party was a party that *was* a party; at least it was so in those far-off days and nothing was ever allowed to stand in the way of it, neither civil wars nor fights for freedom. Abbey parties had been held under armed guards of various political persuasions and as often as not the guards themselves added much to the revelry. Sometimes directors were present; sometimes not; but whatever the company one thing was certain and that, to use the popular phrase, was that a good time was had by all. But what was to be done on this occasion? Obviously, no one could be expected to dress-rehearse at such an unearthly hour as 11.30 a.m. after a party the night before. Indeed, it was as much as some of us could do to put in a sleepy attendance at the 6 a.m. Mass in the Pro-Cathedral down the street. Sean O'Casey or no Sean O'Casey this dress-rehearsal would have to be postponed, that was all about it. Someone approached the directors, and the directors agreed to postponement. The dress-rehearsal of *Juno and the Paycock* would be held at 5 p.m. on the Sunday.

I arrived at the theatre at 4.30 p.m. and found the author there before me looking rather glum and wondering if a rehearsal would take place since so far as he could find out there was no one else in the theatre. I assured him that everything would be all right even though I privately thought otherwise. Sara Allgood, who had spent the night feasting us with song and story, had left the theatre in or around 3 a.m. a very tired woman. I tried to persuade Sean that dress-rehearsals were always like this but he was only half convinced. Although I did not know it at the time he was suffering much pain with his eyes and was attending the Royal Eye and Ear Hospital where he was a patient of the Senior Surgeon, the sensitive and perceptive Mr. Joe Cummins, who took a particular interest in the dramatist and in the theatre.

Gradually the players filed in and quietly went to their dressing-rooms. Lennox Robinson arrived shortly before 5 o'clock and was followed by Yeats and Lady Gregory. Under the direction of Seaghan Barlow the stage staff were putting finishing touches to the setting. Yeats, Lady Gregory and Robinson took seats in the stalls. The author sat a few seats away from them. The curtain rose about 5.36 p.m. So far as I could see and hear while waiting for my cue in the wings the rehearsal seemed to be proceeding smoothly. As soon as I had finished my part of Bentham at the end of the second act I went down into the stalls and sat two seats behind the author. Here for the first time I had an opportunity of seeing something of the play from an objective point of view. I was stunned by the tragic quality of the third act which the magnificent playing of Sara Allgood made almost unbearable. But it was the blistering irony of the final scene which convinced me that this man sitting two seats in front of me was a dramatist of genius, one destined to be spoken of far beyond the confines of the Abbey Theatre.

The third act had been dominated by Allgood's tragic quality even though Barry Fitzgerald and F. J. McCormick were uproariously funny as Captain Boyle and Joxer. This was always so with Allgood in the part of Juno. She had the quality of pinning down preceding laughter to freezing point. When Juno returns from the doctor with Mary the author's simple directions are: 'Mrs. Boyle enters: it is apparent from the serious look on her face that something has happened. She takes off her hat and coat without a word and puts them by. She then sits down near the fire, and there is a few moments pause.' That is all. Yet Sara Allgood's entrance in this scene will never be forgotten by those who saw it. Not a word was spoken: she did not even sigh: her movements were few and simply confined to the author's directions. She seemed to have shrunken from the Juno we saw in Acts 1 and 2 as if reduced by the catalytic effect of her inner consciousness.

We watched the act move on, the furniture removers come and go, the ominous entry of the I.R.A. men, the dragging of Johnny to summary execution, the stilted scene between Jerry Devine and Mary Boyle, and then as with the ensnaring slow impetus of a ninth great wave Allgood's tragic genius rose to an unforgettable climax and drowned the stage in sorrow. Here surely was the very butt and sea-mark of tragedy! But suddenly the curtain rises again: are Fitzgerald and McCormick fooling, letting off steam after the strain of rehearsal? Nothing of the kind; for we in the stalls are suddenly made to freeze in our seats as a note beyond tragedy, a blistering flannel-mouthed irony sears its maudlin way across the stage and slowly drops an exhausted curtain on a world disintegrating in 'chassis'.

I sat there stunned. So, indeed, so far as I could see, did Robinson, Yeats and Lady Gregory. Then Yeats ventured an opinion. He said that the play, particularly in its final scene, reminded him of a Dostoievsky novel. Lady Gregory turned to him and said: 'You know, Willie, you never read a novel by Dostoievsky.' And she promised to amend this deficiency by sending him a copy of *The Idiot*. I turned to O'Casey and found I could only say to him: 'Magnificent, Sean, magnificent.' Then we all quietly went home.

The opening night, Monday March 3rd, was much the same as any other opening night. Everyone was keyed-up. The theatre was fairly full. The play went well with the accent stronger on tragedy than on comedy. This was always to be the effect with Sara Allgood's Juno in the cast. The author was called for and presented himself. The booking next morning was noticeably heavy. It continued to be so.

There was an interesting if unimportant side issue. My part of Bentham had attracted the attention of some theosophists in the audience. They held that what I had to say in the second act left one with a very erroneous impression of theosophy. I spoke to the author about this. He told me that when writing the play he had been at a loss for dialogue for Bentham in this act. One evening when sitting in the Green Room he had listened to Michael J. Dolan holding forth on theosophy. He there and then decided to make Bentham a theosophist and so he jotted down what he had heard Dolan say. Evidently Dolan's theosophy was not of the official kind for the secretary of the Irish Theosophical Society (of which, incidentally, Yeats was the then President) approached the Directors with a view to having this situation remedied. The result was that the crowds pouring into the theatre on the fourth evening of *Juno and the Paycock* saw a poster in the vestibule asking them 'What is Theosophy?' and inviting them to come to South Frederick Street to hear the answer. This surely must be unique in the history of theosophy and the theatre.

Someone said with reference to *Hamlet* that a great play makes question marks of us all. *Juno and the Paycock* raised a wilderness of questions in me. In the first place I was intrigued by this note beyond tragedy which its final scene sounded. In the second place the reactions of the critics made me deeply interested for the first time in the craft of playwriting. For the critics attacked the play's 'cinematic realism' and its 'farcical element'. Its mixture of tragedy and comedy was outrageous, they said. All maintained that the final scene was anti-climax and should be cut. Even the scholarly W. J. Lawrence, writing in *The Irish Statesman* of 15th March 1924, held this view. Yet Lawrence's review was the most favourable of them all and the only one which approached my feelings about the author and his work.
    'Sean O'Casey,' wrote Lawrence:

is at once an iconoclast and a neo-Elizabethan. Years ago, when the Abbey was in its crudely experimental stage, Senator Yeats, in one of those delightful little impromptus with which he used to favour us between the acts, expressed the opinion that the prevailing dramatic moulds had become outworn, and that we in Ireland would have to break them and fashion moulds nearer to the heart's desire. If he is as strong a believer now as he was then in the necessity to go back to first principles he, as chief Director of the Abbey, should be proud of the vogue of Mr. O'Casey's plays . . . He (Sean O'Casey) lures us into the theatre under the pretext of affording us hearty laughter, and he sends us away with tears in our eyes and with the impression of direst tragedy heavy on our hearts. None but a neo-Elizabethan could accomplish this, since the secret of juxtaposing and harmonising the comic with the tragic, and thereby throwing the elements of terror and pathos into greater relief, have been lost to the English-speaking stage for over a couple of centuries. Moreover, one half of the fascination of Mr. O'Casey's work lies in its red-hot throbbing contemporaneity, and that too was a prime trait of Elizabethan drama . . .

So far so good, and so much in accordance with the ideas about this dramatist which were slowly building up in my mind; but to my sorrow Lawrence concluded by declaring that the 'drunken episode' which followed Act 3 was 'artistically indefensible'.

This I was by no means prepared to concede and I told the author so over and over again. What shocked me about the author was that he was by no means as certain as I was about the validity of this scene. Indeed, he left me with the impression that he was by no means as knowledgeable about his play as I was for he seemed to be quietly surprised when I drew attention to what I considered to be this excellence or that. I was to learn in time, of course, that an artist is seldom conscious of the effect of what he has created. I recalled O'Casey's insistence that he was writing a play about a young man called Johnny Boyle. Yet Johnny was only one character amongst other and greater characters. We were seeing much more of each other than formerly and on each occasion *Juno* and the craft of the playwright provided the main talking-point. The critics, public and private, with the exception of Lawrence had used as a whip the mixture of tragedy with comedy. There was some talk of Aristotle and I took my first glance into the *Poetics*. While I was not prepared to agree with O'Casey that 'Aristotle was all balls', I conceded that the Greeks were great in their own time and fashion but that there were great playwrights since that time who had thrown Aristotle's *Poetics* (or rather the misconception derived from them by Italian and French theorists) to the winds. Shakespeare had mixed tragedy and comedy and what had been good enough for Shakespeare ought to be good enough for a 'neo-Elizabethan'.

During one of our conversations he told me that when he submitted *Juno and the Paycock* to the Abbey it had an additional scene which the directors cut. He gave me the impression that he was rather aggrieved at this. I asked him what the scene was and he told me it was the shooting of Johnny Boyle which took place in darkness in a roadside setting. I tried to assure him that the directors were perfectly right and that the shooting of Johnny Boyle was in the imagination of the audience infinitely more terrible in those lines where the Second Irregular asks him: 'Have you your beads?' and Johnny replies, 'Me beads! Why do you ass me that, why do you ass me that?' At this point the audience knows only too well what is going to happen, and hardly needs Johnny's agonised 'Mother o' God, pray for me— be with me now in the agonies o' death . . .' to convince them that judicial murder is afoot. After this an actual shooting scene would be truly anti-climax. After some argument on my part he seemed satisfied. Again it was borne in on me that the artist is not always the best judge of his work.

It was obvious that one of the effects of these conversations was to blunt the remarks of the critics. I still maintained that what made this play something greater than great was its final scene and I repeatedly told him so. The fact was that I couldn't get this play and its author out of my mind. The play itself had stirred up all kinds of problems for me. I suppose in a sense it heralded the birth of a drama critic. I was conscious of the play's faults, the poverty of Bentham as a character, the mawkish artificiality of the scenes between Jerry Devine and Mary Boyle. Yet these faults, and I could find no others, were far outweighed by the play's greatness. One of the critics said that O'Casey knew nothing about the art of construction. On this point what struck me about *Juno* was that its characters came and went without let or hindrance. 'Construction' as it was seen in the work of Abbey dramatists had hitherto consisted of situations in which A, B and C are on stage and the dramatist invents some plausible or (as in most cases) implausible reason to get rid of B in order that A and C may discuss something not intended for B's hearing. If this was 'construction' they could keep it so far as I was concerned, for I reasoned that when one could see a man's framework sticking out there was something wrong with the man. There is nothing particularly attractive about a skeleton and no one wants to see the bones of a play.

I believed I saw the reason why Sean O'Casey was not fully conscious of the value of what he had achieved. This work of his was not art for Art's sake, a phrase very much in fashion in the literary Dublin of those days. It was something much more akin to what Paul Claudel had in mind when he wrote to Jacques

25

Riviere in 1912: 'Do you believe for a moment that Shakespeare or Dostoievsky or Reubens or Titian or Wagner did their work for art's sake? No! They did it to free themselves of a great incubus of living matter, *opus non factum*. And certainly not to colour a cold artificial design by borrowings from reality.' *Juno and the Paycock*, I reflected, was an outstanding example of a play which simply had to be written, which, so to speak, erupted from its author, a fact which gave it that 'red-hot contemporaneity' which Lawrence praised. It pulsed with what Henry James had in mind when he demanded 'felt life' from the writer. No doubt Sean O'Casey sat down consciously to write a play about a tragic young man called Johnny Boyle, but underneath other forces were at work and the total result emerged in a blistering indictment of the stupidity of men and (as I thought then on that March evening in 1924 and think so still) in one of the great tragic masterpieces of our time.

This man Sean O'Casey was attracted towards me (I didn't know why) but from that dress-rehearsal of *Juno and the Paycock* I was forcibly attracted towards him. Like him I was a Dubliner who loved my native city. He had lived most of his years in grinding poverty and I had lived mine on the fringe of it. In *Juno and the Paycock* I had found an overwhelming sense of pity which I myself had sometimes felt but was unable to express. I had also, I believed, found a very great dramatist, one who was destined, I said to him, to write very many great plays. I looked back on my theatre-going experience but could recall nothing which equalled this. The highest peak point in the graph of Abbey Theatre dramaturgy was undoubtedly John Millington Synge's *The Playboy of the Western World. Juno and the Paycock*, I believed, was as high if not higher.

Three

WHEN the spring season of 1924 came to a close it was clear to me that few if any of my colleagues at the Abbey had grasped the fact that *Juno and the Paycock* was a great play. Most of the principal players—and, in particular, Sara Allgood— realised that the author had supplied them with very fine parts. But that was all. They were too involved in the play to see it objectively. From the dress-rehearsal onwards I had made it my business to listen to the play night after night from rise to fall of curtain.

When the season closed I lost contact with Sean O'Casey. Almost all our appointments had been made either for the Abbey's Green Room or its vestibule. We part-timers returned to our now untrammelled daily occupations. The Abbey's professionals had to make what shift they could with casual theatrical engagements. Hence it was that F. J. McCormick might be found touring with a *Paddy The Next Best Thing* company or that Eileen Crowe would visit the Irish 'smalls' in the title role of *Peg O' My Heart*. On this occasion, however, Barry Fitzgerald and I were hardly a week back in our office chairs when the theatre made contact with us and we were asked by Michael J. Dolan to attend a meeting of the company at 5.30 p.m. There we were informed that Sara Allgood proposed backing a venture to take *Juno and the Paycock* to Cork for a week's run. She had the permission of the Abbey directors to use the company for this purpose and the author had given her his play on the usual terms. Could Barry Fitzgerald and I take a week of our annual four-weeks' holiday for this purpose? We could.

Then Michael Dolan told us that we would need a few special rehearsals since we were doing a cut version of *Juno*. A cut version? Yes, a cut version, for we were going to the Palace Theatre at Cork where it was intended, since this was a 'two-houses' management, to present *Juno* twice nightly. But how did he propose to cut *Juno*? Oh, that was easy enough. In the first place the closing scene was completely unnecessary—anti-climax in fact; in the second one could fiddle around with the furniture-removal scene and save a few lines here and there. And there were many other places in the play which, indeed, would benefit from cutting. Then since the setting was the same throughout, a saving could be made by shortening the intervals. Was the author aware of this? I was assured he was.

After putting through the few necessary rehearsals we eventually travelled on a Sunday's slow train to Cork. We duly presented ourselves at the Palace on Monday morning and there in the presence of the manager and (as we were told) the directors of that theatre we dress-rehearsed our twice-nightly *Juno*. After the rehearsal Sara Allgood and Michael Dolan told us that manager and directors had expressed themselves as being very pleased with the performance. *Juno* was a great tragic play and indeed it was a pleasure to make contact with such very fine acting.

We opened that night to a fairly full house but one which was much more in the mood for comedy than for tragedy. This fact considerably upset Sara Allgood who once or twice as the result of unexpected laughter was diverted from her full tragic stride. When the first house was over it was obvious to those of us resting in our dressing-rooms that all was not well outside. Someone said that Miss Allgood had been sent for by the management. After five minutes she appeared back-stage and told Dolan to call a meeting of the players. When we had assembled she told us that the manager had informed her that a director who had not been present at that morning's rehearsal had taken grave moral exception to the play and that he was insisting that something would have to be done about it.

I suggested that since we were in a fairly strong legal position— we had presented the play that morning to the manager and the other directors who had expressed approval—we should return to Dublin and sue the management. This was not listened to, particularly by the professionals, and understandably so, since they were looking forward to a week's salary. Arthur Shields then asked if the offended director had clarified his objections? He had; he objected to the seduction of Mary Boyle. And had Miss

Allgood asked him how this integral part of the play might be altered? Yes; and the director said that we could say that Mary had 'gone into a decline' (the Anglo–Irish euphemism for pulmonary tuberculosis) and that it was for this reason that Bentham had deserted her. At this remove the affair is nothing if not laughable. But it was not so then. A vote was taken. A majority decided to stay and alter the play. There were three main dissenters, Arthur Shields, Barry Fitzgerald and I.

Naturally, Sara Allgood was wholly distraught. With the curtain about to rise sixty seconds from now what lines should she change, and how, in the name of God, should she change them? Somebody told her not to bother until she reached the third act and then meet the lines as they came. I watched her from a sympathetically discreet distance as she stood at the door to take her entrance on her return from the doctor in Act 3. She looked like one demented as, in fact, she almost was. When she went on stage I slipped over to the door and watched through a chink between the flats. Fitzgerald as Boyle was standing still and apprehensive, holding up his moleskin trousers as he asked her what the doctor had to say about Mary. Allgood sat down and tapped the table with nervous fingers saying 'Oh, Jack, Jack . . .' which was rather off script. Something in Fitzgerald's manner made the house titter. Suddenly and to my utter amazement I heard Allgood quickly say: 'Oh, Jack, Jack; d'ye know what Bentham's afther doin' to Mary?' This was capped by the loudest and dirtiest laugh I have ever heard in a theatre.

After that nothing seemed to matter. A great actress had lost her nerve. There was some fiddle-faddle about Mary having T.B., and lines were spoken which had absolutely no bearing whatever on such a situation. Not that this upset an audience out for all the laughs it could get. The rest of the week was like a nightmare. This was how the city of Cork first saw *Juno and the Paycock* in the early summer of 1924. I wondered what its author would think. I made up my mind to discuss it with him on my return to Dublin; and by informing Michael Dolan of this fact I unconsciously laid the foundations of a bitter animosity towards me on the strength of my friendship with O'Casey and my admiration for his play.

It would be much too naïve to look back across thirty-nine years at poor Cork and say: 'Of course, this ought never to have happened!' One may be fairly certain that the theatre director wasn't alone in his attitude towards the play; and, as time was to show, there were other sensitive and shrinking souls who were to voice objections towards it elsewhere.

The Ireland of that time, which is still, though to a far lesser extent, the Ireland of today, was summed up in a public lecture given in Dublin in March 1962 by the Rev. Peter R. Connolly, Professor of English at Maynooth College, in the course of which he pointed out that one of the factors at work in the 20's and 30's was the exalted idealism associated with revolution and independence, and this was nourished on an idealised and wholly ethereal Ireland 'untainted by these frailties which afflict lower regions'. The Rev. Professor then went on to say: 'As it happened the first native writers who spoke from and to the new society came up with the most unflattering picture. The shock of this, more than anything else, seems to have defined the censorship policy towards Irish writers—or at least those who wrote in English.' And he concluded that this patriotic idealism was religious or moral 'only in the most naïve and distorted sense'.

Though *Juno and the Paycock* commanded large audiences one could always meet people—indeed, one still meets them—who like the director in Cork object to the play on moral grounds, and, as some of them say, on national grounds as well. Their case, when they make it, amounts to saying that the writer must not deal with sin, and that Mary Boyle's seduction is just that spread large upon the stage. When it is pointed out to them that the melancholy circumstances into which the action has plunged Mary are far more likely to act as a warning and as a deterrent, they usually veer off on the national tack and say that the situation is not true of any Irish girl and what will visitors to the Abbey Theatre say? And supposing the play should go abroad?

How is it, one asks, that such people seem to be impervious to the pity which the play provokes, that the shooting of Johnny Boyle fails to strike terror to their bones, that they are deaf to the mother's prayer, derived from Ezekiel, that God should change hearts of stone to hearts of flesh, that they fail to see what lies at the play's deep core when Juno silences her daughter's assertion that there isn't a God, otherwise these things wouldn't happen, with the lines:

> 'Mary, Mary, you mustn't say them things. We'll want all the help we can get from God an' His Blessed Mother now! These things have nothin' to do with the Will o' God. Ah, what can God do agen the stupidity o' men!'

Of course, there are historical reasons why this should be so: why some of the Irish had neither eyes nor ears for this new playwright. Ireland was barely emerging from hundreds of years of tyranny of which famine, fever, and the coffin ships of emigration were little more than thirty years from Sean O'Casey's birthday and eighteen years more from mine. One has only to glance through the pages of Cecil Woodham-Smith's *The Great Hunger* to sense the horror of a genocide that with less consciousness of malevolence was yet as thorough as Hitler's. We were still bitterly living or partly living in the aftermath of a civil war the griping effects of which were still being felt. It was an Ireland with much to do and even more to learn and it is little wonder that some of its sons and daughters clung to a patriotic idealism that as Professor Connolly points out was religious or moral 'only in the most naïve or distorted sense'.

I got in touch with O'Casey not long after my return from Cork and we met at our favourite table in the Broadway Soda Fountain Parlour. I told him all that had happened. In the light of my seething indignation I found him remarkably unruffled about the whole affair. He was finishing another play, a one-acter, thinking of calling it *Irish Nannie Passes*. The scene was laid in a little 'dairy' shop. It was a place in Dorset Street which he knew well; he knew the characters too. He used to drop in at night sometimes for a glass of milk. There was a good part in it for me, Joe—a great old Dublin character. We must ramble up there and he would show me the place. We rambled up and we saw it, a small 'dairy' shop on what was the Fire Station side of Dorset Street almost half-way between O'Casey's birthplace and the birthplace of Richard Brinsley Sheridan. The Fire Station is gone now, so is the little shop, and a bank honours the birthplace of Sean O'Casey.

We had many chats and took many rambles that summer. The chats were mostly about Literature and Life. It was O'Casey's contention at that time that Life was being ignored by Literature. The literary people he had met so far knew nothing about life. Most of them were writing in a vacuum. (In the fullness of time this charge was to be levelled at himself.) Now Shakespeare never ignored Life. His plays were full of it; that was why he was such a great playwright. But what did Yeats know about Life? Or George Russell (the poet AE) whose weekly *The Irish Statesman* both of us read. There was Life out there, all around us, Gaby, in fact; but what did these fellows know about it? Sweet damn all!

One evening, walking along a Dublin street, we heard a barrel-organ (it must have been one of the last of its tribe) playing *Santa Lucia*. As the stringy sounds jogged up and down the nostalgic melody, the idea of a barrel-organ let loose a quotation in my mind and turning towards my walking companion I said: 'He heard, deep and rolling, beneath all the trumpets of the pride of life, the drums of the pride of death.' Sean stopped in his tracks. 'Holy God, Gaby' said he: 'Who wrote that?' 'Why?' said I, for I was not certain that I had quoted accurately and thought that Sean was about to correct me. 'God' said he 'I'd give anything to have written that; say it again.' I repeated the quotation and told him that Chesterton had written it. A look of disgust came to his face. 'Ah, Chesterton' he said, 'I've no time for that bloody fellow or for his pal Belloc either.' Now I doubted then if Sean O'Casey had read much of Chesterton, or Belloc either, but the incident stamped itself on my mind and confirmed me in the belief that this man was enamoured of the rolling phrase, that he was a writer who, perhaps dangerously, was very much in love with rhetoric.

As we went on these rambles we often stopped to listen to the racy dialogue which is still to be heard in Dublin's streets, in its shops, on its buses, at its street corners. Whatever took our fancy was noted, memorised, jotted down, examined for possible use. There is a Greek proverb which says that where two go together one sees before the other. It was so with us. As often as not it was: 'Whist, Sean . . . listen . . . the little 'oul fella on your right . . . don't look now, just listen.' Or it might be: 'Wait, Gaby . . . watch th'oul wan that's after crossing the road . . . Look at the way she's holdin' up her skirt . . . She must think she's living in Victoria's days.' Dublin has changed little since then. It is almost impossible to walk half a mile of its streets even now without hearing something that may be described as 'pure O'Casey'. Only a few weeks ago I heard this as it came at a rush from an under-sized citizen who was obviously determined to impress his tall gangling companion. 'I'm tellin' yeh. There's oney wan thing for it. Change over to the *gas*. Now, the secketerry ov our union suffered terribly from the same class o' ting. He was *completely* ulsterated. Yeh'll hardly believe me, but that man ped well over a hundred pouns to a specialist on Merrion Square for his stummick. No use. It was a little jap docthor that gev him the secret.

"What d'ye use for yer cookin' " says the Jap. "Th'electric" says yer man. "Terrible" says the Jap. "Yeh must change over at wanst t' th' *gas*." "Yeh see" says the Jap "there's nothin' like the gas for preserving the neuter-ality ov th' meat." Clever fellas, them Japs.' The tall man seemed impressed.

The blistering irony of that final scene in *Juno and the Paycock* has always impressed me. One day when returning to my office in Dublin Castle I saw an incident which was in almost every respect its counterpart. At that time it was the habit of certain members of the poorer classes to comfort themselves with a potion called 'Red Biddy', a lethal mixture of cheap wine and methylated spirits. Such drinkers were called 'spunkers'. Coming down Stephen Street I saw two ladies sauntering along arm-in-arm in a manner which left no doubt as to what they had been drinking. One of them was humming an undecipherable song while the other was endeavouring to direct her feet through the rhythm which the song suggested. Suddenly the singer sagged at the knees and then slowly and gently subsided until she lay prone on the footpath still arm-gripped by the would-be dancer who now bent solicitously over her. The bending position was obviously too much for this unfortunate who then without releasing the arm-grip slid herself alongside her outstretched companion. As I passed, Levite-like, on the other side the dancer put her mouth close to the ear of the singer, saying (through half-closed teeth) 'Lookit, for the love o' God, Mrs. Maguire, will yeh pull yerself t'gether!'

What an ending for a play, I thought; an ending comparable to the ending of *Juno*. I told Sean about it and urged him to put it in his notebook. About four years ago I met Sean Kenny who had come to Dublin to design and build a setting for a Theatre Festival production of Synge's *Deirdre*. We had a long talk about Sean O'Casey whom Sean Kenny held in high regard. The designer had visited the dramatist at Torquay. I enquired after O'Casey's health and well-being as I usually do whenever I meet anyone who has had contact with him. He was in very good form, Sean Kenny said, and was working on still another play. I said I had at last come to the sad conclusion that the dramatist's material was here and that he was unwise to leave it. The designer did not agree saying that Sean still kept very much in touch with Dublin and, indeed, that he had a rich fund of stories dealing with Dublin characters. 'For instance' said Sean Kenny, 'wait till I tell you this one. There were two Dublin oulwans—

spunkers, there were—coming arm-in-arm down a Dublin street . . .' 'I'm sorry to interrupt you, Sean' said I, 'but will you please allow me to finish it. I think I can tell it even better than Sean told it.' And to Sean Kenny's astonishment I told him the story of Mrs. Maguire and her singing companion.

There is one ramble in particular which I like to recall from those far-off days. It was one of those summer evenings when Dublin looks at her best, when her Georgian buildings, silhouetting a skyscape which, moving through a benediction of primrose, turquoise and orange, hints at some ancient splendour. Where would we go for our ramble? Saying that the heart of a city is said to beat more clearly at her riverside I suggested that we should stroll up the quays as far as the Phoenix Park. Now the view from O'Connell Bridge facing towards the Park is at any time a good view. On a summer's evening a few hours before sunset it is a breath-taking one.

We crossed the bridge and moved slowly along the south side of the river past Webb's, the second-hand bookshop, where Sean and I had bought our volumes of Balzac from Stephen Synott, old Webb's assistant, who knew Sean well, for like him he had been a member of St. Lawrence O'Toole's Pipers Band. From Stephen I had had many an opinion concerning Sean, but I had only half listened to him, for I was taking the dramatist as I found him and was not at that time interested in what others thought of him. We passed the Metal Bridge, or the Halfpenny Bridge as it was called in my early time, when it was a special delight of childhood to watch my mother pay the penny demanded from the two of us by the man at the toll-gate before we were allowed to cross. We discussed the design for the picture gallery which Sir Edward Lutyens had intended should house the Lane Pictures on a new bridge at that spot.

As we strolled along by the low river wall we noticed that the sunset was painting the river and the buildings along its banks with colours of indescribable beauty. Down the middle of the river, heads towards the sea, moved a flotilla of swans. 'The Children of Lir' said Sean. 'More likely the offerings of Gogarty' I replied, referring to the gift which the surgeon-poet-senator had made to the river in thanksgiving for his breast-stroke escape from the bullets of some Civil War 'Irregular'.

Keep you these calm and lovely things,
And float them on your clearest water;

The waters of poor Anna Liffey are seldom clear, but this evening they looked like molten gold. The sky beyond the Phoenix Park was pied with slowly changing colours. We stood there entranced at what we saw. Both of us were affected by this *L'embarras des richesses*. The eye hardly knew what to select, which way to turn in a landscape that was like a transformation scene in some celestial pantomime. All Sean O'Casey's love of colour responded to a scene which some might have held was nothing more than nature behaving like an over-dressed trollop. We walked along slowly, Sean strangely silent, I talking as usual.

Years afterwards the inspiration derived from this particular ramble was to appear in Act 3 of *Red Roses For Me* as 'A part of Dublin City flowering into a street and a bridge across the river Liffey' where the scene brightens and 'bright and lovely colours' are being brought to the group of characters 'by the caress of the setting sun. The houses on the far side of the river now bow to the visible world, decked in mauve and burnished bronze; and the men that have been lounging against them now stand stalwart, looking like fine bronze statues, slashed with scarlet'.

In the first Dublin production of this play—it was presented by Shelah Richards and Michael Walsh at the Olympia Theatre on Monday 15th March 1943—this scene was given all the colour that a modern lighting set could give it. When the play was produced for the second time—by Ria Mooney and Louis Elliman at the Gaiety Theatre during Hitler's war—the same colourful treatment was accorded this scene. When I saw the play at the Mermaid Theatre during the O'Casey Festival in September 1962, I was surprised at the treatment this scene received. I had expected the very fine lighting equipment of the Mermaid (my favourite London theatre) to go into a splendour of action to meet the author's requirements. But this did not happen. Instead, two drapings of what appeared to be butter-muslin were slung from points above the stage and lit in a manner which suggested the Victorian funereality of the Main Hall at Euston enlivened by a couple of shafts of wintry sunlight.

In our talks during the summer of 1924 I assumed that Sean O'Casey if not an habitual Abbey Theatre-goer had attended the theatre fairly regularly. Of course, since the production of *The Gunman* in April 1923, he had been more or less constant in attendance. At all events, I found that no one was more critical than he was of the work of Abbey Theatre dramatists. Perhaps he was judging them by standards derived from Boucicault and Shakespeare. But I, being green in judgment, couldn't for the life of me understand how a man who had written *Juno and the Paycock* should feel the need to criticise writers who in my opinion were very much his inferiors. Yet he constantly hit out at T. C. Murray, Brinsley McNamara, Lennox Robinson, George Shiels and the rest, and, of course, I saw no reason to disagree with him. Put alongside *Juno* most of their plays seemed to me to be completely dwarfed. However, I didn't think the comparison quite fair. In time I was to learn how jealous writers can be of each other—Irish writers particularly. Wasn't it Cyril Connolly who after an expedition into literary Dublin wrote of alligators in an aquarium? And Thornton Wilder, who knows Dublin well and has lectured at its University College, told Brendan and Beatrice Behan on their visit to the United States that while he was very fond of Dublin he wouldn't like to live in it. 'It would be bad for a writer' he said, 'there are too many jealous people.'

In *Inishfallen, Fare Thee Well*, writing of the Abbey's rejection of *The Frost and the Flower*, the first play he submitted to the theatre, Sean O'Casey points out that he had been in the theatre but twice and had seen only *Blight* by Gogarty, *Androcles and the Lion* by Shaw, *The Jackdaw* by Lady Gregory, and another one-act play built up on a short story by James Stephens. Now *Blight*, subtitled *The Tragedy of Dublin*, was billed and programmed as being by 'A and O'. It was given its first production on 11th December 1917. It dealt with tenement life and created something of a stir when it was staged. In literary circles it was known to be the work of Dr. Oliver Gogarty (who wrote a number of plays for the Abbey) and a legal friend of his, O'Connor, who subsequently became a judge. 'A and O', it was said, stood for Alpha and Omega, a typical Gogartian touch. The one-act play based on the Stephens short story was *The Wooing of Julia Elizabeth*, a comedy in a tenement setting; the story is entitled *The Charwoman's Daughter*. An examination of Abbey Theatre programmes reveals that Lady Gregory's *The Rising of the Moon* was presented with *Blight*. The first production of *The Wooing of Julia Elizabeth* took place on 9th August 1920. Two plays were presented along with it—*Maurice Harte* by T. C. Murray and *The Workhouse Ward* by Lady Gregory. The dramatist's reference to *Androcles and the Lion* suggests the possibility of at least a third visit.

One evening Sean and I, returning from one of our rambles,

found ourselves at a spot on the north side of the city known as The Five Lamps. It is a cross-roads at which Seville Place, Portland Row, Amiens Street and the North Strand Road meet; and it is marked by an elaborately ornate cast-iron candelabra-like standard holding five lamps, a typical product of Victorian street furniture. Seville Place marks the main entry to the parishes of St. Laurence O'Toole (R.C.) and St. Barnabas (C. of I.) both of which figure so largely in O'Casey's life and letters. Portland Row rises to become the North Circular Road on the left-hand side of which one eventually comes to No. 422.

The North Strand (true Dubliners never added the word 'Road') leads to Fairview and then on to Dollymount and the sea and before it reaches the former it passes Leinster Avenue, one of the last outposts of the parish of St. Laurence O'Toole. All this is O'Casey country but it is Joyce country too; there is in existence at least one book on Joyce, a pictorial record by Patricia Hutchins, which flaunts on its cover a very fine photograph of The Five Lamps. The author of *Ulysses* knew the North Strand well and invariably walked along it on his way from Grace Park Road (which is up-country from Fairview) to the National University in St. Stephen's Green. It may be of interest to the thesis-makers, particularly those from the U.S., that the North Strand was the stamping-ground of two brothers called Shem and Shawn who worked for an undertaker named Kerrigan (they will find him in *Ulysses*) whose immortelle-laden establishment was about fifty paces from The Five Lamps.

As we stood on this spot that evening—little thinking that in years to come it would change its content if not its form by a visit from one of Hitler's block-busters—we talked about the plays that Sean could, should, and surely would, write. 'Look, Gaby' he said, 'it was here on this very spot that I got the idea that I was going to become a playwright, that I became determined to write plays.' 'One evening' he went on, 'Frank Cahill and I went to the Abbey. We strolled back and we stood here. "D'ye know" said I to Frank "that wasn't such a great play we saw tonight." "Bedad, it wasn't" said Frank; "you, Sean, could write a far better play than that one." "D'ye really think so, Frank" says I. "I'm bloody sure of it, Sean" said Frank. Well, Gaby, I pushed back me cap on me head, looked up at the sky, an' said: "So help me God, Frank; I will!" ' Whether this conversation with Frank Cahill occurred before, or after, his submission of *The Frost and the Flower* to the Abbey, I cannot say. So impressed was I by the significance of the story and by the determination which Frank Cahill's faith in him had so obviously aroused that I even forgot to ask him the name of the play they had seen that night. Was it *Blight* or was it *The Wooing of Julia Elizabeth*? It might have been either. (Ulick O'Connor, Oliver St. John Gogarty's biographer, is convinced it was *Blight*.) It was hardly likely that Frank Cahill believed that Sean could improve on Shaw or that he ought to traffic in Lady Gregory's 'Kiltartan' dialect or that he should emulate T. C. Murray in the writing of tragedy. O'Casey's biographer quotes a letter he received from the dramatist in which he says that he never saw a Synge play till after the production of *The Gunman*. This is very likely indeed. He points out in the letter that he never had the money to go to the Abbey, stating that he went only twice before he wrote plays—once paying for himself in the shilling place; and once through the kindness of a friend to see Shaw's *Androcles and the Lion*. This letter was written about ten years after *Inishfallen, Fare Thee Well*. It is obvious, I think, that the playwright's memory is at fault, that it was even at fault when writing *Inishfallen, Fare Thee Well*. Miss Evelyn Janssen, a graduate of Uppsala University, Sweden, who is working on a doctorate thesis on O'Casey, tells me that she finds it extremely difficult to believe that the dramatist who could write *Juno and the Paycock* had paid only two visits to the Abbey Theatre. Of course she may be overlooking the fact that from the production of *The Gunman* onwards he was seldom out of the theatre.

In his article 'O'Casey's Dramatic Apprenticeship' in the December 1961 issue of *Modern Drama*, published by the University of Kansas, Robert Hogan points out that he has occasionally found the playwright's memory a trifle faulty about minor matters, which is not surprising when one considers that the playwright at this time was facing up to his eightieth birthday. In the same article Mr. Hogan states that *The Frost and the Flower* was a satire 'on Frank Cahill, the founder of St. Lawrence (*sic*) O'Toole Gaelic Club and an early friend of O'Casey'. This is perfectly true; the play was a satire on Frank and when Sean submitted it to the dramatic society attached to the Club on the grounds that it would save the Society the payment of royalties they turned it down saying that the characters in the play would be immediately recognised by the audience and the result would be hurtful to Frank and to others.

In *Inishfallen, Fare Thee Well* Frank Cahill's name is not

The Abbey Theatre.

422 North Circular Road, Dublin.

Sara Allgood as Juno.

mentioned though the author describes the plot of *The Frost and the Flower* which concerns 'Sean's timid friend', a man who was by no means without ability but who lacked confidence in himself. However, he did not lack confidence in Sean. Frank Cahill died in 1957. He was a national teacher in the St. Laurence O'Toole Christian Brothers' School. Though I never met him I knew him well by appearance. A low-sized figure of a man, with a limp, a stick to help the limp, and a cheery smile. A friend said of him: 'He had a natural gift in handling boys—kind, humorous, reproving, too, when necessary, but always building up, making you feel and think that you really amounted to something.'

He was the founder of the St. Laurence O'Toole Pipers Club of which Sean was a member. Tom Clarke and Sean MacDiarmada, two of the executed signatories to the 1916 Proclamation, were his close friends. He was a teacher for fifty years and the head and centre of every national and social movement in the St. Laurence O'Toole parish. His sister, Mrs. Pollard, was a member of the staff of Liberty Hall and a devoted social worker. The Cahill home on the North Strand (until it was demolished by an outsize German bomb) had been an open house for all engaged in the fight for Irish independence. Sean O'Casey spent many an evening there and in his talks with Frank shared the experience of being built up, of being made feel that he really amounted to something. Frank Cahill was loved in the parish of St. Laurence O'Toole which, to prove its love for him, elected him a member of Dail Eireann. It is questionable if it would have done as much for Sean O'Casey who by that time had built a reputation for himself which was spreading far beyond the boundaries of parish and nation. But Frank Cahill never forgot his anything but timid friend and in the corridors of Leinster House (the Irish equivalent of Westminster) could be heard to speak of the playwright with a pride which he might ordinarily bestow on the academic honours of a successful pupil. Nor did Sean O'Casey on his part forget Frank Cahill at least in his many conversations with me before time and distance and the pride of international reputation dimmed memories which others have kept green.

The Abbey was now at the opening of the second half of its 1924 season and we were busy rehearsing Sean's new one-act play *Nannie's Night Out* which had been submitted with the title *Irish Nannie Passes*. Whether the author or the Abbey's directors changed the title I cannot say. He told me that he had had discussions with the directors about the ending of the play. They wanted one ending, he another. Eventually a compromise was reached and it was the compromise we rehearsed. The main action took place in the shop of one Polly Pender who is courted by three elderly beaux of whom I was one. There are minor actions which include the stealing of a doll by a Dublin 'young-wan' which incident the author had actually seen taking place in a shop in Dorset Street. The shop is raided by a gunman in search of money. Poor drunken Nannie alone courageously struggles with the man and is seriously wounded in the struggle. The play closes on Nannie dying on the stage; her corpse being removed on a stretcher by two stalwart ambulance men. But the play does not definitively end at this point. The satiric note dominant in *Kathleen Listens In* is hardly less marked here. *Nannie's Night Out* opens with two ballad singers, a man and a woman, singing off-stage and just before the curtain falls they are heard again. The ballad-singers are a kind of chorus to the general action within the play. The song which the author selected for them was carefully chosen. It was known by its opening line as *When shall the day break in Erin*? and it was not the type of song likely to be found in a ballad-singer's repertoire. When the characters in the play had sheepishly slunk from the scene and the curtain slowly falls on the darkened stage the voices of the ballad-singers are heard through the rainy night lugubriously singing the chorus:

> For Ireland was Ireland through joy and through tears
> Hope never dies through the long weary years
> Each age has seen countless brave hearts pass away
> But the spirit still lives on in the men of today.

The ironic comment of the final line in the light of the action of the play was not lost on certain members of the audience. *Nannie's Night Out* was unique in the fact that it was the first play in which the author's sentiments were publicly hissed. At one point in the play a crippled boy acting as messenger for his mother comes in with a betting-slip which he requests the proprietress to pass on to a bookie. When he leaves the shop it was my cue to suggest that the Government might be better employed in putting food in the young lad's stomach than in stuffing the Irish language down his throat. The first night I spoke this line there were a few hisses; the second night there was a regular barrage of them and a few anti-hiss rounds of applause. The third night hisses and applause were equally divided. Arising out of this attitude in the audience and the sentiment which he had expressed in the play the author, who had himself taught Irish in the Gaelic League and could speak and write the language fluently, indulged in a long and acrimonious correspondence with a Gaelic enthusiast in the columns of *The Irish Statesman*. Quite frankly I was not interested in the discussion. Nor was I at all upset by the ironic comment enshrined in the play. All my interest was concentrated on Sean O'Casey's progress as a playwright.

In *Inishfallen, Fare Thee Well* the author briefly refers to *Nannie's Night Out* as 'a play no-one liked except AE, otherwise known as George Russell, who thought it O'Casey's best work; an opinion that didn't bother Sean, for he knew AE knew nothing about the drama . . .' Robert Hogan in his 'Apprenticeship' article states that in discussing *Nannie* and *Kathleen* with O'Casey he learned that their author still much prefers the latter and that he thinks the former 'rather negligible'. Well, he didn't think a great deal of the play when he wrote it but this I attributed— and still attribute—to the fact that his mind was blindly grappling with bigger things. He had told me of a play which he would write called *The Red Lily* for which the Nannie of this one-act work was merely a prototype. Indeed, two years later he told Lady Gregory that he intended to use Nannie in a new play *The Red Lily* and she recorded this fact in her journal. Unfortunately, she refers to the one-acter as *Lizzie's Night Out*.

For many years the typescripts of *Kathleen Listens In* and *Nannie's Night Out*, with its three endings, were in my sole possession. The *Kathleen* script was the original which had been typed on the second-hand typewriter in '422'. It had been sent to me at the author's request some years after I had left the Abbey Theatre. The Abbey never intended to revive the play and therefore it forgot that the script was still in my possession. This saved it from being consumed with other valuable scripts when the theatre went on fire in 1951. The *Nannie* script was sent me by the author himself. The story of the return through Robert Hogan will have to be held over to a later chapter. However, the effect of *Nannie* on Robert Hogan deserves to be noted here. The concluding paragraph of his 'Apprenticeship' article reads as follows: 'Directing the play merely confirmed for me the conclusion that I had reached after reading the manuscript (*sic*) and preparing it for the printer: *Nannie's Night Out* is one of the superb one-act plays of the modern stage, and it must take place next to the great one-acts of O'Casey's colleagues—Strindberg, Synge and Shaw.' This is a judgment with which I find myself in complete disagreement. My immediate reaction to *Nannie* was to urge the dramatist to 'get on with the next', an opinion delivered to him in front of 'the big fire in 422', for it was while we were rehearsing *Nannie* that the invitation to visit him came.

Four

YES, to get on with the next play. That was the main subject of our opening talks at '422'. He had plans for a number of plays, he said. First of all he wanted to write a play called *The Red Lily*. It would be written around a prostitute. Some are inclined to think that he achieved this objective in *Within the Gates* with the character of 'The Young Whore'.

Yes; and he wanted, too, to write a play called *The Castaway*. Its central character would be based upon Philip Francis Little, a member of a distinguished family and a poet whom Yeats has described in his *Later Essays and Introductions* as a man 'devout and Catholic . . . who became unbalanced, wandering about Dublin in clothes of sackcloth stitched by his own unskilful hands, full of queer tricks to gather an audience for his moral exhortations'. Sean and I knew him well by appearance as, indeed, all Dublin did. He was one of its favourite characters. But the title—*The Castaway*—how did this apply? Surely I knew my St. Paul? I was forced to confess that I didn't know him that well. Well, I would find it in 1 Cor. 9, 27:

> But I chastise my body and bring it into subjection: lest, perhaps, when I have preached to others, I myself should become a castaway.

So that was it—*The Castaway*. Poor Philip Francis Little. Lines from his *Thermopylae and Other Poems* published (by John Long) in 1915 have found their way into several anthologies. His one-sentence 'Foreword' has a touch of pixilation about it: 'The aim that all we poets have in writing is of pleasing ourselves, which is the object each one has when he is sneezing.' He has long since gone to rest beneath his three poplars:

> I shall have three grey poplar trees above me when I sleep;
> the poplars will not sway or swing, nor like the willow weep,
> but upright as the staff of one, who watcheth o'er his sheep.

43

But the play *The Castaway*, which promised so well when we talked it over in front of the big fire, was never written.

Then he wanted to write a play about railway working. He would call it *The Signal Light* or *The Red and the Green*; he wasn't certain which. He had worked as a labourer on the Great Northern Railway. Indeed, when that Railway had been taken over by Coras Iompar Eireann, Ireland's general rail and road transport body, and documents were being transferred in 1959, a number of time-sheets bearing the name 'J. O'Casey' were found among the records of the engineering department.

Some of the characters of subsequent plays were based on 'characters' he had met when working on the railway. One of them was the prototype of Captain Boyle. He referred to him as Jack. Jack was a know-all, a chancer, a walking 'Boney's Oraculum'. No matter what topic found its way into the conversation, which generally took place at a tea-break round the forge, Jack knew it 'from backside to breakfast time'.

On one occasion a group was discussing the meaning of the word 'anthem'. 'Sure anyone knows what an anthem is' said the bold Jack. 'Well, tell us, Jack' cried one of the group.

Jack put on a professional air. 'Well, now,' said he, 'supposin' I was to say to one of yous—"han' me over that hammer"—now that's not an anthem.'

The group began to listen intently. Jack went on: 'But if I was t' ask for it this way.' Jack proceeded to clear his throat, and striking the highest note he could reach began to make his demand in the form of an operatic cadenza: 'Ha-aa-nd-me-eh-ee-oh-o-o-ver' etc. Puffing and blowing at the end of his endeavours he barely managed to splutter out 'Now . . . that's . . . that's an anthem!'

Sean had many exciting stories to tell of railway work, some of them relating to the Great Northern's crack engine drivers. He had one very gripping story about a fireman who, when oiling an engine standing in steam, found that he couldn't withdraw his arm from between the spokes of one of its driving wheels.

The man called for assistance and a group of his comrades quickly gathered. They gave him encouragement and advice and tried to extract his arm by gently pulling him away from the engine beside which he was fearfully squatting, the oil-can still gripped in his right hand which was hidden somewhere in the engine's undercarriage.

A hurried consultation was held and it was decided that the

only thing to do was to get the man's mate, the engine driver, to mount the footplate and move the engine about one inch. Sean saw drops of perspiration on the driver's forehead as he stepped into the cabin to perform this delicate operation. In the meantime, members of the group placed themselves in strategic positions with a view to pulling the fireman clear the very second the engine moved. One of them arranged to signal the driver to move the engine.

Suddenly the signal is given. The engine moves; the men pull, and the fireman is free. The remarkable thing is that nobody fainted. It was incidents like these that marked his life as a labourer on the Great Northern Railway and made him want to write a play with a railway background. The nearest he got to it is to be found in the setting for the opening of *Red Roses For Me* where through the large tall window one can see 'the top of a railway signal, with transverse arms, showing green and red lights' while 'occasionally in the distance can be heard the whistle of an engine, followed by its strenuous puffing as it pulls at a heavy rake of goods wagons'. The atmosphere of the railway is there but the play itself never materialised.

He used to tell me stories from his railway days of a remarkable character called Johnny Rankin, a stonemason with whom he worked on some station buildings in north County Dublin. Johnny was a deeply religious man who spoke in a high falsetto voice. There is a Richard Rankin, a mason, in *The Bishop's Bonfire* who speaks in a 'high falsetto voice', but this character is merely a shadow of the man who flitted through the railway stories told round the fire of '422'.

One evening I described to him a scene which a colleague in the office had described to me. It concerned two Dubliners, one very drunk and the other half-sober, who arrived in a cab at a sub-post office. The half-sober one led the drunk inside and acting as guide and interpreter for his companion tried to get him to sign a form to obtain a pound on demand from his post-office account. The drunk's signature proved to be as indecipherable as his speech was past understanding and the post office clerk refused to honour the demand. The result was a right royal row and both had to be removed from the premises, the half-drunk swearing that his companion's money would be immediately removed from Post Office custody.

Sean thought that this story had in it the makings of a good one-act comedy. I didn't think so. But many years later when he

45

wrote *A Pound on Demand* he asked me to accept half the royalties he received from it, telling me that it was my story. It was kind of him, but I refused. There was talk of other possible plays and titles for them, but none came to fruition. But he was thinking of one at the moment in which he might make use of some material from an earlier script *The Crimson and the Tricolour* which had been rejected by the Abbey. And to remind himself of the task in hand he had written on a large piece of pasteboard which he placed on his mantel-piece: GET ON WITH THE BLOODY PLAY.

Now at the Abbey Theatre at this time there was a particular activity which was to have a marked effect on Sean O'Casey's career as a dramatist. It was called the Dublin Drama League. The idea of the League began in talks between Yeats, Lennox Robinson and the poet James Stephens, at the end of the first World War. The aim of the League was 'To secure the production of plays which, in the ordinary course of events, would not be likely to be seen in Dublin'. The League's two-night performances, about five a season, took place in the Abbey Theatre on Sunday and Monday nights. Its players and producers were drawn mainly from the Abbey Theatre company and supplemented with amateurs drawn from the League's members of whom Denis Johnston was probably the most productive so far as the theatre is concerned. The authors whose major works were presented by the League included the following: Leonid Andreyev, H. L. Lenormand, Paul Claudel, Wiers Jensen, Anatole France, Luigi Pirandello, Jacinto Benevente, Ernst Toller, Jules Romains, Georg Kaiser, August Strindberg, Franz Molnar, Arthur Schnitzler, E. Martinez Sierra and Anton Checkhov. In addition the League presented contemporary works by English and American authors including Eugene O'Neill, Susan Glaspell, Henry James, Richard Hughes, G. K. Chesterton, J. E. Flecker and Bernard Shaw; and even one by a Japanese author, Kakuchi Kwan, called *The House-top Madman*. Mention of the latter, in which I played the title role, brings me an intriguing recollection of myself, kimono-clad, perched perilously on a flat mid-way between stage-level and the flies.

I produced a number of these plays and played in most of them. The League activities began in 1919 and lasted for ten years. Sean O'Casey saw at least six seasons of its major presentations. We discussed the plays in great detail during the evenings

46

following their production. Some impressed him; some did not. He was particularly attracted by Strindberg and the work of the German expressionists. He professed, too, a great regard for Strindberg's *The Dream Play* which he had read but which the League had not done. For me, at that time, any dramatist who was different whetted my curiosity. I was stricken by that disease of the 'twenties which was marked by an almost pathological craving to break away from the conventions of fourth-wall realism. I was twenty-five at the time and in many respects much younger than my years. I shall never forget my excitement on seeing Pirandello's *Six Characters in Search of an Author*, an excitement which lasted into the early 'thirties but faded after that. Strindberg appealed merely to the actor in me. I had made something of a stir by my performance as Old Hummel in *The Spook Sonata*, being invited as a reward to dinner at the exclusive monthly-dining Thirteen Club of which Yeats was a leading member. To the astonishment of some of its members I brushed aside their compliments by saying that to any actor with a sense of theatre playing in Strindberg was as easy as falling off a log. As for the play itself I didn't understand a word of it and I doubted if they did either. Lennox Robinson, who played the Student in the same production, agreed with me in this.

But Sean O'Casey, who was obviously impressed by the play, professed to understand it ten minutes after its performance, when I found him waiting for me as usual in the Green Room. We walked home together but when I questioned him closely about the characters and action of the play all I could get out of him was: 'It's a great criticism of life.' Perhaps it was, but I didn't see it that way; some of my difficulty being, no doubt, that I was involved in the play's presentation. But the play in the Drama League's repertoire which had a lasting (and some say a blasting) effect on Sean O'Casey's career as a dramatist was undoubtedly Toller's *Masse Mensch* which was presented at the Abbey Theatre under the title *Masses and Man*; and it was the form even more than the content of the play that appealed to him.

I took the play to mean in essence a condemnation of violence under any circumstances, a defence of the person against the class, an indictment of our so-called civilisation. Here again I was handicapped by the fact that I was playing in the play and had little or no opportunity of seeing it objectively. But from what I saw of it at rehearsals I thought that the working out of its theme

47

was erratic and laboured with the result that the play's general outlines were rather blurred. However, as usual, it was a relief to get away from fourth-wall realism and peasant dialogue and to listen to and to speak such lines as these:

THE MAN:	. . . this is treason To the State.
THE WOMAN:	Your State makes war, Your State betrays the people, Your State robs, stifles and oppresses The disinherited, The People.
VOICE:	Munition factories Are offered At one fifty.
VOICE:	Liquid-fire-thrower Trust On offer.
VOICE:	War-prayerbook Limited On offer.
THE WOMAN:	O way through fields of ripened wheat In August days . . . Rambles over winter mountains . . . O little cricket in the hush of noon . . . O world . . .

Looking back from this remove it is difficult to see how one could have felt unduly elated by this sort of thing. Ah, youth, youth. But to Sean O'Casey who was taking it all in very quietly this was to mean for good or ill a tocsin heralding his ultimate break with realism; and a few years later when he sent me the type-script of *The Silver Tassie* and I came to its second act my mind flew back to the Dublin Drama League and its production of Toller's *Masses and Man*.

There is a passage in *Inishfallen, Fare Thee Well* in which its author describes a conversation between himself and Lennox Robinson who had invited him to one of the Thirteen Club's dinners. Robinson is alleged to have asked Sean O'Casey if he had seen Andreyev's *The Life of Man* or Giacosa's *Falling Leaves* or Maeterlinck's *Monna Vanna* and *Joyzelle* or Benevente's *Passion Flower* or Pirandello's *Right You Are (If You Think So)*. No he had not then seen nor had he read them. But he retorted with the names of Shaw, Strindberg, Dion Boucicault, Shakespeare, Webster, Forde and Massinger, to the alleged astonishment and partial horror of Robinson. There is, of course, some truth in this felicitous piece of hind-sight. Andreyev's *The Life of Man* was one of the earliest of the Drama League's productions. Sean couldn't have seen it; but I am fairly certain he saw Benevente's *The Passion Flower* just as I am certain that he saw at least sixty per cent of the League's productions.

From the beginning of our talks on current dramatists I made it clear to Sean that like James Agate (then nothing more than a name to Sean O'Casey) I was almost entirely allergic to Shaw. Like Agate I was prepared to admit that Shaw's was possibly the greatest brain that the theatre had known since Shakespeare but it was a brain that was using the theatre for its own purposes. Shaw was much *too* didactic for my taste. Sean, of course, violently disagreed with me as did many another of my friends and neighbours. I had played in Shaw and I had produced a couple of his plays. I had a soft corner for *Candida* (in my opinion almost a play); I liked the melodrama of *The Devil's Disciple* and I was prepared to accept *St. Joan* (without the epilogue) as Shaw's nearest approach to great tragedy. But generally Shaw bored me by being much too much didactic for my taste in theatre.

In this I felt inclined to subscribe to Yeats's dictum that art should be a revelation not a criticism. Possibly Yeats was suffering from something like my Shavian boredom when he described G.B.S. as a 'smiling sewing-machine'. Anyway I held that the greatest plays are those which show truth revealed by an analysis of life—in which category I placed *Juno and the Paycock* —and not life constructed to fit in with the principles of truth— or as in Shaw's case a very personal philosophy—already established. Of course, Sean O'Casey would not agree. Shaw was the greatest genius in the British theatre. I replied that I would go further than that and say that Shaw was in effect the British theatre, a veritable colossus before whom the rest, though nearer true theatre, were puny whipsters. And then I added: 'So much the worse for the British theatre!'

Of course we didn't reach agreement about Shaw and in fact we never could. But just as I had noted the danger of too much rhetoric so far as Sean O'Casey was concerned I noted also the danger of didactism. Yet thinking of *Juno and the Paycock* I felt that its author would be true to the genius that moved him to this great work, and that such dangers as I had envisaged would but touch him lightly or pass him by.

One evening I arrived at '422' to find that its now famous occupant had, as he put it, wasted his day. He had spent it reading two plays by Noel Coward—*The Vortex* and *Hay Fever*. 'The bloody fellow is not a dramatist at all' he said. I tried to put in a word for Noel by saying he was at least a great man-of-the-theatre. I was promptly told that Shakespeare was a man-of-the-theatre but this fellow was not. His work was nothing more than 'codology'— yes, that was it, 'Noel Coward codology'. I suggested that this criticism was rather harsh. I was told that the characters in these two plays were not people, had neither flesh nor blood in their make-up. I tried to point out that they might possibly be the kind of people that Coward knew, people that a certain famous dramatist and I, were not, thank God, acquainted with. It was no use. This was awful bloody stuff and had nothing whatever to do with the theatre, I was told. With the British theatre? I queried. Yes indeed with the British theatre, for the British theatre, be it known to all and sundry, was the theatre of Shakespeare! I was surprised that he didn't add Shaw.

Shakespeare provided the cue for a respite from poor Coward and going to that bookshelf on which he kept this author's works in twelve volumes I dumped them on the settee. Then began an entertainment with which we filled many an odd evening. I picked a volume at random and handed one to him. We flicked through the pages in silence and then suddenly it would begin—'Eh, listen to this, Gaby!'

CLOWN: Yonder man is carried to prison.
BAWD: Well: what has he done?
CLOWN: A woman.

'God, that's good. "What has he done? A woman"!'

BAWD: But what's his offence?
CLOWN: Groping for trouts in a peculiar river.

When Sean O'Casey laughed it was a whole-hearted affair; loud, long, gargantuan laughter. 'Groping for trouts in a peculiar river'! 'Grouping for . . .' and he was still laughing, laughing, laughing. Looking over his shoulder I urged him to go on with the passage.

BAWD: What! is there a maid with child by him?
CLOWN: No; but there's a woman with maid by him . . .

And still laughing he spluttered a loud emphasis on 'woman' and 'maid'.

Then my turn would come and having the second part of *King Henry IV* open at Act 3, Scene 2 we would recruit with Falstaff after talking over old times with Shallow and Silence.

SILENCE: This Sir John, cousin, that comes hither anon about soldiers?

SHALLOW: The same Sir John, the very same. I saw him break Skojan's head at the court gate when he was but a crack not this high: and the very same day did I fight with one Sampson Stockfish, a fruiterer, behind Gray's-inn. Jesu, Jesu, the mad days I have spent! and to see how many of my old acquaintances are dead!

SILENCE: We shall all follow, cousin.

SHALLOW: Certain, 'tis certain; very sure, very sure: death, as the Psalmist saith, is certain to all, all shall die— How a good yoke of bullocks at Stamford fair?

At this Sean would bellow forth in laughter again. 'Ah, yes . . . very sure, very sure . . . as the Psalmist saith . . . But, all the same . . . How a good yoke of bullocks at Stamford fair?'

One evening when we were at this game he opened *Henry V* at Act 4, Scene 1 at the entrance of Bates, Court and Williams.

COURT: Brother John Bates, is not that the morning which breaks yonder?

BATES: I think it be; but we have no great cause to desire the approach of day.

WILLIAMS: We see yonder the beginning of the day, but I think we shall never see the end of it—Who goes there?

K. HENRY: A friend.

He went on with the scene until he came to a speech by Williams, and then said very solemnly: 'Now, Gaby, listen to this.'

WILLIAMS: But if the cause be not good, the King himself hath a heavy reckoning to make when all those legs and arms and heads, chopped off in a battle, shall join together at the latter day and cry all, We died at such a place; some swearing; some crying for a surgeon; some upon their wives left poor behind them; some upon the debts they owe; some upon their children rawly left. I am afeared there are few die well that die in a battle; for how can they charitably dispose of anything when blood is their argument? . . .

That the man was strangely moved by this passage there was not the slightest doubt. It was to create its full effect a few years later when in the comfortable surroundings of 19 Woronzow Road, St. John's Wood, London N.W.8 he sat down and typed:

'Act II (In the war zone: a scene of jagged and lacerated ruin . . .)'. He went on then to put into the mouth of 'The Croucher':

> And the hand of the Lord was upon me, and carried me out in the spirit of the Lord, and set me down in the midst of a valley.
> And I looked and saw a great multitude that stood upon their feet, an exceeding great army.
> And he said unto me, Son of Man, can this exceeding great army become a valley of dry bones?
> And I answered, O Lord God, thou knowest. And he said, prophesy and say unto the wind, come from the four winds a breath and breathe upon these living that they may die.

Thus the opening of the second act of *The Silver Tassie*. Surely one of the greatest indictments of war written in our time.

'Come on, Gaby, I'll walk a bit of the way home with you.' I waited for him to change from slippers to boots, to put on his cap, to buckle the belt of his trench-coat. 'You can leave that open' I said, 'for it is a fine balmy night.' He didn't; he was particularly sensitive to cold, though, Heaven knows, the weather was anything but that. We walked down the North Circular Road in the direction of the Five Lamps. There were few people about for the hour was late. Not that we noticed this fact for we were oblivious to our surroundings as, heads down and hands in pockets, we plodded slowly along, talking, talking and sometimes stopping to emphasise all the more what each had to say.

He was on to Coward again whom I grudgingly though gallantly continued to defend. You can't compare Coward with Shakespeare, I said, you can only compare Coward with Coward. To compare Coward with Shakespeare is to ignore Coward completely. I suppose, then, he retorted, you can only compare O'Casey with O'Casey. Exactly, I replied. Very likely there are people who are comparing you with Lennox Robinson or T. C. Murray—actually some of your critics are doing that—but they're wrong. You are not Robinson or Murray and Coward is not Shakespeare. A writer must remain faithful to the laws of his own universe. Anyway, why should you worry about Coward? You have written a play which within its own field is vastly superior to anything written by Robinson or Murray or Coward in theirs. Your job is to go on being Sean O'Casey to the top of your bent; to be true to yourself only, to exhaust your own potential, without trying to exceed it. Look at what is happening to Robinson in his efforts to become one of the Coward school, to write plays which will be acceptable in London's West End. But by the time we reached the Five Lamps he was still not satisfied.

'Come on, I'll walk back some of the way with you', I said. We turned in our tracks. He was off now on play-writing. I quoted Yeats:

My curse on plays
That have to be set up in fifty ways.

Someone had told Sean to read William Archer's *Play Making*. 'O, holy God' he said, 'I never read so much rubbish in all my life.' I hadn't read the book and had no intention of reading it. 'But surely' I said, 'it's as simple as this—either a man has a play to write, a play which simply demands to be written, or he hasn't; surely Yeats's difficulty suggests that whatever else he may be—and he is a very great poet—he is not a born playwright.' Sean didn't think it was as simple as all that though he was prepared to concede that Yeats, unlike Shaw and Shakespeare, was anything but a born playwright. I immediately pounced on Shaw. Now look here, Sean, I said, Shaw is primarily a philosopher and a sociologist who uses the theatre, sometimes brilliantly, sometimes not, to further the ends of his sociology and philosophy. Shakespeare had only one purpose, that of writing plays to entertain his penny public. He left the Shavian end of the game to Ben Jonson. 'You stick to Shakespeare, Sean' I said, 'and never mind about Shaw.'

By this time we were back at the intersection of Dorset Street and the North Circular Road within sight of '422'; so, of course, there was nothing for it but that Sean should go back 'a bit of the way home' with me. This time we walked along Dorset Street and turned down the straight almost mile-long Clonliffe Road with its memories of the notorious eighteenth-century Buck Jones who lived here and whose ghost was said to haunt the place. But the divil a ghost we saw; and if the ghost saw us it surely would have wondered what two such seemingly ill-assorted companions were doing abroad at such an hour. We arrived finally at Ballybough where a stone bridge crosses the Tolka River not far from the spot where King Brian Boru routed the Danes at Clontarf. Again the talk was of war.

Many of my office companions had been lucky enough to escape death in Flanders in 1914–1918 though I had a theory that life stopped for them at 11 a.m. on November 11th of that final year. Office work apart, they could talk of little else than their experiences in water-logged trenches, estaminets behind the lines, or when the Jerries came over the top in March '18. Some of their stories I retailed to Sean, who had known his own survivors from that dreadful holocaust. We sat on the parapet of the bridge, seemingly alone in the world, and reluctant to part company. Suddenly I thought of the office with its attendance deadline at 9.30 a.m. sharp. I looked at my watch. It was almost 2.45 a.m. 'Brother John Bates' I said, 'is not that the morning which breaks yonder?' 'O, holy God' replied Sean, 'I believe you're right. Come on; let's scoot!' And so we scooted.

That morning I failed to make the attendance book. The failure perturbed me; not indeed that I was an habitual late comer; far from it, but with such an outside interest as the Abbey Theatre one couldn't afford to take chances so far as the Civil Service was concerned. For some time past my office colleague and theatre dressing-room companion, Barry Fitzgerald, had been urging me to share a flat with him on St. Stephen's Green. This would bring us both much nearer to the office and would ensure that Barry, who found it difficult to rise in the mornings, would have a human alarm clock as well as a mechanical one. At lunch that day I told him that I had decided to move in with him and would make the change-over in a week's time.

In the evening on my way home I called into Webbs, the second-hand book shop on Aston Quay, to pick up a copy of Anatole France's *The Crime of Sylvester Bonnard* which Stephen Sinnot was holding for me. He motioned me to the back of the shop saying: 'I have something down here which ought to interest you.' He handed me a copy of a slim paper-bound book published by the defunct firm of Maunsell & Co., Dublin. It was entitled *The Story of the Irish Citizen Army* by one P. O'Cathasaigh. 'That's your friend Sean O'Casey' said Stephen, 'the "P" was a misprint.' Now Stephen was a member of the St. Laurence O'Toole's Pipers' Club, a good gaelic footballer, who knew Sean O'Casey, the man, much better than I did. He was proud of Sean's success as a dramatist but he seemed to have some misgivings about the man himself. This was an attitude which I was to encounter in many of Sean's old friends. Perhaps jealousy had a hand in it. I couldn't say; and truth to tell I didn't care. I reminded myself again that I was taking this man as I found him.

One of the first photographs (probably the first) of the author of *Juno and the Paycock*, at 28 Claude Rd., Dublin, the home of the Allgood Family. *Left to right:* Joan Allgood, Gabriel Fallon, F. J. McCormick, Mrs Allgood (mother of Sara Allgood and Maire O'Neill), Sara Allgood. Sean O'Casey.

Shivaun O'Casey, the Author, Arthur Shields (brother of Barry Fitzgerald).

FIVE
IRISH PLAYS

JUNO AND THE PAYCOCK
THE SHADOW OF A GUNMAN
THE PLOUGH AND THE STARS
THE END OF THE BEGINNING
A POUND ON DEMAND

To Gaby Fallon
from

SEAN O'CASEY

His sure and Best Wise.
Sean O'Casey

With all the old affection.
1936

WITH A PORTRAIT OF THE AUTHOR

MACMILLAN AND CO., LIMITED
ST. MARTIN'S STREET, LONDON

1935

To Gaby Fallon,
first piece in
Literature of the Drama,
is Renew name of
many important ai at
pleasant Lamo

THE STORY OF THE
IRISH CITIZEN ARMY

Living cracked in
part of the Big Five
i. 422. North Circular Road.

from

Sean O'Casey

(P. O. Cathasaigh)

That night I read the seventy-two pages of *The Story of the Citizen Army*. I learned that Sean had been the secretary of that army, a position which is possibly unique so far as armies are concerned. The book conveys perfectly the atmosphere of the period it deals with—the period of the 1913–14 strike and lock-out when James Larkin, that great labour leader, taught the wage-slaves of Dublin to rise from their knees and walk erect as men. I had heard Larkin speak over and over again. He was the finest street orator Dublin has ever had. My father, though a white-collar worker (he was a legal accountant), used to refer to Larkin as a 'Heaven-sent man' much to the discomfiture of my mother who was inclined to take the blind clerical view of the man and his activities which was then prevalent. Every week it had been my duty to purchase for my father a copy of *The Irish Worker*. This I invariably got from the grey-haired and bespectacled old Fenian, Tom Clarke, smiling at me from behind the counter of his newspaper and tobacconist shop at the Five Lamps end of Amiens Street. Tom Clarke, a signatory to the Proclamation of 1916 was, with other leaders, executed by firing squad in Kilmainham Gaol.

It was clear from *The Story of the Citizen Army* that Sean O'Casey worshipped the fiery Jim Larkin and that he liked James Connolly (who took over leadership of the labour movement when Larkin went to America) to a far lesser degree. He believed that Connolly mixed nationalism with his labour politics and that he was more interested in freeing Ireland than in breaking the chains that bound labour. But the passage in this book that caught and held my attention was that in which the soldier-secretary mused as follows as he sat on the grass in Croydon Park, Fairview, the headquarters of the Citizen Army:

> The surrounding trees were swaying clumps of melody which sprang from the swelling throats of numerous finches and linnets, and some-times, one was forced to ask the question, was all the strife with which man's life was coloured a shining light or a gloomy shade? . . .
> . . . Here with one's head in the bosom of Nature, to what a small compass shrinks even the Constitution of the Irish Citizen Army. How horrible is a glistening oily rifle to one of the tiny daisies that cowers in a rosy sleep at my very feet, happy in itself, and giving to the world to which it has been born the fullest beauty and fragrance that its simple nature has to give.

Here was proof, if proof were needed, that this man was a pacifist. And yet according to this book he continued to associate with men who were preparing themselves for battle. This I could not understand. After all, Shaw was much more logical when he defined his position in *Common Sense about the War*:

> In my own case, the question of conscientious objection did not arise: I was past military age. I did not counsel others to object, and should not have objected myself if I had been liable to serve: for intensely as I loathed the war, and free as I was from any illusion as to its character, and from the patriotic urge (patriotism in my native country taking an implacable hostility to England), I knew that when war is once let loose, and it becomes a question of kill or being killed, there is no stopping to argue about it: one must just stand by one's neighbours and take a hand with the rest.

Well, that was that—*The Story of the Citizen Army* by its secretary, Sean O'Casey, a confirmed pacifist, a story written after that army had gone into action in the Rebellion of 1916, after its leader James Connolly, wounded in the defence of the General Post Office, had been taken strapped to a stretcher to the prison yard of Kilmainham Gaol and there summarily shot with his volunteer comrades. There was an anomaly here in the life of the dramatist which I was to encounter again and again in a variety of forms. But did this matter? The man had written a great play and would no doubt write many another surpassing that one in greatness. His warm persuasive personality was beginning to get the better of me, to wrap me round like a cloak. Dropping the book from my hand I sought refuge in the reflection that this man's past didn't matter, that it was his present and his future that I was most concerned with.

Nevertheless, I found it difficult to escape from a few nagging thoughts. Shaw was right when he defined Irish patriotism of that time as being an implacable hostility to England. And Sean O'Casey was never behind the door in expressing in copious prose and verse the very head and front of that implacable hostility. Wasn't it he who wanted the Irish people 'to carve the epitaph of Robert Emmet with their naked swords on the hearts of their ancient foes?' And hadn't he written 'poems' of which the following verse presents a typical example:

> Beneath thy flag fresh hopes we feel,
> Ireland, dear Ireland.
> We'll gild its folds with glint of steel,
> And rifle's flame, dear Ireland.
> In garish day, 'neath night's damp dew,
> Its green and white and orange hue
> Shall signal death to England's crew
> And hope to thee, dear Ireland.

How did he reconcile this stuff with pacifism, with a horror of war which seemed to me to be perfectly genuine? From what he had told me already I knew that like the rest of us he had experienced the glint of steel and the rifle's flame of Easter 1916 from a reasonably safe remove. Could there be something deeper than the character of Philip Francis Little in the proposed play *The Castaway*? Was something stirring in the subconscious mind of Sean O'Casey which made him consider his part in the fight for independence in the light of St. Paul's admonition to those who preach to others? Again I said to myself: 'What the hell does it matter? The man is a great playwright.' And with that I fell asleep.

Five

THERE is a passage in Sean O'Casey's *Rose and Crown* in which the author describes his fireside conversations 'away in a house in the deep green country' with a friar of a Roman Catholic Order who puts him in mind of a young Catholic layman whom he had known in the now-to-be-forgotten past. According to the author this young layman had a much keener mind than the friar with whom he was of an age. Unlike the friar the layman was a man of liberal opinions, and an absentee from the practices of his Church. But for all that, in the author's no doubt tranquilly revised view, he had lacked the courage of accepting that estimate of life which would allow him to say with Claudio in *Measure for Measure*:

> If I must die
> I will encounter darkness as a bride,
> And hug it in my arms.

And so this young man, much to the regret of the author whose first friend in literature he had been, retreated in his cowardice to that Church whose theories he had often quizzically rejected, the Church which would give him an assurance of life in that undiscovered country from whose bourne no traveller returns.

Fair enough. It would be difficult, if not impossible, for Sean O'Casey to see it otherwise. Yet when I sat with him in front of the big fire in '422' comparing notes on life and listening to 'the still sad music of humanity' I was to some extent rather like Pietro Spina of Ignazio Silone's *Bread and Wine*: 'His real reason for leaving the Church while still so young had not been because he had grown out of it spiritually or criticized it intellectually, but because of the profound disgust with which he reacted to the abyss which he perceived between its practical actions and the

58

words that it preached.' There were other reasons, of course; one of them being the stifling effects of a code morality, with its rule-of-thumb prescriptions for virtue, illsuited to a questioning personality that had not yet learned to equate Beauty with Truth. What Sean did not then, and even now cannot, realise, is that while one may criticise the Church intellectually, or react with disgust to its real or fancied shortcomings, it is next to impossible to grow out of it spiritually. For twenty years or more Francois Mauriac did not practice his faith; nor, as he tells us did he give any particular thought to it, but he assures us that during that period of apparent indifference he had not ceased to be a Catholic; that, indeed, he always knew he could never be anything else.

The Trappist monk, Fr. Thomas Merton, maintains that James Joyce, whom he holds to be the best writer of this century, made the mistake that the people who hate him have always made: that of making no distinction whatever between the culture of the Irish middle-class and the sacramental life of the Church. 'He is always attacking the former, and very rarely the latter' he writes in his *Secular Journal*, 'but he makes so little distinction between them that when he makes fun of the Irish middle-class, he leaves it to be clearly understood that he is including everything they might possibly want to believe in. But to the people who hate him, the middle-class is as sacred as the Mystical Body of Christ and indistinguishable from it, so *everything* he says seems to be blasphemy.' Many a young Irishman in his twenties —and I was such—has wrestled with this Joycean problem. And it is not always possible at this age to see with blazing clarity— however dimly one may feel it to be so—that Christ suffers in his Church, and that everything that happens to the poor, the meek, the desolate, the mourners and the despised, happens to Christ.

I at that time hated the culture of the Irish middle-class as much as O'Casey did. Like O'Casey I found myself on the side of the poor, the meek, the desolate, the mourners and the despised, and that was not the side taken by the Church in Ireland when in spite of Pope Leo XIII's encyclical issued in 1891 its ministers thundered against James Larkin and his struggle to emancipate the worker from economic serfdom in 1913.

On those occasions on which Sean talked about religion I was always struck by his knowledge of Roman Catholic doctrine, which sometimes exceeded mine. I knew, of course, that almost all his friends in the St. Laurence O'Toole Club were Catholics; I knew, too, that he had been friendly with the Parish Priest of St. Lawrence O'Toole's parish, Canon Brady, whom he condescended to describe as 'a great soldier of Christ'. A few years afterwards when Sean had gone to London and I was about to marry I had a chat with the Canon. It was clear that he knew the dramatist well and that he held him in high regard as a man. Just when I was about to leave he said to me. 'My dear friend, God's ways are mysterious ways; that dear man, Sean O'Casey, might have become a Catholic if it hadn't been for his great love of his mother.'

This could well be true. Sean's love for his mother was one of the ruling passions of his life. It is true that when I met him he had loved another woman—that Maura to whom, with the Abbey Theatre, he had dedicated his first two plays. He had read me reams of verse written to, and under the inspiration of, this Maura; verse which so patently lacked the one thing necessary, what George Russell (AE) would no doubt have described as the 'divine afflatus', that I was constrained to take refuge in wrapping up my opinion of the verses in the remark that 'Well, Sean, it just lacks some little thing—I can't say what—to make you another Robbie Burns.' Such are the pitiful subterfuges to which friendship unwillingly drives us.

Yet one evening he spoke a prose sentence which seemed to enshrine all the love and indeed all the poetry which his verses lacked. He had been talking of his mother, and of the great sense of humour which he believed he had inherited from her. He told me that on returning home on the evening on which she died he had distinctly heard her laughing when he was still some way off from the house. He would dedicate the play he was writing, he said: 'To the gay laugh of my mother at the gate of the grave.' Silence descended until one could hear the fall of a cinder as it left the glowing fire and dropped amongst its fellows in the grate. There was a long pause before he said: 'I loved her so much, Gaby, that she is a living presence with me still.' As another and another cinder fell one could have sworn that there was a third person in the room.

Sean's first love among the arts was painting. His plays hold much evidence of an infatuation with colour. He told me he had always wanted to be a painter. From time to time he had picked up in the second-hand bookshop on the Quays reproductions of such masters as Raphael and Fra Angelico. On one occasion he happened to bring home a very fine reproduction of a Raphael Madonna. His good mother on finding it was very perturbed about her son and frankly said that she would be better pleased if he would put such an idolatrous representation on the back of the fire. Sean tried to assure her that his interest in the reproduction was purely aesthetic and that there was no need for her Irish Protestant susceptibilities to be offended. But the poor woman was only half convinced.

Yes, he wanted to be a painter but his defective eyesight ruled against it. Oh, he had tried; little water-colours. At Christmas with little or no money to purchase cards—'they're all a cod anyway!'—he used to buy plain post-cards and do little water-colours on them with cheap paints. Wait now, he might have one of them somewhere. Yes, here it was—look, this sort of thing. Yes, indeed, here it was, a post-card with a tiny landscape of the type that might have enshrined 'The Stag at Bay'. May I keep this, Sean? Of course. Wait now, you'll have to sign it for me. This he did; and consequently I can boast that I have in my possession what is possibly the only existing water-colour painted by the young O'Casey.

One evening, still talking about religion, he told me that he had been in the habit of attending high church services. He specifically mentioned the Church of All Souls, at Grangegorman, where, incidentally, the then Rector, the Rev. Bewley, was a godly man affectionately known to the Roman Catholic children of the neighbourhood—for whom he had always a pat on the head and a couple of sweets—as 'Father Bewley'. Sean professed to be scandalised at the behaviour of certain dissidents who purposely attended the services at this Church in order to create trouble. He told me it was no uncommon thing for these gentlemen profanely to interrupt the service whenever the ritual seemed to them to move in the direction of Rome. Echoes of their behaviour are to be found in the concluding act of *Red Roses for Me*. In telling me this he never gave me the impression that he himself attended as a serious worshipper. He left me to understand that he merely went there to observe the commotion whenever the dissidents protested.

Years afterwards I was to learn another side to this story from Ernest Blythe, the present managing-director of the Abbey Theatre, formerly Ireland's first Minister for Finance, and one of

Sean's earliest friends. Sean had told me of this friendship saying that one evening when hurling in the Phoenix Park he saw a young man about his own age who, like Sean himself, seemed to be very much on his own. He struck up an acquaintance with him and they walked home together. On the way they discovered they had one thing in common—a love of Ireland and the Irish language. Sean at that time was a member of the secret organisation pledged to secure Ireland's freedom—the Irish Republican Brotherhood. It didn't take much persuasion on Sean's part to urge the young Ernest to become a member and Sean himself officiated at Ernest's swearing-in ceremony. Inevitably they saw much of each other.

In time, of course, Sean left the I.R.B. for reasons best known to himself. Ernest soldiered on, resigned from the British civil service, organised the Irish volunteers up and down the country and was jailed frequently. He was deported to Britain early in 1916. Consequently he missed the Rising but he returned to be one of a number of deadly gunmen in our war of independence and a ruthless opponent in our civil war. Retired from politics and managing the Abbey Theatre, he still has plenty of fighting on his hands.

In his autobiographical *Trasna na Boinne* (Across the Boyne) Ernest describes the O'Casey he knew when they first met. Sean seemed to be dissatisfied with Irish Protestantism as practised. He wanted something which would go as near as practicable, without perhaps going the whole way, to the religion of Rome. He actually carried a rosary beads on his person and was all for devotion to the Virgin Mary, believing that a religion lacking a motherly figure was only half a religion. This, of course, intrigued and amused the Ulster Presbyterian in Blythe. When Ernest told me this (he was working on his book at the time) I found it impossible to reconcile it with the Sean I had known in '422'. That particular Sean had obviously parted company with the idea of a Virgin Mother. One evening he elected to discuss Lourdes. My attitude towards Lourdes at the time could have been described as one of beneficent neutrality. I have never believed that the best way to keep one's candle alight is to blow out the candle which is being held by one's neighbour.

Anyway, Sean professed to be annoyed at the number of people who were running off to Lourdes, to Lourdes, to Lourdes. I contented myself by saying that if in order to make the journey they were leaving the grocer's or the butcher's bills unpaid they were simply defrauding their neighbour, and instead of going a-pilgrimage they were simply going a-pilfering. Ah, but did I believe in miracles? Well, why not? And then he said a subtle and a surprising thing. 'Don't you know perfectly well that a far greater miracle takes place every morning when on the altar at Mass the priest changes the bread and wine into the Body and Blood of Christ?' Now he said this with such conviction that I felt he really believed it. Of course at that time I had not the wisdom much less the grace of the young French peasant Bernadette to say to him what she said when asked after her First Communion which made her happier—receiving God into her heart or talking to Our Lady at the grotto? She replied: 'The two things go together and can't be compared with one another.'

Sean has never hesitated to tell mutual friends, even sometimes mere acquaintances, that he 'gave Gaby Fallon back to the Church'. There is a sense in which this is perfectly true; and although some might think that his saying so was not in the best of taste, I have never resented it. Why should I? Each of us has a role to play in the scheme of things. As Paul Claudel points out in *The Satin Slipper* '*All* things minister to a divine purpose and so to one another. Even the falterings of circumstance and the patternings of personality, *sin and falsehood*, are made to serve truth and justice, and above all salvation, in the long run.'

Of course we didn't spend all our time talking about religion. Why should we? There was life and there was literature, brother, and a void to be filled with plays and still more plays, all to be written by the author of *Juno and the Paycock*. I had been fairly busy at the Abbey after my 'discovery' of *The Story of the Citizen Army*. We were meeting as usual over cups of coffee in the vestibule or cups of tea in the Broadway. The next time I was free to go to '422' I took a copy of the book with me. I had noted that he wasn't over-enthusiastic when I first mentioned the book to him. I got the impression that he would like to forget it. However, he thawed out somewhat in '422'. It wasn't his first attempt at publication, he said. He had written three essays which he put together under the title *Three Shouts on a Hill*. These he had sent to George Bernard Shaw requesting him to write an introduction. He had received a reply from Shaw saying that he had no doubt whatever that the essays would sell if he agreed to write an introduction. However, he suggested it would be much better for the writer to market his work at its own value. This was interesting. I regret I never asked Sean to show me the Shaw letter—surely a thing to be treasured. I suppose my natural antipathy towards Shaw prevented me from doing so.

That evening on my arrival he had complained: 'I've done nothing today.' I retorted with Montaigne's 'What! Have you not *lived*? That is not only the most fundamental, but the most illustrious of your occupations.' He was not satisfied; he had no time for Montaigne. Glancing ruefully at the mantel-piece with its admonishing notice 'Get on with the bloody play' he confessed he had been reading Arthur Quiller Couch's Cambridge lectures published in two volumes under the titles *The Art of Reading* and *The Art of Writing*. He had found them to be good, very good. Soon enough, such is the force of example, I was to find them even better than very good. When I read them a few weeks later I found them to be excellent.

I had always been a reader and I had hopes some day of being a writer. I felt these lectures were just what I needed. In what Stevenson calls the bright troubled period of boyhood I had read omnivorously. I was what is called an inveterate reader by those who seem to feel that this kind of reading is something of which one ought to be ashamed. Like Coleridge I could confess that with a book in hand 'my whole being was, with eyes closed to every object of present sense, to crumple myself up in a sunny corner, and read, read, read'. Sean, too, was such a reader but with what a difference. His sight defect was such that the book or paper had to be brought to within two inches of his eyes; when typing he had, and still has, to lower his eyes to within two inches of the machine's keys. His good mother had taught him his letters. For a number of years of his young life his eyes had to be protected from the light by a bandage. When his normal-sighted brothers and sisters returned from school he would seize upon their books and go off to a corner where, lifting the bandage from his eyes, he would poke out what information he could from the well-thumbed pages. This proved, at times, to be the source of minor family disturbances for he would sometimes question the other members of his family and find them sadly wanting in their school studies.

Shakespeare and Irish writers apart the authors we mainly discussed in '422' were Balzac, Anatole France, Milton, and Thomas Hardy. I had begun to read Hardy at Sean's request and starting with *Tess of the Durbervilles* I made my way through

64

everything that this author had written, not forgetting the poems and that strange and difficult play *The Dynasts*. Sean's favourites were *Tess* and *Jude the Obscure*. One passage in the latter seemed to have a strange fascination for him. It is the last chapter in the book and is entitled 'At Christminster Again'. I had read it and noted the passage but he insisted on reading it aloud for me. It is the scene in which the dying Jude hears through his open bedroom window the shouts and hurrahs floating up from the direction of the river, as in the warm and cloudless day the Remembrance games take place. While Jude whispers the terrifying words from the Book of Job each passage is punctuated with an 'Hurrah!':

> Let the day perish wherein I was born, and the night in which it was said, There is a man child conceived
> ('Hurrah!')
> Let that day be darkness; let not God regard it from above, neither let the light shine upon it. Lo, let that night be solitary, let no joyful voice come therein.
> ('Hurrah!')

And so on.

Agreeing that the passage was a powerful one, I could only guess at its attraction for him. Was it the dramatic quality intensified by the juxtaposition of joy with desolation? Or did he, like Jude, feel that he had been wrongfully deprived of university education?

Yet Sean O'Casey professed to despise universities. When I told him I regretted that circumstances compelled me to by-pass the university for the civil service he assured me that I was much better off, that I hadn't missed anything. At this time a young Irish poet, a close friend of mine, John Lyle Donaghy, was planning a production of Marlowe's *Faustus*. Rehearsals were taking place in Trinity College where Donaghy spent much time dodging lectures. Poetry was all that mattered to him; he was the finest speaker of verse I have ever heard. I invited Sean to a rehearsal which took place on the ground floor of the Engineering School. Unless I am very much mistaken this was the first occasion on which the dramatist entered the portals of the College. In *Inishfallen, Fare Thee Well* he speaks of his being brought round the place by Professor Rudmose Brown. That may—or may not—have been later. I know I brought him to the *Faustus* rehearsal and am almost certain that it was Donaghy

65

and not Rudmose Brown who showed him the model of the planetary system in the Engineering School. It hardly matters. For Sean, as he tells us, found his own imaginary creation of the universe to be a far mightier thing than these puny toys. He appears to have missed or misunderstood the scale.

Sean seems to have been unfortunate in his experiences with universities, at least with those on this side of the Atlantic. In *Sunset and Evening Star* he describes in a chapter headed 'Cambridge' a night spent in St. John's College. The reviewer of this volume in *The New Statesman and Nation* of 30th October 1954, who was an undergraduate at St. John's at the time of Sean's visit, describes Sean's picture of Cambridge as 'a ludicrously distorted one'. On the other hand Sean himself might feel inclined to accuse his reviewer of ludicrous distortion, for it is a far more biting review than any ever penned by those to whom Sean constantly refers as his 'lousy Irish critics'. Its opening paragraph reads as follows:

> Through four volumes—this is the concluding one—Mr. O'Casey has been building up, touch by repulsive touch, his portrait of 'Sean'. It is a curious fascinatingly horrid work, a labour of hate, one might say. 'Sean' is Sean O'Casey minus O'Casey—minus, that is, all the qualities that made the superb dramatist, minus compassion, minus humour, minus generosity, minus understanding, minus even the acute ear and eye. Sean is a tiresome, opinionated, ill-mannered boor, a creature so soaked in hate that he can't see the world around him as it is, but only as a reflection of his raw and ugly dislikes. 'Sean', let us hope, has never really existed, but Mr. O'Casey is a brilliant enough writer almost to convince us that he has.

Well, the Lord between us and all harm, as we say, but that's a hair-raising indictment! Not that time and the four volumes of 'Sean' have failed to make me aware of the existence of this strange ambivalence. I can only plead that the great dramatist I knew in my youth was one Sean O'Casey. He was a kindly man if a proud one. I never knew this 'Sean' until I encountered him within the pages of this mastadonic autobiography. However, as the novelists of our fathers' time used to say: Let's not anticipate.

It was certainly to Sean O'Casey and not to 'Sean' that a young French professor called Raymond Brugère, on exchange from L'École Normale to Trinity College, wrote in the middle 'twenties asking if he might come to see him. Making certain that I would be available on the evening in question Sean invited him to '422' where he was received with customary warm hospitality. The only *gaffe* of the evening occurred when Raymond told us he was a Gascon. Sean immediately responded with: 'Ah, D'Artagnan!' and I unwittingly said 'Yes, one of the Corkmen of France!' Turning on me rather coldly Raymond replied: 'Yes, I know exactly what you mean—and I don't like it!' For all that we three became the best of friends and went on walks and excursions together. Raymond professed to be a communist but in reality he was nothing of the kind—he only liked to think he was, was Sean's verdict. Little did Sean know it at the time but I was thinking exactly the same thing about Sean. The Frenchman—like many of his race—had a brilliant mind and for a man who had been attending the Abbey Theatre for little more than three months had completed a strikingly accurate assessment of the entire Irish dramatic movement.

One Saturday in summer the three of us went on a visit to Liam O'Flaherty who at that time was living in a mountain cottage up beyond Enniskerry. We returned at about six in the afternoon and feeling hungry from our four hours in the high Wicklow air I suggested that we should go to a restaurant for a meal. However, nothing would do Brugère but that we should go to his rooms in college and partake of what food his 'Skip' or man-servant had left for him. When we got there Sean showed a keen interest in the surroundings. The rooms, a sitting-room-cum-study and a bedroom off that, were as comfortable and as well-furnished as any young exchange professor might desire.

Hanging on the wall of the sitting-room were Raymond's professorial gown and 'mortar-board' cap. Sean now asked what they were; and, having told him, I suggested he should try them on. This he did much to the amusement of Raymond who had returned with the startling news that all the food his 'Skip' had left him consisted of six eggs and a mutton chop which we would have to cook ourselves. He apologised most profusely for the absence of his man-servant. I assured him that this would present no difficulty. Sean, now in great fettle, and complete with cap and gown, asked where the cooking was to be done. Raymond led us to a gas stove in the corner of a landing outside his sitting-room. From an adjacent cupboard he produced a pan. And there in the dim-lit corner we fried the mutton chop and after it the six eggs, with the be-gowned Sean holding the pan, the professorial headgear cocked over one eye; I all the while lighting matches to see if chop or egg had been fully cooked. I have always regretted the fact that I had not got a camera with me on that occasion. At one point Sean, bringing the sizzling pan to an open window across the landing, stuck his head out demanding the whereabouts of the Provost declaring that he wished to lodge a complaint about the cooking arrangements.

It was all good simple fun, and after regaling ourselves, I on the chop, they on the six eggs, as well as two pots of strong tea, Sean and I walked home together. He was strangely moody, almost depressed. Most of the journey was spent by him in indicting universities and all their works and pomps, declaring that Brugère's living conditions were worse than those of a tenement, and that the idea of wearing such things as caps and gowns was a ridiculous one anyway; the custom ought to be abolished. I couldn't make head or tail of this sudden change of mood but when I left '422' that night I thought of 'Christminster' and the dying Jude and wondered if Sean, in some remote corner of his mind, felt as Jude felt about universities. There is a strangely foreshortened version of this affair in *Inishfallen, Fare Thee Well* in which the chop and eggs become kidneys and rashers, the matches are still matches, and Raymond becomes simply 'a Lecturer' from whose rooms the light had been cut off. This, of course, is not true. The last time I heard of Raymond he was on the staff of a university in Iowa. If this should ever meet his eye he will surely remember the six eggs and the chop.

When I discussed *The Story of the Citizen Army* with Sean O'Casey I did not tell him that I felt the work revealed him to be a pacifist. What I did tell him was that nothing I had ever read so revealed the background and the atmosphere of that time. I had lived through every minute of it as a sympathetic onlooker; I moved and had my being in a district in which most of the events took place. Thanks to my father's interest I was soaked in the fighting vituperative contents of *The Irish Worker* and whenever the opportunity presented itself I was to be found on the fringe of Jim Larkin's many meetings. I had attended what must surely have been Ireland's first military tattoo in the grounds of Larkin's headquarters at Croydon Park, Fairview, where the Army after a display of figure-marching and arms drill, staged when night fell what was imaginatively described as 'an attack on the stockade'. What fifteen-year-old, fresh from reading volume after volume of G. A. Henty, could ask for more than this seen through colours which were slowly changing from red and blue to green and gold?

Some years ago when our young short-story writer, James Plunkett, was preparing to write a play on James Larkin (subsequently produced at the Abbey Theatre) he came to me in order to discuss the form and pressure of that stirring time. I saved myself much talking breath by presenting him with my copy of *The Story of the Citizen Army* saying as I did so: 'You'll find it all in that!' But before giving it to him I carefully extracted the frontispiece, for it was on that sheet, to prove that P. S. O'Cathasaigh was indeed Sean O'Casey, that the latter had written his laudatory tribute to his 'first friend in literature and the drama'.

The evening he wrote it was the only evening he made reference to the rebellion of Easter 1916. He had been convalescing, he said, following an operation by a surgeon at St. Vincent's Hospital in which some glands had been removed from the side of his neck. With most of the men in his district he had been rounded up by the British Military, who had been suffering excessively from snipers in the St. Lawrence O'Toole area, and had been incarcerated for the night in a large grain store at the North Wall. He complained that the dust from the grain on which most of the prisoners were lying found its way into the incompletely healed wounds in his neck and caused him considerable discomfort. One can find an echo of this round-up in *The Plough and the Stars* where Fluther and the rest are imprisoned in a church.

Before the operation he had been attending the hospital as an outpatient. He was reluctant to face up to the operation, telling the doctor concerned, who insisted that there was nothing for it but the knife, that he, Sean O'Casey, knew the three things that would cure him. 'And what are these?' asked the doctor. 'Fresh air, good food, and rest' replied Sean, consciously or unconsciously confronting the doctor with what his profession knows as the Therapeutic Triad. I could get plenty of the first and third, said Sean to me, for the simple reason that I couldn't get the second—'I was out of a job at the time'.

Eventually he agreed to enter St. Vincent's for the operation. The hospital is run by the nursing section of the Irish Sisters of Charity. Some time before he had told me that my parish priest, Canon Brady, had been trying to persuade him to enter the Hospital saying that he would arrange to get him a bed there. This offer, Sean told me, he gratefully but stoutly refused. I can well imagine him doing so for he is a proud man in such matters. Nevertheless, I suspect that it was through the good offices of the Canon that he eventually got a bed there.

In St. Vincent's at that time, as in every other Dublin hospital, there were wounded from the 1914–18 War. When a well-intentioned nun on one occasion mistook him for a soldier he insisted on maintaining this status, saying that he was a soldier wounded in the great industrial war. That he was impressed by these days and nights in St. Vincent's there is not the slightest doubt. There is plenty of evidence of this in *The Silver Tassie*. Long before the writing of this play ever occurred to him he spoke to me of the eerie experience of lying awake at night, the only light in the ward coming from the red lamp flickering below the large crucifix and lighting up every detail of the tortured figure. Now and again the silence would be broken by a nebulous moan from a near-by bed or the more positive screams from a neighbouring ward of some of the war-haunted wounded. Indeed the third act of *The Silver Tassie*, as I felt when I read it, holds much that arises from this basic experience of being a patient in St. Vincent's. He closes this act with the Sisters of the hospital moving to the chapel where they can be heard singing the *Salve Regina*. This hymn the author quotes in full from its opening line *Salve Regina, mater misericordiae* until its close *O clemens, o pia, O dulcis Virgo Maria!*

Coming from a man who deplored the attraction of Lourdes, who has so frequently and so bitterly written about Catholic devotion to the Virgin Mary, this use of one of the greatest hymns ever written to the Mother of God may appear to some minds to be passing strange. Some may see in it the ambivalence of 'Sean' and 'Sean O'Casey'. For myself, I am constantly faced with the fact that while the forebears of this man were Roman Catholics he was the favourite son of a well-loved Protestant mother. One feels he could say as Hamlet said of himself in another context:

'In my heart there was a kind of fighting that would not let me sleep.'

Six

EVENTUALLY the evening came when Sean told me that he was fairly satisfied with the new play. He would call it *The Plough and the Stars* he said. This was the name given to the flag of the Citizen Army which bore on a blue background the seven stars of the heavenly plough. I had seen the flag but had never grasped its symbolism. Earthly plough to heavenly plough; well, Ireland was and indeed still is an agricultural country, though its industrial wheels today are many and merrily whirring. Sean told me that the symbolism for the flag had been suggested by the poet and economist George Russell 'AE'. Since Russell's economic interests lay almost solely in a rural direction this possibly accounts for the plough.

But labour owed another debt to Russell. His famous open letter to the Masters of Dublin on behalf of labour written in October 1913 was not without effect.

> I address this warning to you, the aristocracy of industry in this city, because, like all aristocracies, you tend to grow blind in long authority, and to be unaware that you and your class and its every action are being considered and judged day by day by those who have the power to shake or overturn the whole social order, and whose restlessness in poverty today is making our industrial civilisation stir like a quaking bog . . .

And so it went on.

> . . . You may succeed in your policy and ensure your own damnation by your victory. The men whose manhood you have broken will loathe you, and will always be brooding and scheming to strike a fresh blow. The children will be taught to curse you. The infant being moulded in the womb will have breathed into its starved body the vitality of hate. It is not they—it is you who are blind Samsons pulling down the pillars of the social order. You are sounding the death knell of autocracy in industry . . .

71

Labour in Ireland has not forgotten its debt to George Russell. But on the head of a petty quarrel in Russell's paper *The Irish Statesman* Sean O'Casey saw fit to lampoon the poet savagely in the *Inishfallen, Fare Thee Well* volume of his autobiography under the heading 'Dublin's Glittering Guy'.

However, that was yet to come. *The Plough and the Stars* was the title of the new play and it would deal with Easter 1916. I suspected it would deal with it from the pacifist point of view; and I was right. How could it be otherwise in view of that revealing paragraph in *The Story of the Citizen Army* and the fact that Sean O'Casey took no active part in the rising? However, this aspect of the play didn't interest me one whit. How did it stand theatrically? That's what I wanted to know.

Evening after evening he read passages of the play to me. So far as I could judge it was dramatically as good as *Juno and the Paycock*. In some respects it seemed to surpass the earlier play. However, he wasn't quite satisfied with the script; he still had a number of things to do with it. There was the Bessie Burgess death scene for instance. 'Now, had Bessie been a Catholic,' he said 'she would, knowing she was at death's door, say an "Act of Contrition". But what would a Protestant do? That's my problem. The other day it occurred to me that Bessie might say a hymn—this hymn, a rather nice one by the same token.' And then, in a clear but quavering voice he sang:

> I do believe, I will believe
> That Jesus died for me
> That on th' cross He shed His blood,
> From sin to set me free . . .

I said it seemed most appropriate. 'Ay, I feel it's just possible', he said 'that the words of this hymn might return to the semi-consciousness of the dying Bessie.'

One of his biggest worries was that he had written the part of Bessie for Sara Allgood who was now in London and would not be available for the Dublin production of the new play. I told him that Sara was corresponding with me and that she had written to say that while she would give anything to play Bessie she felt that Maureen Delany would make a good job of it though naturally she wouldn't play it half as well as she, Sara, could play it. This proved to be cold comfort to him. He was worried, too, about the part of Rosie Redmond, the young prostitute in Act 2. 'I don't think that there is an actress in the Abbey who could play this part.' I was able to cheer him up slightly on this point by drawing his attention to young Ria Mooney, a new-comer. From what I had seen of her work I thought she was ideally equipped to give the part what it required. He seemed a little happier. 'Barry Fitzgerald', he mused, 'would be first-class as Fluther Good; F. J. McCormick excellent as The Covey; Shelah Richards and P. J. Carolan good as the Clitheroes; Eileen Crowe will be all right as Mrs. Gogan; and, of course, you, Gaby, ought to play Peter Flynn.' Circumstances—and Lennox Robinson—were to make some drastic changes in this casting.

A few evenings later he was still worried about the play though this time his worries were not technical ones. I had told him that, in my opinion, one of the finest scenes in the play was that in the second act where the fiery patriotism of 'The Voice of the Man' outside the window is pitched against the rich scenes of comedy inside the public house, and then lifted in a dramatic crescendo by the entry of the three officers carrying the Tri-colour and the flag of *The Plough and the Stars*. It was this scene which was causing him to worry. The words which he had given The Voice were, he said, taken from speeches made by Padraic Pearse. 'Well, what about it?' I said. 'Did you ever hear Pearse speak, Gaby?' I had to confess I hadn't, though I had heard Larkin speak time out of mind. 'Well' said Sean, 'there will probably be many in the audience who heard Pearse speak and they might easily be offended at my use of his words.' Now this, at the time, was quite beyond me; had I been 'in the movement', as we say, I might have given deeper thought to his point. As it was, I told him plump and plainly that I felt that any alteration of the scene would certainly destroy it. He seemed satisfied.

Nevertheless, I couldn't get this worry of his out of my mind, though I failed to see the situation from his point of view. I didn't know then that the old Fenian, Tom Clarke, one of the executed signatories to the 1916 Proclamation, had in 1914 written to his brother Fenian, John Devoy, in America: ' 'Tis good to be alive in Ireland these times . . . although . . . Larkin's people for some time past have been making war on the Irish Volunteers. I think this is largely inspired by a disgruntled fellow named O'Casey.' Clarke's reference was to Sean O'Casey and a campaign in *The Irish Worker* which ceased when James Connolly took over the paper late in 1914. There were rumours, too, at that time of a raid alleged to have been made either by members of the Irish Volunteers or the Citizen Army on the revolutionary publishing premises of Whelan & Son of Upper Ormond Quay in the course of which copies of Sean's *Story of the Citizen Army* were said to have been removed from the premises. Since Sean had never discussed matters of this nature with me, beyond hinting at the fact that he loved Larkin and thoroughly disliked James Connolly, I could not understand his obvious apprehensiveness about the play. I knew, of course, that he could not forgive Connolly for having, as he alleged, deflected the course of the Citizen Army by leading it into the fight for Irish Freedom. But there may have been personal reasons also. Connolly, like Sean, wrote patriotic verse and this, according to Sean, reeked with sentimentality; but to me it didn't seem to be any less sentimental than the verses Sean himself was writing at that time. Sean quoted the chorus of Connolly's *The Watchword of Labour* as a typical sample of the kind of stuff he meant:

> Then send it aloft on the breeze boys!
> That watch-word the grandest we've known.
> That labour must rise from its knees, boys!
> And claim the broad earth as its own.

Well, there was nothing particularly sentimental about a badly wounded man, strapped to a stretcher, boldly facing a British firing-squad in the yard of Kilmainham Gaol. That was my vision of Connolly at that time although I didn't disturb Sean by presenting him with it.

However, in or around this time something happened which was due to have a particularly deleterious effect on the production of *The Plough and the Stars*. The incident is very briefly referred to in *Inishfallen, Fare Thee Well* and recorded as if it happened after *The Plough*. The whole point of the incident is that it occurred *before* that event. F. J. McCormick and Sean O'Casey were still great friends though they were not seeing as much of each other as they did before and after *The Gunman*. One reason for this was that McCormick was the Abbey's leading whole-time actor and as such was in constant employment. It was very rarely indeed that F. J. had a week to spare. The other reason was that I had taken over in Sean's company where F. J. had left off, and not without some slight resentment on F. J.'s side.

We had just opened a season with a revival of *Man and Superman* directed by Michael J. Dolan. In my opinion it was anything but a worthwhile presentation of Shaw's play. Accustomed as we were to the weekly grind of peasant comedy and tragedy we lacked the style and sparkle, particularly in speech, which a play of this nature demands. The only Shaw plays in which the Abbey company of that time really excelled were *John Bull's Other Island*, *The Devil's Disciple*, and *The Shewing Up of Blanco Posnet*. Our approach to *Man and Superman* was a totally naturalistic one whereas most of Shaw's plays call for players who having made a gift of their personalities to the characters in the play are then willing and able to turn themselves into efficient talking machines. In this particular production only F. J. McCormick as John Tanner was giving anything like a worth-while interpretation of Shaw. Barry Fitzgerald was playing a Roebuck Ramsden which was more or less what his director, Dolan, demanded from him. Unfortunately, the more was Barry and the less was Shaw. Having played old Malone in an earlier presentation, and a succession of successful old men in between, Dolan now cast me in the part of old Malone's son Hector. (Barry Fitzgerald was right. It didn't do under Mr. Dolan's régime for a young actor to be too successful in old men's parts.)

Sean O'Casey was present on the opening night and came up to the Green Room after the performance. He sat on a couch in ominous silence, his head in his hands, always a bad sign. Barry Fitzgerald and I were there, and after preliminary greetings I broke the silence. 'Well, Sean,' I said, 'what did you think of the show?' He replied with two very effective words: 'Bloody awful!' 'Oh!' said Barry Fitzgerald, 'I suppose I was awful too?' Sean soft-pedalled his reply: 'Well, you were not good, Barry!' Barry said nothing, but simply went on looking uncomfortable. Then I noticed that Michael Dolan had quietly entered the room. It was obvious that he had been there for some time and had heard much if not all of the conversation. When I looked in his direction he slipped out quickly and quietly and went upstairs towards the dressing-rooms. There was an awkward silence.

I knew that Sean was perfectly right. So I said to him with a half-grin and in mock-obsequious tones. 'And would you have any objection, Mister O'Casey, to accompanying two "bloody awful" actors upstairs to their dressing-room for it's to that place we'll be going in order to wipe the honest sweat of Shaw from our disreputable persons?' Up he went with us. On the way he volunteered the opinion that the only worth-while performance in the play was F. J. McCormick's John Tanner. We were hardly inside the dressing-room when the door opened

75

and Dolan and McCormick walked in, the former suspiciously quiet, the latter strangely excited and still wiping the grease-paint from his face with a towel. I began to smell trouble. 'I believe, Sean,' said F.J., in increasingly provocative tones, 'that our little presentation of Shaw wasn't good enough for a big shot like yourself.' Sean's voice was ice-cold as he replied: 'I thought, and I said, that it was bloody awful, Peter.' 'And what right, may I ask' said McCormick (Peter Judge) 'have you to sit in front while we sweat on the stage and then to come barging around here with your "derogatory" opinions, which, incidentally, we don't bloody well want!' 'I have the right of paying for my seat, Peter' replied Sean, 'I have the right of visiting my friends; I have the right of answering a question when asked: the right of expressing an opinion; the right of giving words to whatever truth that is in me!' I could see that O'Casey's temper was steadily rising. Poor F.J. was almost ready to explode. Dolan quietly stood there and said nothing.

I thought it time to intervene. 'Look, Peter' I said to McCormick, 'it's only a few moments ago since Sean said to both Barry and myself that the only worthwhile performance in the play was your own Jack Tanner.' 'I don't give a damn what he said' replied McCormick, 'I'm not thinking of myself; I'm thinking of the rest of the company.' O'Casey replied slowly and with deliberate emphasis. 'You're thinking of yourself, Peter; and, what's more, you've been egged on to think of yourself by the gentleman in the corner who is saying nothing.' 'He's not thinking of himself' lamely interjected Dolan, 'he's thinking of the company.' O'Casey drew himself up to his full height and turned towards Dolan. Sean was at any time a fine figure of a man. It was but a few months since he had given up strenuous manual labour. Had it come to a fight he could have finished any three of us. I saw the colour slowly mounting up the side of his neck. I knew it was a bad sign. 'Look' he thundered at Dolan, you may think that Peter's not thinking of himself; Barry may think that Peter's not thinking of himself; Gaby may think that Peter's not thinking of himself; but I, Sean O'Casey (and here he roared) not only think, but firmly believe, that Peter Judge, otherwise known as F. J. McCormick, is thinking and thinking and thinking of himself, and that you, Michael J. Dolan, put him up to it.'

It was time to break it up. I rushed Peter out of the room. Dolan slunk behind us. My friendship with O'Casey was already a sore point with the Abbey's manager. This affair would make it an open wound. That night as Sean and I walked home I suggested to him that it might be better for both of us if we met only at his place or in the vestibule at the far side of the Theatre. He said he was thinking along the same lines. But Michael Dolan was doing some thinking too and had issued orders to the stage manager to the effect that Sean O'Casey was to be banned from the Green Room. He then consoled himself for Sean's severe criticism of *Man and Superman* by telling the company that O'Casey was half-blind anyway and couldn't possibly have seen the play as a normally-sighted person would have seen it. For myself, I didn't care a rap about what happened to *Man and Superman* but I had grave fears concerning the attitude the company might adopt towards Sean's new play *The Plough and the Stars*.

This unfortunate incident did more than affect the coming play. It severed the connection between the dramatist and the 'theatre workshop'. Most Irish dramatists, particularly the earlier ones, had access to the Abbey's back-stage departments, including the Green Room, and were on terms of close friendship with the players. This, at first sight, may not seem to be of much importance; but it did bring about conditions comparable with those in which Shakespeare worked. Apart from whatever advice and assistance the directors of the Abbey—all of them dramatists—could afford the working dramatist, his close contact with the players had an inspirational value for him. It was a well-known fact that the part of Juno Boyle was written with Sara Allgood in mind; Captain Boyle and Joxer Daly were tailored to fit Barry Fitzgerald and F. J. McCormick respectively. There is not a doubt that Sean's friendship with the players played an important part in his creation of these characters. One has only to contrast the earlier plays, particularly *Juno* and *The Plough*, with some of the later works, written, so to speak, *in vacuo*, in order to assess the value of close contact with a repertory theatre to the work of a dramatist of quality.

The next time I visited him at '422' he seemed to have forgotten the incident at the theatre. He was in much better form, too, about the new play. We went over bits of the first act and played the scene of 'Georgina: The Sleepin' Vennis'—Oh, that's a terrible picture; oh, that's a shockin' picture! Oh, th' one that got that taken, she must have been a prime lassie!' The idea for this scene had been suggested to him in an odd way. I had given him a framed photograph of a Thorwaldsen Venus which he placed on his mantelpiece over the big fire. Tired of doing the job himself and being now a man of affluence with royalties to the tune of £200 a year he had hired a woman, a neighbour glad to earn a few shillings, to tidy and dust his room. This she religiously did, 'religiously' being the operative word, for every time she dusted the mantelpiece she turned the Thorwaldsen Venus face to the wall!

On the £200—it varied, of course, and was sometimes below that figure—he lived in frugal comfort in his tenement room. He did his own cooking which amounted to boiling eggs and brewing tea. His tea was 'always the best', two and a half tea-spoonfuls of the most expensive Indian tea 'bought in Kelly's of O'Connell Street, with the big Chinaman over the front door'. The rest of his diet at this time consisted of fruit, tomatoes, biscuits and Bovril. His appetite seemed to have lessened with his giving up manual labour. He told me how in the old days at his breakfast he would as often as not eat the best part of a two-pound loaf and wash it down with a pint of cocoa, or water, if cocoa was not available. 'Never use the word "hunger"' he said to me on one occasion, 'until you have gone without food for three whole days. Otherwise, you don't know its meaning.' One evening when we were about to set out on one of our many 'rambles' I asked him why he was not wearing his newly-bought flannel trousers. 'Why d'ye think?' he replied. 'Where is it?' I asked. 'Well, where the hell d'ye think it is? It's in me Uncle's; pawned, popped, up the spout!' A delayed royalty cheque had led to this predicament. It took me some time to get this informa-tion from him. A word to the Abbey's secretary, Johnny Perrin, soon remedied the situation. The incident is another indication of Sean O'Casey's pride which would not allow him to hint, even to a 'buttie', that he was short of cash. The story reached Lady Gregory's ears and she duly noted it in her *Journal*.

At the dress rehearsal of *Juno* I had come to the conclusion that its author was destined to be heard of in a much larger world than Ireland and its Abbey Theatre. With this in mind I urged him to approach a local photographer and have the interior of '422' photographed. I could see that he thought the request a strange one but I pressed my point and gave him my reasons for doing so. 'Look' I said, 'some day the world will want to know all about this place, this room in which *Juno* and *The Plough* and your other plays were written.' The next evening I called he told me that the job had been done and he presented me with a signed copy of the photograph. It now appears as a frontispiece to *Inishfallen, Fare Thee Well*. Over the fireplace is a photograph of F. J. McCormick as Joxer Daly and on the mantelpiece beside the Thorwaldsen Venus is a photograph of the present writer as the old doctor in Martinez-Sierra's *The Two Shepherds*.

One evening after a visit—the only one as it happened—of Liam O'Flaherty to '422' Sean rebuked me for telling too many good stories. 'O'Flaherty is a writer' he said, 'all's fair in love and literature; he'll use them and they are really your property.' I brushed the matter aside on two grounds, the first being that the stories weren't in Liam's particular line of country, the second being that there were many more where these had been found. He wasn't satisfied. 'These stories are yours' he said, 'and you should write them.' He strongly advised me to keep a notebook and to jot down everything I saw and heard that happened to take my fancy. 'Never trust your memory' he said, 'You never know the minute it will let you down.' He pointed to a slate over the head of his bed. 'Look' he said, 'I keep that there for a purpose. It might happen an odd time that I'd wake up in the middle of the night and think of something worth while. If I didn't jot it down right away it would be gone by morning. No, never trust your memory.'

I told him I hadn't quite made up my mind about the writing game. It was a time of 'movements' in writing; I was fascinated by Joyce and the odd copies of *transition* that came my way. Miss Stein's simplification appealed to me with its attack on order and meaning in favour of sound. Something might be accomplished in this direction, I said, by beating out characters in rhythm. I was at an age when these things seemed to matter; indeed, I was a rather late starter for that particular age. I showed him a sketch which Middleton Murry, then editing *The Adelphi*, had been kind enough to pat on the head with words of critical praise. 'Yeh, good' said Sean, 'but not good enough. Forget the theories; most of them are bloody rot, anyway; just go on writing. Remember, you've put your hand to the plough; don't look back.' Some time later when my first experiment in what I fondly believed was a new manner, *Merry-Go-Round*, appeared in *The Irish Statesman*, Sean was as pleased about it as if it had been his own. And he repeated his advice: 'Plough on, don't look back!' Many years after we had quarrelled he was heard to refer to this early effort of mine and to say to a young man in whose company he seemed to be re-living our former friendship: 'What a pity he chucked the creative stuff and went in for all this damned criticism!'

On a summer evening in 1925 Sean O'Casey told me he had just sent his new play *The Plough and the Stars* to the Abbey. From all I knew of it—though he hadn't read it to me in its entirety— I felt certain of its acceptance, and told him so. 'Well' he replied, 'you never know.' A few weeks later he received an invitation from Lady Gregory to visit her at her home at Coole Park, Co. Galway. Now this was something which didn't happen to every Abbey dramatist. Actually, Sean was unique in this respect. Lady Gregory had taken kindly to him from their first meeting. Off Sean went, arriving at Coole Park to find that his play had got there just before him, having been posted from Switzerland by Lennox Robinson who had read the play there to W. B. Yeats. A covering letter stated that in their opinion it was 'probably the best thing that O'Casey has done'.

This visit to Coole was undoubtedly Sean's first contact with rural surroundings and he thoroughly revelled in it. His love of flowers, plants and trees, inherited from his mother, had in these surroundings full scope to spread itself lavishly on all that he saw. The trees of the Seven Woods were nearing their autumnal beauty. The lake from which the poet Yeats saw nine and fifty swans suddenly mount 'and scatter wheeling in great broken rings' fascinated Sean. He spent much of his time wandering along its edge listening to the murmuring of the wood pigeons in the sun-drenched woods. He was impressed by many things— the magnificent avenue of arching Ilex, like some cathedral nave, that marks the entrance to Coole; the lawn facing the house on which so many cricket matches had been played—Gort v. The Rest, the famous W. G. Grace on more than one occasion being content to face the bowling of the local butcher; the great autograph tree on which he was privileged to carve his initials. They can be seen there today, deeply cut into the bark, not far from the widely-spread W.B.Y. and the almost three-feet high G.B.S. One had to be of the privileged few to be allowed, knife in hand, to creep under the earth-sweeping foliage of this gigantic copper-beech and begin the carving act. Nothing less than a clear invitation from 'Her Ladyship' would suffice.

Sean wrote to me twice during his ten-day stay in Coole and

when he returned he filled in the details. He was greatly impressed with the thoughtfulness of Lady Gregory's hospitality. Knowing that his sight was bad she had fixed up a special arrangement of shaving mirrors for him. Worrying about his food she told him he must ignore the formal table arrangements of the house and order his own particular likes—if he wanted poached eggs for dinner or tomatoes and fruit for lunch then these he must have and that was all about it. So far as the house and its surroundings were concerned he must wander at will; the whole territory was his to explore. In short, she fussed over him just as she fussed over Yeats in the days before the foundation of the Abbey Theatre.

The evening of his arrival Lady Gregory slipped away after dinner and read the first act of *The Plough and the Stars*, leaving Sean in the library with Jack Yeats and his wife. Finding the play very much to her liking she returned to the library and read the rest of it to her guests, never flinching for a moment at the bawdy song sung by Rosie Redmond in the second act. This impressed Sean very much. But trouble was looming ahead although neither he nor Lady Gregory knew it at the time. Two years ago I had a long conversation with the last of Lady Gregory's coachmen—an old man of eighty-one—about the many visitors to Coole. I asked him about Sean. He summed him up in a sentence which beneath its colloquialism brims up with the highest praise: 'The likes of him' he said, 'never came to Coole before nor since!'

Sean treats of this visit in his own very personal way in *Inishfallen, Fare Thee Well*. However, there is a passage in the chapter 'Dublin's Gods and Half-Gods' which rather pointedly reminds me of something which he discussed with me on his return from Coole Park. It is that passage in which he indicts Lady Gregory as well as the poets James Stephens and George Russell on the grounds of reading 'Blood and Thunder' novels. He refers to returning with Lady Gregory on one occasion from Coole to Dublin (as if there had been other occasions) and being compelled to wait at Athenry Junction. Lady Gregory sat on a platform bench while Sean strolled off to have a look at the town and incidentally to see things in his own autobiographical fashion. When he returned to the railway station he saw Lady Gregory reading a book. When she heard Sean coming she closed it quickly but not before Sean had time to see it was *Peg O' My Heart*.

I thought this incident paid an extraordinary tribute to Sean's strangely improving eye-sight, for I felt that even my sight which is perfectly normal would not be capable of such a smart piece of detection. In the same chapter he tells something which he told me with much gusto when I stayed with him some years later in St. John's Wood, how his wife Eileen, seeing a book protruding from Oliver Gogarty's suitcase, bent down and snatched it before Oliver could stop her, and Sean, to his horror, saw that its author was Edgar Wallace. When he told me this I privately considered that Eileen's action was a remarkable piece of rudeness. But his earlier references to Lady Gregory and to Yeats—who read detective stories provided they had a love interest—led me to suspect the beginnings of an intellectual snobbery. What did it matter what they read, I argued, provided their own creative work was something worth while, as it undoubtedly was? John Keats may have fed on the thinnest of porridge. No, that wouldn't do Sean O'Casey. *Peg O' My Heart* was rubbish, so were detective stories, so was the stuff turned out by Edgar Wallace. I told him that I derived some of the greatest pleasure my reading life has ever held from Conan Doyle's Sherlock Holmes and from a defunct weekly called the *Union Jack* which dealt with the adventures of one Sexton Blake. I told him, too, that I would read anything today that would give me the pleasure that these had given me. No, no, it was all wrong; it wouldn't do; these things were nothing but rubbish and no man (or woman either) interested in Literature should have anything to do with them. I let it go with him. But I thought, and still think, that if he really felt that way about such books—if it wasn't merely a snobbish pose with him—that he might have spared Lady Gregory his indignation at her frailty.

I began to wonder about Sean. Had my idol feet of clay? I couldn't understand this growing intolerance in a man whose sympathy with the human condition was otherwise so broad and deep. Was he merely being naïve? There was that evening when I took him to the Theatre Royal—his first experience of vaude-ville—where Barry Fitzgerald and I, whenever the occasion permitted us to do so, went to rejoice in the art of such great music-hall artistes as Lauder, Lashwood, Nellie Wallace, Gertie Gitana, Rob Wilton, Dorothy Ward, Shaun Glenville and a host of others. On the occasion of my visit with Sean he was obviously interested in the surroundings of a theatre other than the Abbey.

But when the conductor of the orchestra, opening the second house of the evening, briskly ascended his podium and casually waved the orchestra into a brassy version of 'The Entry of the Gladiators' Sean turned to me and with the greatest solemnity said: 'You know, Gaby, *that* is not music!' To which, of course, the only possible reply was: 'Who the hell ever claimed it to be?'

Things were beginning to thrive with him now. The royalties from J. B. Fagan's London production of *Juno* were merrily rolling in. He had joined the Society of Authors. There were some changes to be seen in '422'. Many of the old second-hand books were going out; expensive new ones were coming in. In place of the wooden shelves there was a spanking new glass-fronted bookcase. Copies of the *Theatre Arts Monthly* of that time, a more seriously sober production than it is now, were to be seen on the work-table or the new settee. There were some fine new chairs. Strangely enough, it never occurred to him to buy a new typewriter.

One evening he told me that he was expecting a visitor, a friend from the past, a member of the O'Toole Club, a great Gaelic footballer—Paddy MacDonnell. I knew MacDonnell by sight, a magnificent specimen of Irish athletic manhood with a handsome face crowned with a head of black curls. He and his brother John as well as John and Stephen Synott (Stephen worked in Webb's the booksellers on Aston Quay) were all old friends of Sean's. On 21st November 1920, still known in Irish history as 'Bloody Sunday', the MacDonnells and the Synotts were playing for Dublin in an All-Ireland final at Croke Park when the ground was surrounded by Black and Tans who, with rifles and machine-guns, calmly proceeded to shoot at everyone in sight as a reprisal for shootings of members of the British forces by Michael Collins's gunmen which had taken place in another part of the city that morning. One player and eleven spectators were killed and many more were injured in the stampede that followed.

Well, Paddy MacDonnell arrived on time, and I—never the athletic type—was thrilled to hear Sean and Paddy talk of famous hurling and football games in the course of which they covered a good deal of the history of Sean's former membership of the O'Toole Club. I was interested, too, to get from Paddy a first-hand description of the 'Bloody Sunday' affair. All-in-all it was one of the most interesting evenings I had spent in '422'. Paddy MacDonnell left fairly early and Sean, who had been elated

83

enough while Paddy was there, seemed caught in a mood of depression after he had gone. Thinking it might be the memory of times past that weighed heavily on Sean I ventured to cheer him up by telling him how thoroughly I had enjoyed their conversation since it introduced me to a world which was completely foreign to me. I had just commented on MacDonnell's fine physique when Sean stopped me with the remark: 'Ah, but you see, Gaby, he knows nothing whatever about art or literature!' This was something of a shock. Heavens above, was a man to be judged solely on his knowledge of art and literature? I said nothing; but I thought a lot. Was this the result of new fame, increasing affluence, the London production, the invitation to Coole Park? Was it a part of the antipathy towards poets and playwrights who filled in their leisure reading detective stories? Was it intellectual snobbery of the worst type, an attempt to become the exlusive artist, a determination to cultivate that love of Bach which casteth out Puccini? Only time could tell.

Seven

❦

IN MID-JANUARY, 1926, the Abbey Theatre Company was invited by Senator and Mrs. Parkinson to their house and training-stables on the wide wind-swept Curragh of Kildare. The purpose of the invitation was the presentation of *The Shadow of a Gunman* in the gymnasium of the Curragh Military Camp, the proceeds being in aid of St. Joseph's Young Priests' Society of which educationally charitable body Senator Parkinson's wife was a member.

William Butler Yeats, also a senator of the Irish Free State, accompanied us on the visit. After the performance, the players, who had been entertained royally throughout the day, assembled in the Parkinson drawing-room. Much of the conversation concerned horses, jockeys, races and trainers prompted by an extensive visit to the Parkinson stables which had taken place between lunch and the performance at the gymnasium.

Yeats, whose knowledge of racing was as negligible as mine, sat in a high-backed chair beside the fireplace. It happened that I sat opposite to him chatting with the youngest daughter of the Parkinson household who hoped that the poet might be persuaded to write some verse in her autograph book. I knew by the gleam in the poet's eye that he was in good talking form and would need little encouragement to make himself heard above the din of pedigrees, weights, and distances, that crowded in upon us from every side. Seeing that Miss Parkinson and I were whispering together (about the poet as it happened) he elected to scent an amorous intrigue and leaned forward in our direction with a knowing smile. 'Fallon' he said, 'an old farmer in the West of Ireland once said to me: "There were eighteen of them, and I loved any one of them better than the woman I married".' This set him off. Miss Parkinson was delighted. I got him to talk about the Rhymer's Club, about Ernest Dowson, Lionel Johnson and Oscar Wilde. His stories about Wilde were fittingly tempered to Miss Parkinson's hearing. I encouraged him to speak about Mrs. Pat Campbell, who had played in his *Deirdre*. He described her as having 'an ego like a raging tooth' and spoke of her habit of 'throwing tantrums' at rehearsals. On one occasion after a particularly wild 'tantrum' she walked to the footlights and peered out at Yeats who was pacing up and down the stalls of the Abbey Theatre. 'I'd give anything to know what you're thinking' shouted Mrs. Pat. 'I'm thinking,' replied Yeats, 'of that master of a wayside Indian railway-station who sent a message to his Company's headquarters saying: "Tigress on the line; wire instructions".'

I lured him on to Synge and *The Playboy* and the rioting at the first production. Here he was in his element as he re-lived his fight before a growing audience, for some of the players had dropped their racing talk and had brought their chairs nearer to Yeats and the fireplace. His eyes shone as he concluded his story of the fight with the remark: 'I *fought* them, Fallon; my father did a finer thing—he *forgot* them.' At this point Barry Fitzgerald's brother, Arthur Shields, suddenly asked what I thought was a very pointless question. 'I wonder, Mr. Yeats,' he said, in that soft, persuasive, slightly unctuous voice of his, 'I wonder if we will ever see scenes like that in the theatre again?' The question seemed to prick Yeats into increased vitality as a rider's spurs prick a lagging horse. He rose in his seat and lifting his right hand in its familiar pontifical gesture he smiled broadly as he said: 'Shields, I shall tell you that in a fortnight's time!'

'In a fortnight's time?' Good Lord! In a fortnight's time—on February 8th—we were to open with *The Plough and the Stars*. My mind raced back to Sean O'Casey's qualms about the second act and the speech outside the window. I had dismissed these doubts of his as being unimportant, assuring him that the entire scene was a magnificent piece of theatre and that it would be ruinous to interfere with it. But here was Yeats actually looking forward to trouble. Could it be, I wondered, that in his role of Free State Senator he was hoping to use O'Casey's play to score over his Republican enemies? It certainly looked as if something like that was afoot. The following evening I went to 422 North Circular Road and told the author of *The Plough* about Yeats's remark. It didn't seem to worry him unduly. There was some talk of his wanting to make changes in the script and of Yeats

Lady Gregory.

Sean's skill as a caricaturist. *Above:* In this, done in his pre-Abbey days,
he is wearing a beard, following glandular trouble.
Below: The 'Will' here referred to is Barry Fitzgerald (William Shields).

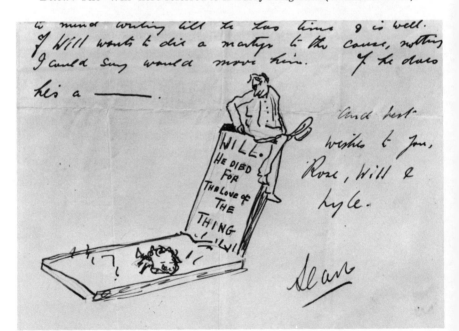

refusing to allow him to do so. I didn't pursue the matter any further. We were in the throes of rehearsal and Sean had other things to worry him.

One of these was that Lennox Robinson had invited himself to '422' to discuss the casting of the play. Sean insisted on my being present and so I went, though I wasn't feeling very happy about it since I knew that Lennox would prefer to be alone with Sean. I was already familiar with Sean's casting. He wanted P. J. Carolan to play the part of Clitheroe. Carolan was a forthright upstanding figure of an actor with a fine commanding voice and presence. His Clitheroe, had he played the part, would have gone down in flames in the General Post Office without the slightest suggestion of nervous hysteria being a part of the character. Sean had written the part of The Covey for F. J. McCormick, who had served him so well as Seumas Shields in *The Gunman,* and as Joxer Daly in *Juno.* He had already told McCormick about The Covey and the actor was understandably looking forward with some relish to the part.

Sean had written the part of Bessie Burgess for Sara Allgood but since Sara was playing in London in *Juno* he was satisfied to accept Maureen Delany as a substitute. He wanted Eileen Crowe to play Mrs. Gogan, Shelah Richards to play Nora Clitheroe, Ria Mooney to play Rosie Redmond, and Kitty Curling (who had just joined the company) to play Mollser. He was particularly anxious that I should play Peter Flynn. Outside of this casting he didn't care who played what. That evening Lennox was in his most skittishly quarrelsome mood. He wouldn't hear of Carolan playing Clitheroe. That part was simply crying out, he said, for F. J. McCormick. Sean protested, but it was no use. Lennox politely pointed out that it was he, and not O'Casey, who would have to direct the play. Who then would play The Covey, Sean asked. Lennox insisted that the part should be played by Michael J. Dolan. This infuriated Sean, but there was little he could do about it. He might have taken the matter up with Lady Gregory who, no doubt, would have seen the casting problem from his angle, but it never occurred to him to do so. There is not a doubt, of course, that Lennox knew at the time that Dolan was O'Casey's greatest enemy. The subsequent publication of Lady Gregory's *Journals,* edited by Lennox himself, have proved this up to the hilt. When the casting had reached this point I could see that I was not likely to get Peter Flynn. Lennox gave the part to Eric Gorman who, incidentally, made an unforgettable characterisation of it. Having made these radical changes in O'Casey's plans for his play Lennox abruptly left.

When I had time to think things over I began to consider that, consciously or unconsciously, Lennox was out to damage O'Casey's play. After all, he was then aware of the fact (unknown to most of us until the publication of Lady Gregory's *Journals*) that Dolan, who was still the manager of the Abbey, was doing his damnedest to prejudice the newly-appointed Government Director, Professor George O'Brien, against the play. He must have known, too, that Dublin was seething with rumours (as had happened before Synge's *The Playboy*) that the Abbey was about to stage one of the most 'immoral' plays in its history. Incidentally, it is interesting to note that in a letter to Lady Gregory published in the *Journals* Dolan attempts to assure her that 'a heated argument about the production of *Man and Superman*' had nothing whatever to do with his attitude to the play. He then went on to say: 'As a matter of fact, when and if it is read to the company, I feel there will be a real difficulty in getting them to play in it. You can rely on me not to try to influence them in any way. Let them judge and decide for themselves.'

Of course, there had been pro- and anti-Sean O'Casey parties in the company even before the *Man and Superman* affair, and well Mr. Dolan knew it. The anti-O'Casey party was the larger of the two. The pro-O'Casey party consisted of Barry Fitzgerald, his brother Arthur Shields, Shelah Richards and myself. There were a few neutrals as well, on the grounds that, after all, a part is a part. This was the atmosphere into which Lennox Robinson's casting of the play dropped to create more discontent. I had told Sean that I would play the minor role of Captain Brennan of the Irish Citizen Army. I knew that Lennox would give it to me for the asking: which, of course, he did. Though the role was a minor one I still maintain that it is a key part in the play and I was particularly anxious to try my talent on that scene of suppressed hysteria when Brennan, having managed to escape from the burning Post Office, returns to the tenement to tell Mrs. Clitheroe of her husband's death. My choosing this part was made solely in the best interests of the author and his play, though Sean's slight reference to it in his autobiography might leave one with the impression that my refusal to face Lennox Robinson, and insist on getting Peter Flynn, arose partly out of timorousness and partly out of disloyalty to him.

Rehearsals of *The Plough* began in an atmosphere of tension, suspicion and distrust. The difficulty of rehearsing part-time and whole-time players together kept Barry Fitzgerald and myself away from some of the distressing 'scenes' that marked the early rehearsals. We heard of course that Eileen Crowe had refused to play Mrs. Gogan 'on moral grounds' and that the part had been given to May Craig. We were not told at the time precisely what those moral grounds were. According to Yeats's letter quoted in Lady Gregory's *Journals*, Miss Crowe objected to say the concluding line in a speech in which Jinnie Gogan protests that 'any kid, livin' or dead, that Jinnie Gogan had since (her marriage) was got between th' bordhers of th' Ten Commandments'. Since the line is a perfectly moral one it is difficult to believe, as stated in the letter, that Miss Crowe's refusal was made 'after consultation with her priest'. No priest in his senses could condemn that line on moral grounds. F. J. McCormick's refusal to use the word 'snotty' in the line: 'Oh, well, if we're goin' to be snotty!' sparked off an unpleasant scene between himself and the author. It seemed hopeless to explain to this sensitive and highly-strung actor that 'snotty', particularly in this context, meant 'short-tempered, annoyed' and that this meaning was confirmed by the Oxford English Dictionary. F. J. McCormick was just as much aware of this fact as Sean O'Casey was, but his irrational refusal was merely a part of the atmosphere of uncooperativeness verging upon hostility in which the rehearsals were held. Since Michael Dolan's attempt to have the play rejected had failed (and Lady Gregory's *Journals* show the length to which he went in this attempt) there was still the possibility that a series of objections by the players might compel the directors to re-consider their decision. There can be little doubt, I think, that Michael Dolan played no small part in trying to bring this situation about, but in face of the directors' determination to stage the play he was bound to fail. Yeats in his letter to Lady Gregory referred to the whole affair as 'an aggravating comedy' and declared that F. J. McCormick would be allowed to leave out the word 'snotty' since Miss Richards, who played Nora Clitheroe and had to use the word in her reply, certainly meant to use it. F. J. McCormick, much against the feelings of Sean O'Casey, substituted 'nosey' for 'snotty' and the directors compromised.

It was after three weeks of this kind of 'aggravating comedy' that the dress rehearsal was held. On the whole it was a rather subdued affair. Lennox Robinson had not over exerted himself so far as the production was concerned. The reason for this is now clear. He must have been familiar at that time (which most of the players were not) with Dolan's attempt to have the play rejected. Very likely, too, he was perturbed by the action of F. J. McCormick (for whom like the rest of us he had a high regard) and by Miss Crowe's refusal to play Jinnie Gogan. For Miss Crowe was at that time his favourite actress. That night when Barry Fitzgerald and I discussed, in our St. Stephen's Green flat, the chances of the play's success, we came to the conclusion that it was impossible to say what might happen. The play might be as great a success as *Juno*; on the other hand it might be a flop. I had told him about the casting conference at '422' and he agreed that Sean's casting was infinitely better. He felt, as I did, that since Sean had written 'The Covey' for F. J. McCormick, that actor should have been given the part. At the dress rehearsal McCormick's Clitheroe had been uncertain and ragged. The actor was clearly overwrought, with the result that the characterisation lost much in manliness, which was possibly not what the author intended. We talked, too, about the fact that Dublin was rife with rumours about the 'immorality' of the play and we agreed that the manager as well as some of the players and back-stage staff were responsible for this state of affairs. We concluded that so far as the Abbey Theatre was concerned Sean O'Casey had few friends. Pensively we went to bed.

On the following evening, Monday February 8th, *The Plough and the Stars* opened at the Abbey Theatre to a 'booked out' house. That evening Senator Yeats had invited to dinner certain members of the Executive Council of the Irish Free State, including its Vice-President, its Finance Minister, and its Lord Chief Justice. They accompanied him to the theatre and occupied seats in the stalls. The play seemed to go reasonably well though a number of us thought we detected a certain air of over-tenseness in the auditorium. At the second interval Yeats led his party of Ministers to the Green Room to meet the players. As they mounted the stairway on the left-hand side of the stalls leading to the pass-door, Joseph Holloway, that inveterate theatre-goer whose diaries are now in our National Library, was heard to voice his Republican sympathies in the clearly audible remark: 'There they go, the bloody murderers!' Otherwise things went as they usually do on a first night. There was generous applause at the end. The author was called for and appeared.

On the Tuesday night there was a certain amount of hissing the purpose of which we couldn't accurately determine. On the Wednesday night the hissing was louder in volume and seemed to be directed against the young prostitute, Rosie Redmond. On Thursday night, February 11th, the storm broke in earnest. Only one reasonably accurate version of the main events of this night ever reached the public eye. In *The Observer* of Sunday, 14th February 1926, Stephen Gwynn published an eye-witness's account sent to him by a friend who was present. This account opens as follows: 'Back from a very rowdy evening, having heard with difficulty two acts (first and last of the four that there are) and much of a Republican demonstration, curiously illogical, headed by Mrs. Sheehy-Skeffington, and also a threat that the Abbey might be blown up, as a cinema was, on the charge of Free State propaganda.'

Various accounts have been written about what took place that evening. Some of these have been magnified beyond recognition. Listening to them I have been reminded of the Duke of Wellington's reaction to another's description of Waterloo, 'My God, was I there at all?' I have had to lend my ears to exciting recitals by people who were not even within the vicinity of the theatre on the evening in question. Incidentally, most of these Gadshill-like descriptions referred to 'the riot which broke out the *second* night of *The Plough*'. But it was the *fourth* night not the second.

Realising that I was, so to speak, right in the middle of history in the making, I decided to note down the important things and to forget the rest. Michael Dolan's quiet delight that the riot had taken place was understandable; so, too, was his order to lower the curtain. F. J. McCormick's attack of neurosis in which he spoke to the audience and protested that the author was to blame and not the players was no surprise to anyone who understood his temperament and realised the strain under which he had unsympathetically rehearsed and played another's part. Barry Fitzgerald's well-aimed blow to the chin of the male rioter who succeeded in mounting the stage; Shelah Richards clawing the hair of the female rioter who accompanied him: these things did happen, but after all, were not so important.

What was important, however, was the attitude of Yeats to the whole affair. Lady Gregory was at her home in Coole, Co. Galway. Lennox Robinson was—well, no one knew where

Lennox was; a fact which now occurs to me as not being without significance since he had directed the play and this was merely its fourth performance. Yeats, I was told, was already on his way to the theatre. I made up my mind to note everything he said and did.

One would imagine that the senior director of a theatre at which rioting was taking place would have looked somewhat perturbed on arriving there in the middle of the riot. Not so Yeats. He was smiling broadly as he came through the stage door and down the seven wooden steps leading to the stage itself. I happened to be standing at the centre of the stage curtain which had been lowered on Michael Dolan's instruction. Yeats began to pace up and down the stage, his eyes gleaming behind their glasses. From the auditorium came a confused medley of sound in which it was possible to distinguish such words as 'shame', 'scandal' and 'insult'. Earlier in the rioting it was obvious that the rioters were divided on the issue at stake. The politicals, led by Hannah Sheehy-Skeffington, were objecting to the play on 'national' grounds—contending that it was a studied insult of the heroes of Easter 1916. Their sticking-post was that point in the play towards the end of the second act where Clitheroe, Lieutenant Langan and Captain Brennan excitedly enter the public house, carrying the banner of The Plough and the Stars, and a green, white and orange Tricolour. This, seemingly, was considered to be an outrage perpetrated on the national flag. Another party, inflamed by the consideration that this was obviously a public row in which anyone could join, decided to make a protest on moral grounds. Poor Rosie Redmond became the target of this particular group. I can still hear the Joxer-Daly-like accents of that fruity Dublin voice that wanted 'that wumman taken offa th' stay-age'.

When Yeats stopped his pacing I said to him: 'This looks like a rather serious state of affairs, Mr. Yeats; what do you propose should be done about it?' He threw back his head, ran his hands through his flowing white hair, looked at me with the light of battle in his eyes, smiled and said: 'Fallon, I am sending for the police; and *this time* it will be *their own* police!' The significance of this emphasis was not lost on me. The old war-horse was hearing once again trumpets sounding the vindication of Synge. This time, too, he was going to fight the rioters, however much his father's memory might have counselled him to forget them.

By now the author of *The Plough* was in the vestibule of the theatre surrounded by a crowd of patriotic women to whom he was appealing for 'one at a time, please; one at a time'. The upshot of their clamour was that they were begging him to write plays that would honour Ireland's heroes not defame them. Knowing that he would be violently opposed to the idea of sending for the police I managed to get word to him that Yeats had already taken that step. Leaving the women in the midst of their clamour he made his way back-stage and told Yeats that he did not want police protection for his play. Yeats pointed out that such protection was needed for the theatre. In any case Sean's protest came too late. The police were already on their way.

As coolly as if he were pacing his eighteenth-century drawing-room in Merrion Square, Yeats walked up and down the stage still smiling to himself, apparently oblivious of the pandemonium that raged beyond the curtain. Suddenly he approached me and said: 'Tell O'Malley (the stage electrician) to raise the curtain the very moment I give the signal.' I told O'Malley. Yeats then placed himself close to the curtain opening and after a moment's pause gave the signal. Actors are trained by instinct and experience in gesture, tempo, and the effective rise and fall of intonations. Armed with such technique they meet dramatic situations on the stage and transmute them for an audience into unforgettable shining moments. That night at the Abbey Theatre even the finest of actors would have stood transfixed in admiration of Yeats's performance. Every gesture, every pause, every inflection, was geared to a tolerance calculated to meet an angry mob. From his well-considered opening, with flashing eyes and upraised arm: 'You have disgraced yourselves again!' to the final hammer-blow: 'This is his (O'Casey's) apotheosis!' it was a performance of genius; regally contemptuous, an emperor rebuking slaves.

Truly magnificent, but what of the author of *The Plough and the Stars*? In the evenings that followed, with their police-protected crowded houses, their smell of quietly-crushed stink bombs, their occasional outbursts of Green Room excitement, I saw little of him. For the first time in the history of the Abbey Theatre audiences were given permission to smoke, this in an attempt to counteract the obnoxious fumes of sulphuretted hydrogen or whatever it was that emerged from the small glass capsules that were to be found splintered each morning under every third or fourth seat. Protestors (mostly students) were still coming to the play. Police in plain-clothes came to the theatre each evening. They had to stand in the aisles; every seat had been booked days in advance. There was no further rioting. Even the hissing had ceased. No arrests were made.

On the Friday night of the first week of *The Plough*, that is the night following the riot, Barry Fitzgerald casually mentioned that he was going to a dance and that he would not be back for supper at our St. Stephen's Green flat. He did not appear for breakfast the next morning. There was nothing unusual in this. Most likely, I considered, he had spent the sleeping end of the night, or morning rather, at his family home at Seafield Road, Clontarf. I went to the office as usual. About noon Barry came to my room accompanied by a police-sergeant. According to the sergeant there had been an I.R.A. raid on the house at Seafield Road in an attempt to capture Barry. But Barry wasn't there. The sergeant had instructions from his superiors to supply us with police protection and to escort us to the Abbey Theatre for the matinee performance.

For more reasons than one the plan didn't appeal to me. Barry didn't seem to be in love with it either. We told the sergeant we intended to go to lunch as usual at the Bonne Bouche restaurant in Dawson Street. From there we would walk to the Abbey. But we didn't want police protection. The sergeant said that in that event the responsibility for what might happen would be ours not his. We agreed to accept the responsibility. It was a fine day with more than a hint of spring in the air. The prospect of playing a matinee and after that a smoke-laden, stink-bombed, evening performance, did not particularly appeal to me. The kidnapping scheme was obviously intended to keep the play from going on. Its organisers probably considered that *The Plough* without Fluther Good would be *Hamlet* without the Prince. As Barry and I slowly walked towards Dawson Street the thought occurred to me that it would be nice to have a few weeks' rest in a cottage in the mountains, somewhere deep in the Synge country, above Glenasmole, maybe, 'listening to the larks and the big thrushes when the days are warm'.

I shared these thoughts with Barry as we walked along, occasionally glancing behind in the hope I might see two or three young men in caps and trench-coats, each man with his right-hand thrust ominously into his trench-coat pocket. Barry was not amused. 'They wouldn't kill us' I argued; 'they merely want to keep us out of the way; and we could both do with a rest.' I failed to arouse his interest. We lunched and walked on to the

94

theatre. The place had an air of being in a state of siege. The police were there, of course; and we were received with much head-shaking at our foolhardiness in walking abroad without protection. Alas for my hopes of a mountain holiday. We were not allowed to leave the theatre in the interval between the matinee and the night show. Walter Rummel, who had been playing at a Celebrity Concert in the Theatre Royal, came across to the Abbey and, following a Green Room tea, entertained us with a recital of Chopin and Beethoven. For all that, I would have preferred to be drinking from a can in a well-guarded cottage in the Wicklow hills and listening to the wind outside 'crying out in the bits of broken trees left from the great storm, and the streams roaring with the rain'.

During the second week of the play I heard a rumour to the effect that one of the Societies (the Literary and Historical, I think) attached to University College, Dublin, proposed to have a debate on *The Plough and the Stars*. I didn't ask for details since I didn't think the affair important enough to bother about. However, Sean told me he knew about it and that he intended to be present. I strongly advised him not to go. I said he would be letting himself down, that in going he would be playing right into the hands of his enemies, that he had written his play, had said what he had to say, and that he should leave it at that. If they wanted to have a debate, let them have a debate, and to hell with them. But Sean didn't see it that way. Happening to meet Yeats in the Green Room I told him that Sean intended to go to the debate and asked him if he or any of the other directors would be there to support him. He said that the directors would not attend and that he had already advised O'Casey to ignore the affair. For some reason or other the debate did not take place in the College. For all I know the College authorities may have banned it on official grounds. It took place instead in the hall attached to Mills' Restaurant in Merrion Row, a venue much favoured for whist drives and dances. I managed to persuade Shelah Richards and Arthur Shields to come with me to represent the Abbey. If Sean was going to go I felt it was up to us to give him at least some moral support. Barry Fitzgerald, I found, had another engagement. I also asked my poet friend, Lyle Donaghy of Trinity College, to come. Lyle was an excellent speaker, was much in favour of the play, and had done some hefty chucking-out on the night of the riot.

When we got to Mills Hall the place was crowded, mostly with undergraduates. There was a small—a very small—sprinkling of theatre folk. Over all there was a flamboyant 'Up the I.R.A.' atmosphere. A Professor Clery of U.C.D. presided. On the platform sat Mrs. Sheehy-Skeffington and near it, if not actually on it, sat Maud Gonne McBride, the once beautiful first love of William Butler Yeats. I could see no sign of Donaghy but I managed to get a glimpse of Sean sitting in the front row to the left of the platform, cap off, head slightly bowed. Undergraduates and others were attempting to crowd into the already crowded hall with the result that the atmosphere was oppressive and the excitement tense.

Mrs. Sheehy-Skeffington led off for the rioters. There was nothing unusual about theatre riots, she said, there were the famous O.P. riots, etc., etc. But the bringing of the national flag into a public house, this was an insult to the men of 1916 who had lain down their lives that this flag might fly in freedom over the Irish people. And there was much more in this strain. When Mrs. Skeffington had brought her defence of the theatre protest to an end the Chairman called on Sean O'Casey. Sean rose from his seat. His face was white and drawn and I noticed that he was attempting to shade his eyes from the light with his right hand. He began to speak—slowly, then hesitantly. I sensed what was wrong. He should have been wearing his cap. The peak of that cap was the only thing that could stand guard between his eyes and the light that penetrated them with agony. He stumbled in his speech; then paused. There was a tense silence. He spoke again. 'I'm sorry' he said. 'I'm . . . I'm not well . . . I can't . . . I can't go on.' There was an audible murmur of sympathy; and then a hubbub from the back of the hall.

I looked around in time to see Lyle Donaghy flailing his way through the crowded centre passage until he reached the platform. 'Mr. Chairman' he said, in a loud clear voice that had both dignity and poetry in its tones, 'with your permission, Sir, I will speak for Sean O'Casey.' He did. In a speech which was a judicious blend of reason and rhetoric he defended *The Plough and the Stars* as a work of art of which the Irish people ought to be justly proud. Then Madame McBride spoke, complaining, rather irrelevantly, I thought, that General Maxwell in command of the British Forces at Easter 1916 had been entertained to tea in the Abbey Theatre Green Room by the actress, Maire O'Neill. This was news to me. Then Sean O'Casey signalled the

Chairman and rose to his feet. He began a speech in which he swiftly and directly turned upon his enemies. He mocked them, laughed at them, ridiculed them, using every weapon in the armoury of satire to pierce their pompous patriotism. It was a speech which in another country might have earned him sudden death yet he resumed his seat to a round of applause every bit as loud, as deep and as sincere, as that which had greeted each of his opponents. I turned to Shelah Richards and said: 'There's Ireland for you!'

Shelah and Arthur Shields had been nudging me to speak but knowing that an actor always needs other people's words to make him sound effective, I was very reluctant to do so. However, after a particularly severe bout of nudging I managed to get on my feet and lamely said something about the impropriety of rioting in a theatre and the danger of creating a panic in which innocent people might be injured, even lose their lives. 'After all' I said, 'protests could be made just as effectively and without danger to an audience in letters written to newspapers.' At this point I was interrupted by Mrs. Sheehy-Skeffington who asked me if I was aware that any letters written by her to the *Irish Times* invariably found their way into the editor's waste-paper basket, while those she sent to *The Irish Independent* were always censored. I proceeded then to say something derogatory about both these newspapers, linking the second of the two with certain of the executions which took place in 1916. As I did so I noticed quite an amount of fuss at the press table. I then rather lamely sat down. It was my first public speech; I swore it would be my last. Next morning, with unbelievable magnanimity. *The Irish Independent* said: 'Mr. G. Fallon also spoke.'

When the meeting, or the debate, or whatever it was, was over, I noticed Mrs. Sheehy-Skeffington in deep conversation with the dramatist. She was explaining to him that only that day someone had placed in her hands a copy of *The Story of the Citizen Army* by P. O'Cathasaigh, telling her that its author was none other than Sean O'Casey. She had been deeply moved by this book; and, no wonder, for in it O'Casey had declared that the real hero of Easter 1916 was not Pearse or Connolly or MacDonagh or McBride, or any of the other signatories of the Proclamation, but Francis Sheehy-Skeffington:

He (Sheehy-Skeffington) was the living antithesis of the Easter Insurrection: a spirit of peace enveloped in the flame and rage and hatred of the contending elements, absolutely free from all its terrifying madness; and yet he was the purified soul of revolt against not only one nation's injustice to another, but he was also the soul of revolt against man's inhumanity to man. And in this blazing pyre of national differences his beautiful nature, as far as this world is concerned, was consumed, leaving behind a hallowed and inspiring memory of the perfect love that casteth out fear, against which there can be no law.

Francis Sheehy-Skeffington, pacifist, had been arrested and shot on orders issued by the strange Major Bowen Colthurst, and his memory had been somewhat overshadowed by the execution of the rebel leaders. There were tears in his widow's eyes when she parted from Sean O'Casey.

As we made our way from the hall Shelah Richards invited Arthur Shields and myself to supper at her home in Fitzwilliam Place. She wanted Sean to come too. We tried to get him but he was caught in conversation with various groups, still standing and arguing, as we moved out into the clear night air. We waited for some moments but he did not appear. Two nights later I called to '422' and there made an interesting discovery. Some weeks previously James Bernard Fagan who was presenting *Juno and the Paycock* at the Fortune Theatre, London, and was anxious to follow it with *The Plough and the Stars*, had written to Sean inviting him over, enclosing a boat and rail ticket with his letter. I had then pressed him to accept the invitation but he was strangely reluctant to do so. He didn't like travelling, he said, he was sure he'd dislike London; of course, on the other hand he might grow to like it and if he grew to like it, he might come to love it, in which event he might never want to come back to Erin. So his argument ran. 'Never mind about that' I said, 'the thing is to go. After all, you've no financial worries now and you can keep this place at little cost *in case* you want to return.' 'Don't be a fool, Gaby' he replied, 'don't you know *damned well* I'd want to return.' For all that, I couldn't persuade him to take the initial step.

However, when I saw him after the Mills Hall affair I found, to my surprise, that all had been settled. It appeared that he had been driven home from the Hall by Frank Hugh O'Donnell. Frank was a successful businessman of Republican sympathies who had tried but failed to become a successful Abbey playwright. Two of his plays had been presented there but neither of them had set the Liffey on fire. A kindly soul, Frank, and free from the corroding jealousy that one too frequently finds amongst literary folk. He subsequently became a Senator during Mr. De Valera's régime and at the moment I write is valiantly carrying on his still successful agency business despite the handicap of partial paralysis. Well, Frank had succeeded where I had failed. Sean was going to London.

When I left him that night—or rather early the next morning —for I know he 'saw me home' and I 'saw him back' again—I reflected that he might well be going among friends and away from enemies. Lady Gregory, I knew, was staunchly on his side, but it was obvious that Robinson was growing jealous of him, and Yeats, if not in the same category, was clearly using O'Casey for his own ends. The attitude of the literary fraternity to Sean was anything but fraternal. When crowds thronged the Abbey Theatre to see his plays the poet, F. R. Higgins (who some years afterwards became the Abbey's first Managing-Director), declared that the place had been 'given over to the mob'. Novelist Liam O'Flaherty in a letter to *The Irish Statesman* stated that in his opinion *The Plough and the Stars* was a bad play and added that 'it would be quite in order for an audience to hiss it as a bad play'. The poet Austin Clarke in a letter to the same journal said that 'several writers of the Irish school believe that Mr. O'Casey's work is a crude exploitation of our poorer people in an Anglo-Irish tradition that is now moribund'.

Some of the ordinary run-of-the-mill criticism had described Sean's plays as photographic realism, the work of a man who knew nothing about dramatic construction. Rumour had it that Sean O'Casey was obviously 'ghosting' for someone else, that an unlettered labourer couldn't possibly have written these plays, that very likely some of the Abbey actors had a hand in the task; one particular piece of gossip went so far as to hint that the plays were written by me, prompted, no doubt, by the fact that Sean and I were to be continually seen in each other's company. His friends among the Abbey players were now reduced to three at most but so far as Abbey audiences were concerned, it was only too obvious from the booking queues that they were solidly behind the author of *Juno* and *The Plough*. But Sean was scarcely thinking of these things as he packed his bag in '422' and made arrangements for a neighbour to look after his room and books during his absence. If he was thinking of anything at all he was thinking that he was about to embark on a strange exciting adventure. He had never been out of Ireland. Indeed, he wasn't much of a traveller in his own country. Understandably, he was feeling nervous at the prospect before him.

I met him by arrangement and travelled with him on the boat-train from Westland Row to Dun Laoghaire. It was said by Tony Quinn, one of my Abbey Theatre colleagues and now an actor living in London, that I accompanied Sean in order to ensure that he wouldn't attempt to jump from the train at one of the intervening stations. There was an element of truth in this piece of humour. Even as the train moved out from Westland Row Sean was protesting his reluctance to leave Ireland, his fear that he might grow to like London, the possibility that he might never return to Ireland again. I paid little heed to this now familiar dirge of his. The thing was to get the author of *Juno* and *The Plough* to the pulsing centre of things, to put this genius of a dramatist, as I believed him to be, right into the theatrical shop-window of the world. It would be one up for the Abbey and one up for Ireland, not to mention several up for Sean O'Casey. For this man, I held, had it in him to write many great plays, indeed was destined to be a great world dramatist.

However, he looked like anything but what I thought a great world dramatist ought to look like as he leaned over the hand-rail of the mail boat and gazed sadly shorewards, wearing his heavy boots, his trench-coat and cap; a woollen muffler concealing his knitted black-and-amber tie. 'You'll write, Gaby?' Of course I would write. 'And you'll write, too, Sean?' To be sure, he would. The seagulls screamed and whirled, and whirled and screamed. The ship's siren gave forth a deep shuddering groan. The water churned as the propellers revolved in their first slow deliberate strokes. The vessel began to move slowly away from the anything-but-quiet land of Erin.' Good-bye, Gaby!' 'Good-bye, Sean; and good luck!' As the vessel, gathering speed, clove the waters of the harbour the seagulls whirled their wildest whirls, screaming their most agitated screams. Another deep groan from the siren, as the vessel, passing the lighthouse at the harbour's mouth, performed a graceful turn, and then, pausing for a moment, fixed its course for Holyhead and for what the future might hold for Sean O'Casey. In what seemed a little while it was nothing but a smudge of smoke on the horizon.

Eight

L EFT to myself I reflected that it was just as well that Sean had finally agreed to go to London. I hadn't told him that early in February I had a letter from Sara Allgood in which the following rather ominous passage had appeared:

> Things seem to be going pretty well here, although I got a hint that we might expect to see the usual fortnight's notice go up as soon as they are not doing as well as they want. Of course managers give me the eternal hump. Unless a play is playing for ever to capacity they are ready at a moment's notice to take the play off. However, quite between ourselves, I don't care if it does come off. They are beginning to get a bit cheap—the players, I mean, and Fagan never calls a rehearsal.

Obviously Sean had just gone in time. His personal appearance would certainly give the play a new lease of life and would possibly have the effect of disciplining the players. Much would depend on how he got on with James Bernard Fagan. Sara had written in the same letter:

> I heard the other day that Sean is getting a swelled head. He was very haughty with Fagan over the rights of *The Plough*. He said to J.B. that his offer was as much use to him as a half lettuce to a starving man. That's a funny thing to say, isn't it? Oh, I do hope that Sean isn't going to become 'difficult'. It's one fault I have to find with the majority of Irish people. The minute they have a little success it seems to go straight to their heads. I did think Sean was different.

Well, perhaps he was, and perhaps he wasn't; I couldn't quite make up my mind. In any case his arrival in London had sounded the trumpet-note of a big success, not a little one. The night he appeared on the stage of the Fortune Theatre it became obvious that the presentation of *Juno* had taken on a new life. He made a speech which was followed by tumultuous applause during which an excited and enthusiastic audience threw flowers at the cast. James Bernard Fagan and his wife, the distinguished London actress Mary Grey, were delighted; as well they might be. *Juno* settled down into a steady run. Then began London's lionising of its author. He was besieged by photographers, newspapermen and radio reporters. He had barely arrived when he was interviewed on the B.B.C. This was followed by special press interviews.

Photogenically and in interview he made first-class copy; his appearance, background, and originality in reply to questions, saw to that. He was slightly bewildered by London's lifts, taxicabs, restaurants and by seeing his photograph almost everywhere he went. It's not every week of the year or year of the century that London finds a tenement-dweller, ex-labourer genius. The Fagans, partly through kindness, no doubt, and partly to bask in reflected glory, attempted to take him into protective custody, to direct his steps in the way they thought they should go through London's West End. Little did they know our Sean, God help them! They might as well have tried to lead a tiger on a string. Anyway, he was making his own friends in London, bigger fry than the Fagans. Lady Gregory had crossed to London a few days after Sean had arrived there. After paying a visit to the Fortune Theatre and assuring herself that, her beloved Sara Allgood excepted, this *Juno* wasn't half as good as the Abbey's presentation, she invited Sean to lunch. She was anxious, no doubt, to make certain that in the first place Sean was thoroughly comfortable in his new surroundings, and, in the second, that whatever happened he would not neglect to write more plays for her little Abbey Theatre.

Sean was able to tell Her Ladyship that on the following night he was going to see Boughton's *The Immortal Hour* in the company of Lady Londonderry at whose drawing-rooms he had become the quizzical and quietly outstanding attraction if one is to accept all he tells us in his *Rose and Crown*.

Before the end of the month he had been elected a member of The Garrick Club and could preen himself on the fact that he had had to ¦make Maurice Macmillan (of the publishing firm who had a great regard for Sean) wait a whole fortnight for a luncheon appointment. There seemed to be no end to the interviews but he took them all in his stride. One of those who interviewed Sean at that time was the young Beverley Nichols, who subsequently published his 'Profile' along with others in his book entitled, I think, *Twenty-five*. Writing a few years ago about

The Plough and the Stars Act (II)
Left to right:
Patrick Layde (The Covey),
Eileen Crowe (Bessie Burgess),
Michael O'Brien (Barman),
Marie Kean (Mrs Gogan),
Philip O'Flynn (Fluther Good).

Eileen Reynolds Carey.

this interview in an issue of *Woman's Own* Nichols said that he asked the dramatist 'to tea at a Corner House, partly because I was broke and partly because, even if I hadn't been, I couldn't somehow visualise him at the Ritz'. Nichols pointed out that years later in his autobiography Sean recalled that tea party in the most scathing terms. 'Apparently, I had given him the impression of a la-dee-dah socialite, and he was particularly scornful about the fact that I was wearing a smart pair of gloves.' Nichols then adds: 'Dear Sean O'Casey, for your information, I have never worn or even carried a pair of gloves in my life, and never shall unless you count the gardening variety, which are useful when one's dealing with nettles.'

Sean was appalled at the 'ignorance' of this prim, good-looking product of Marlborough School and Oxford University. For he tells us in his autobiography that there was 'not a word from this gem-like lad about England's greater children. Shakespeare unmentioned; Shelley apparently forgotten; Milton ignored: neither could Sean see a sign of a scene from a Constable or a Cotman livening the iris of his boyish eye.' Which despite Marlborough and Oxford was expecting rather much from a young and impecunious journalist across the marble-topped table of a London Corner House. But perhaps Nichols wasn't the particular kind of la-dee-dah socialite, gloved or ungloved, that Sean was keen on meeting at that time. After all he was beginning to get the feel of the rich carpets of Londonderry House under his feet, walking 'where the wines were rare and the fittings gorgeous; where the vast rooms were flounced and friezed by the gorgeous gowns of many ladies, floors patterning elegantly with sandalled shoes of crimson satin or filigree of gold, the air swooning with the moist sweetness of affectionate perfumes and all was lit up by jewelled orders looking alive on the coats of costly men.' Certainly '422' was never like this; neither was the Abbey Theatre vestibule nor the Broadway Soda Fountain Parlour in O'Connell Street; even Lady Gregory's beloved Coole with the Lake and the Seven Woods thrown in must have seemed shabby by comparison.

Yet he was finding at times that London could be a lonely city, that people in it were so damned busy that they hadn't time to make friends. But the mood was merely a passing one, for the first night of *The Plough* which, in the middle of May, followed *Juno*, was an outstanding success, and in the midst of added laurels Sean found himself sitting for his portrait to that 'fine, simple, and great man' Augustus John. What is more, Father Kearney, the beloved Parish Priest of Maiden Lane (the 'Actors' Church') had sat through the entire dress rehearsal of *The Plough* and found it to be 'wonderful, wonderful and intensely Catholic'. Let Dublin's 'Holy Joes' put that in their hymn books and sing it. And now here he was shifting digs from W.C.1 to S.W.3, flitting from Bloomsbury to Chelsea, and thinking of stopping in London till God called him away. Sometimes though he is tired and a little weary of many things. His eyes still give him trouble yet he has no difficulty in focusing them in order to see the beauty of that darlin' girl, Margaret Burke Sheridan, who had come from a worshipping Milan to sing in Covent Garden. Margaret had gone to see her old friends Sara Allgood and Maire O'Neill in *The Plough* and left the theatre feeling proud not only of these great actresses but of Ireland's new dramatist.

He thinks he might possibly go over to Dublin for a few days; on the other hand he might not. He has lots of things to do in London, for instance to speak in a few days' time at a London Critics' dinner, to have lunch next week with Bernard Shaw and Augustus John. John's portrait has turned out to be a magnificent piece of work, embarrassingly vivid, a face wearing a look of (to Sean) shuddering agony. John slaps him on the back and praises him for breaking every damned rule of the stage. His eyes are giving him hell; but he allows himself to be persuaded to visit the specialist, Bishop Harman, with the result that he is now wearing spectacles, no less. He is hurt by the fact that F. J. McCormick and Eileen Crowe have been visiting London and haven't called to see him, haven't even asked after him. He is worried too by the fact that except for letters to him I have been neglecting the writing trade. And why did I leave my St. Stephen's Green flat and the comradeship of Barry Fitzgerald? (The fact is, of course—though I haven't told Sean—that I am thinking of getting married. Indeed preparations are well on the way to that event.) I have a feeling that Dublin is not likely to see Sean for a long time. Well, perhaps this is only as it should be; he is much too big a fish for our little Abbey pond. I shall miss him all the same; and unless I am very much mistaken he will miss Dublin. He may even miss me.

I knew it was bound to happen; Sean has broken with the Fagans. Some trouble over the Fortune Theatre and now *The*

Plough is to be transferred to the New Theatre. In any case the Fagans are comparatively small fry from the theatrical point of view and he is the author of what James Agate called 'two blazing masterpieces . . . the greatest since the Elizabethans'. And so he has taken matters into his own hands and is coming to Dublin as soon as he can to bring over his things for residence in London. So there it is: 'Goodbye the Abbey Theatre, farewell N.C. Rd., it's a long way to S.W. London, but my heart's right there!' Had this anything to do, I wonder, with my writing to him to say that I intended to get married on July 1st? I wonder. Isn't it strange, he reflects, that all his Irish friends have so quickly faded from his memory—'all except you'. Well, the poor fellow hadn't very many Irish friends if one disregards the thousands who flocked and are still flocking to his plays here.

And now here he is in person just for a few days to gather up a handful of things, to say goodbye for ever to '422' and, incidentally, to meet Mrs. Fallon. Perhaps we were a little shy of each other, somewhat subdued; at all events there was none of the old boisterousness in this meeting. Perhaps, too, we lacked the time to thaw out; perhaps the presence of a third party made things difficult. After all, he had only been four months away; and then he was here merely to be gone again. He thought I had done the right thing in getting married; but I mustn't neglect writing. 'You have it in you to write; and don't forget what happens to the man who puts his hand to the plough and then looks back.' Well, what writing had he done in London? Damn all; but then, like Martha, he had been busy about many things. He had ideas for a play, however; no, he wouldn't talk about that now. Had he met anyone of the opposite sex in London that he felt attracted towards? No, not one. Was all his talk about being a 'great man for the wimmin' just idle boasting? I had long suspected that it was, just something with which to scandalise the 'holy Joes'. And these he loved to scandalise. Well, it was a short visit and, on both sides, a rather self-conscious one. We seemed to be closer to each other on paper now than face to face.

It was well into August 1926 before he got things straightened out in his South Kensington flat. Many tasks had to be faced. His typewriter had to be set up where the light would fall favourably; his books—he had invested in a complete set of Maupassant—had to be shelved in proper order; his recently purchased copy of Georgione's *Sleeping Venus* ('Oh, that's a shockin' picture!') hung in a place of honour. *The Plough* finished its West End run at the beginning of September and the company took *Juno* on a tour of the English provinces. By the end of the month he had found a good opening for the first act of a new play, with the ideas for each succeeding act already spaced out in his mind. By January of the following year the play—in which two major characters insisted on shadowing the main theme—was going well. It was building itself around a song he had heard sung by a Scotsman in whose blood ran the salt of a thousand seas. But he still had to deal with many other things, requests from Russia, Germany and Sweden for translation rights for the 'blazing masterpieces'. Why wouldn't I go over for a few days? I could assure Mrs. Fallon that he wouldn't lead me into any trouble. We could have a quiet time and a gentle talk. He himself might hop over to Dublin for a few days later on. Could I recommend comfortable accommodation, a room in which to sleep and one in which to receive friends? It was difficult, if not impossible, to express oneself in letters. It would have to be a talk or nothing.

Now what did this all add up to? Was the man feeling lonely? Did he hanker to be back again among Shaw's 'granite rocks and magenta heather' and the dreaming, dreaming, dreaming? 'I know' said Aeschylus in 500 B.C. 'how men in exile feed on dreams.' Let him come home then and, renting a comfortable flat in Dublin, finish his play here. Nothing of the kind. I was completely off-centre or egotistically on it in asking him to return. The invitation was kind and grand but selfish. No, he would tell me all, or nearly all, when he'd see me. Well, there was no chance of his seeing me, at all events in London, for my annual leave in the Service was three weeks and most of this was already committed. After all I was a married man now with all the responsibilities attached to that situation. The mystery—if it was a mystery—would have to wait. I was content to accept his assurance that he was *not* longing to return to Dublin and that he was *not* hankering after London's fleshpots either, that Sean here was just the same as Sean there, and that having finished the first act he was now starting the second act of the new play.

It was four months before the mystery unfolded itself and by that time, following a new idea for the second act of his play, he had completely re-written it. He was now off on the third act and giving it all the attention he could spare, for there were distractions, or rather there was an attraction; for, would you believe it, he had been 'keeping company' with a 'pretty' girl and it was possible that Dublin might see the two of them for a week some day soon. Well, of course, Dublin did; and Dublin saw them as Mr. and Mrs. Sean O'Casey. Surgeon-poet Oliver St. John Gogarty very kindly met them at Dun Laoghaire and drove them in his Bentley to the Claremont Hotel, Howth. Across the bay in Killiney where I was now living I received a message asking me to call at the Claremont. Well, here he was, or, rather, here they were. 'Pretty' was hardly the right word for Mrs. O'Casey; Eileen Reynolds Carey was decidedly beautiful. Of Irish stock, though London born, Eileen was a Roman Catholic and the marriage had taken place in the Church of the Most Holy Redeemer in Chelsea. It was obvious that the newly-weds were very much in love with each other. A dinner party for the Fallons was arranged by the O'Casey's at Jammet's celebrated restaurant. Sean was in his old boisterous form again. He insisted on the four of us driving 'in style' on an 'outside car' when we arrived at Amiens Street Station on the train from Howth. As we passed up Abbey Street at a right spanking pace—the mare had just had a feed of oats—Sean asked the jarvey what building that was on the left. 'That's the Abbey The-atre, sorr; where they do be puttin' on the plays?' 'Would you believe that now!' replied the dramatist. The week went all too quickly. Sean and Eileen returned to London; she to look for a suitable house, he to get on with his new play and arrange for an American tour of *The Plough*.

Since the company was to sail on November 10th there was a hurried conference concerning the cast. Sean would like some of the Abbey players to join forces with Allgood, O'Neill, Sinclair and the rest. Eventually Shelah Richards and Ria Mooney went in their original roles (Nora Clitheroe and Rosie Redmond) and Michael Scott, teetering on the threshold of his architectural career—he is the designer, with the French architect, Pierre Sonrel, of the new Abbey Theatre—went with a twofold purpose, to feast his eyes on U.S. architecture, and to play the part of Commandant Jack Clitheroe. By December Sean was putting the finishing touches to the final pages of his new play preparatory to selecting and re-modelling the whole. After Christmas Eileen and he hoped to take up residence in St. John's Wood, at 19 Woronzow Road, to which end he hoped the Lord would be kind enough to send him some American dollars.

Towards the end of 1927 I was beginning to feel that I'd had enough of the Abbey Theatre. Being a part-time actor was sufficiently arduous when one lived within convenient distance of Dublin Castle and its daily 9.30 a.m. to 5 p.m. of Civil Servicing. Having to commute to and from Killiney was a different matter. As often as not now I found myself leaving home at 8.15 in the morning and returning by the last train from Westland Row station with the ground-work of my make-up still showing some of its traces on face and collar and the main meal of the day facing me a few moments short of midnight. Besides I had another reason. I was thoroughly fed-up with playing in plays that Lady Gregory in her *Journals* courageously described as 'rubbish'. This second reason was stronger than the first and so I sent in my resignation to Lennox Robinson making it quite clear that the Abbey's 'rubbish' was at the heart of the matter. Lennox sent me a charming acknowledgment telling me what a fine actor I was, how much the Abbey would miss me, an hoping I would change my mind and return there *as soon as I was better*. A typical Lennox touch this to counteract the 'rubbish' charge. Illness was no part of my reason.

However illness wasn't too far off for in February of the following year I went down rather badly with sinus trouble. Strongly advised by my doctor to see a specialist I presented myself to the one specialist I knew, Oliver St. John Gogarty. Oliver was regularly visiting London and calling at 19 Woronzow Road whose occupant had described him as a great skin and a good surgeon. I needed no assurance about Oliver. I had known him a little longer than Sean and knew things about his surgical skill and his broad charitable outlook that few who knew him knew. Nevertheless it was kind of Sean to warn Oliver that I was no Rockefeller. Anyway, Oliver sharpened up his knives and gadgets; the job was done, and I felt much the better of it. Since acting was no longer my suit I decided to study the theatre from every possible angle, and in the meantime—from sheer financial necessity—to take up any jobs of play production that the amateur theatre offered. I had now a wife and a son to consider.

Suddenly word came from across the water that the title of the new play was *The Silver Tassie*, that its author had been studying Plainsong and Gregorian chant, that it had been sent for final typing and would I like to play a part in it even though I had left the Abbey. Yes, he was as certain of acceptance as that; and so, indeed, was I. But *Silver Tassie* or no, I felt I just couldn't face the Abbey again and I told him so. On St. Patrick's Day, 17th March 1928, he sent his play to the Abbey at the same time sending the rough copy to me with the remark: 'I think it is by far the best work I have yet done.' And so, indeed, did I. I read the play at least six times to various groups of friends who were in complete agreement with the author's opinion of it. It's second act held a particular fascination for me. Surely, I thought, this must be the most blistering condemnation of war written in our time. I could sense the influence of Toller and the clear indication that O'Casey was determined to break away from the conventions of naturalism. I remembered what he told me about the idea which struck him in the middle of writing the second act which led him to reconsider and completely re-write the act. From one point of view I thought it a pity that he hadn't re-written the entire play, treating the whole thing in an expressionistic manner (for there are very definite touches of expressionism in Acts 1, 3 and 4); and yet on second thoughts he was quite right to frame his war scene with, as Granville Barker has noted, 'its symbolism of sense and character and its choric rhythms of speech and movement' with three acts of naturalism. The total effect is that the war scene stands out with striking horror which was, no doubt, what the subconscious dramatist in O'Casey intended. Anyway, the problem—if problem it was—could be resolved by a sensitive director by which I mean one with a sincere feeling for the play.

To say that the Abbey's rejection of the play shocked me is to put the matter very mildly indeed. Even if the play was a bad one—which it most certainly was not—I considered that the theatre owed it to O'Casey to allow the audience to decide for itself. When the correspondence between the theatre directors and the author finally emerged (Sean sent me copies of the letters before publication) it became all too clear that, so to speak, the villain of the piece was Yeats. Lady Gregory, though only partly in love with the play, was obviously in sympathy with the dramatist. Lennox Robinson was at liberty to side with either of his fellow-directors. He elected to vote with Yeats. It is Sean O'Casey's contention that Yeats was influenced in his decision by Robinson but this I refuse to believe for a single moment. Yeats was wholly his own master in such matters. The idea that he acted as pennyboy for Lennox is part of the salve which the author of *The Silver Tassie* finds necessary to apply to the deep and still-open wound inflicted by the rejection. That Robinson may have been pleased at Yeats's decision is another matter; that he was prepared to support it goes without saying: but that he moved Yeats to it is as likely as that he moved the rock of Gibraltar.

Whatever about Lady Gregory's personal feelings towards Sean O'Casey it is clear from her published *Journals* that her opinion of the play was exactly the same as Lennox Robinson's. She writes: 'Sean O'Casey's play came yesterday. I read it through. Well, I absolutely agree with Lennox Robinson's criticism, the beginning fine, the first two acts; then such a falling off, especially in the last, the "persons" lost in "rowdiness".' She then goes on to say: 'I must have written something like this to Lennox Robinson for he writes in return: "I was very relieved to get your letter today and to find that you agreed with me about O'Casey's play. If you had disagreed with me I should have suspected myself of all sorts of horrid subconscious feelings".' That last sentence should clear Lennox of any suspicion of jealousy. His letter to Lady Gregory continues: 'I shall send the play at once to W. B. Yeats and avoid writing to Sean until he has read it.'

Well Yeats read the play and sent 'Dear Casey' his opinion of it not even realising that his omission of the 'O' in O'Casey was in itself an insult. Lady Gregory's comment on it was as follows:

Yesterday Yeats's letter came with his criticism of Sean O'Casey's play. I've made a copy of it. It shows him in full (mental) health again. I have now sent it to Sean. Of course, it must be a severe blow, but I believe he will feel its force, its 'integrity', and be grateful in the end. I have sent him also Lennox Robinson's less forcible outcries . . . But I had a bad night or early morning thinking of the disappointment and shock he will feel.

Lady Gregory was right though she underestimated the disappointment and the shock. Sean felt the force of Yeats's letter though not in Lady Gregory's sense. It was indeed a severe blow and in some respects a mortal one, for it stabilised his exile, deprived him of the theatre workshop he had in the Abbey, and ultimately left him to experiment *in vacuo* with an expressionistic technique of which he was never the complete master. To a great extent it killed that inner confidence in himself as a dramatist which the success of *Juno* and *The Plough* had helped to build. There was little I could do to staunch the wound though I did what I could. I was furiously in disagreement with the Abbey's directors. With all its faults thick upon it *The Silver Tassie* was the work of a master and the Abbey owed it to Sean O'Casey to put it on and let the audiences judge it for themselves. There was a fourth opinion but it was one that hardly mattered. George O'Brien, the director who objected to *The Plough and the Stars*, resigned from the Abbey Theatre directorate in February 1927, and was replaced by the Trinity College Professor, Walter Fitzwilliam Starkie, who acted on the Board as government director. Starkie, professing annoyance that his opinion had not been sought by his fellow-directors (he was in Spain at the time) published a belated report suggesting that the play should be produced. In the course of this he wrote: 'I feel that the author had a great idea at the back of his mind and fugitive symbols presented themselves to him but he was not able to create, as he did before, living men and women. The play seems to me to decline act by act from the beginning . . .' words which were not likely to endear him to Sean O'Casey who swept aside as of no importance this Mr. Facing-Both-Ways attitude. Ernest Blythe, the Free State Minister of Finance (and now Managing Director of the Abbey Theatre) wrote to him to say that he couldn't understand the rejection of *The Silver Tassie* by the Abbey, adding that he thought it a powerful and moving play; which shows, said Sean, that Ernest Blythe knows more about drama than Yeats or Robinson or Starkie or Lady Gregory. But the words of Yeats's letter had eaten their way into the dramatist's soul and as Sean's Mr. Grigson would say 'there was no blottin' them out'.

Students of theatre would do well to examine Yeats's and O'Casey's letters, for each of them, though written in opposition, contain important fundamentals of theatre. So far as these are concerned Yeats is right but O'Casey is by no means wrong. Yeats opposes didacticism, declaring that dramatic action must burn up the author's opinions. 'While he is writing he has no business to know anything that is not a portion of that action.' And then he goes on to say this:

Do you suppose for one moment that Shakespeare educated Hamlet and King Lear by telling them what he thought and believed? As I see it Hamlet and Lear educated Shakespeare, and I have no doubt that in the process of that education he found out that he was an altogether different man to what he thought himself, and had altogether different beliefs. A dramatist can help his characters to educate him by

III

thinking and studying everything that gives them the language they are groping for through his hands and eyes, but the control must be theirs, and that is why the ancient philosophers thought a poet or a dramatist Daemon-possessed.

Now this was particularly interesting to me because I had watched at first hand the process by which the characters in *Juno* (and to some extent those in *The Plough*) were educating Sean O'Casey, at least in the sense in which he set out to do one thing while they were intent on doing another. Again, too, in his total unawareness of their effect and stature even after seeing them in action on the stage. Those who will go to the trouble of comparing the militant patriot revealed in the collection of writings in *Feathers from the Green Crow* with the man whose deep sympathy for the human condition reveals itself in *Juno* and *The Plough* (and indeed in *The Silver Tassie*) will grasp what Yeats was getting at when he made the point that in the process of creating characters in action the dramatist often finds that he is an altogether different man to what he thought himself, and has altogether different beliefs. Certainly in *Juno* and *The Plough* (and again I add *The Silver Tassie*) Sean O'Casey was fulfilling Yeats's dictum that a dramatist helps the characters to educate him by thinking and studying everything that gives them the language they are groping for through his hands and eyes.

That Sean was stunned and hurt and angry when he received Yeats's letter is to put it very mildly indeed. He had every reason to feel that way; for he had almost finished the play when he received a visit from Lennox Robinson who had called on him in his flat in South Kensington to check up on rumours running round Dublin that Sean's new play would not be given to the Abbey Theatre. I knew that these rumours were false and I had told many of my former colleagues at the Abbey that Sean had no intention of turning his back on the theatre to which he owed so much and which owed so much more to him. But the directors were not assured. And so some time after Robinson's visit Yeats appeared at the London Court Theatre during the run of an O'Casey play and asked to see Sean who happened to be in the office. He told Sean that he had come specifically to ask if the new play would be given to the Abbey. He made the point that it would be a great pity if O'Casey decided to ignore the Abbey. Sean assured Yeats that this was not likely to happen. Yeats seemed pleased and asked Sean what the new play was about. Was it set in Dublin? Sean had given him an outline of each of the four acts and emphasised the fact that the second act took place 'Behind the trenches, in the Rest Camps, out in France'. 'And not a word or a suggestion from him then that I wasn't interested in the Great War.'

Well, Sean hit back, and made certain that he was hitting hard. Every phrase in his letter was geared to topple Yeats off the pedestal from which he had proffered his dramaturgic advice to the author of *Juno* and *The Plough*. I had told Sean at the time that someone close to the Abbey had said that *The Silver Tassie* was 'just not an O'Casey play'. To this he had replied that if the play was not an O'Casey play his letter to Yeats was an O'Casey letter. It certainly was; from its opening gambit in which he hangs the preliminaries of Yeats's letter 'up on the stars' until towards the end he refers to Yeats's theories of drama as infants which he has held in his (O'Casey's) arms 'a thousand times and they are all the same—fat, lifeless, wrinkled things that give one a pain in the belly looking at them'. He thrust home with vehemence on the question of an author's 'opinions' which Yeats held should be consumed in the fire of dramatic action by pointing out that the Abbey Theatre had produced plays that 'were packed skin-tight with the author's opinions—the plays of Shaw, for instance'.

Answering the major charge that he was not interested in the Great War; 'You never stood on its battlefields' Yeats had written; he questioned the writer's seriousness. 'Were you serious when you dictated that—really serious now? Was Shakespeare at Actium or Phillipi; was G. B. Shaw in the boats with the French, or in the forts with the British when St. Joan and Dunois made the attack that relieved Orleans?' And, indeed had he thought of it he might have added the instance of Stephen Crane and *The Red Badge of Courage*. But with Sean in anger the temptation to ridicule is never too far away, and so he added: 'And someone, I think, wrote a poem about Tir nan nog who never took a header into the Land of Youth.' However he condescended to tell Yeats about some of the contacts from which his interest in the Great War came. 'I have talked and walked and smoked and sung with the blue-suited wounded men fresh from the front. I've been with the armless, the legless, the blind, the gassed, and the shell-shocked; with one with a head bored by shrapnel who had to tack east and tack west before he could reach the point he wished to get to; with one whose head rocked like a frantic moving pendulum . . .' I, too, had had contact with such men through membership of the British Red Cross, though my duties (mostly on hospital trains and ships) had never taken me to France. Sean and I had often discussed such cases around the fire in '422'. Indeed, it was after one of these evenings that he again turned to that passage in Shakespeare's *Henry V* from which the germ of the idea for *The Silver Tassie* first sprouted. Most of my colleagues in the Civil Service were men who were fortunate to have survived that 1914–1918 holocaust, men who never tired of talking of their experiences. Indeed, I had a theory which I expounded to Sean that life ceased for these men at 11 a.m. on the 11th November 1918, that the only reality they knew was that in which death had walked continually by their side. There was very little about those years in France which I did not know and Sean and I had often swapped our knowledge.

The rejection of *The Silver Tassie* was a blow to my belief in the judgment of the Abbey Theatre, at least in that expressed by the directors. The upshot of the rejection was that a number of people saw in it an opportunity of making some ready money and perhaps a little distinction for themselves by producing the play in another Dublin theatre. The result was that I received many requests from professional and amateur theatre organisations to use my influence with the author to secure the rights of presentation. These I refused. So far as Sean was concerned he refused to be sympathised with. He protested that the rejection was not such a terrible blow after all, that it was more than partly expected, that in his own 'peculiar, canny way' he had sensed all that was going to happen. This attitude on Sean's part led me to suspect a touch of maliciousness in Yeats's rejection. Did he think that Sean had become a little too big for his boots, bigger at all events than the theatre that had given him birth? Or was he annoyed at the fact that negotiations for the London production of the play had been set on foot *before* the Abbey Theatre had given its opinion of it? Sir Barry Jackson had asked for a first glimpse at the script, but declaring it to be 'a fine play . . . a terrible play' felt that he dare not put it on—'an English audience couldn't stand it.' Then C. B. Cochran became interested and his interest held, despite the Abbey's rejection, for Sean put the rejection letters before him as soon as they came.

Rumours of the Cochran interest had reached Dublin. Had these influenced Yeats? It is difficult to say. When he met Sean in London and had asked about the new play he had just given a lecture to the Irish Literary Society there in which he had pleaded for a new direction in Irish drama. Well, here was a new direction coming from one of the greatest of the Abbey's playwrights and here was Yeats turning it down. Here, too, was Sean saying that he had suspected all along the line that this was going to happen. Here was a problem having a sniff of skulduggery about it. For knowing how I felt about the rejection and that I was likely to join in the controversy which followed it Sean warned me to keep out of the row 'for you'd never know how it might affect you in your job'. Since my 'job' was in the Civil Service this warning might seem at first sight wholly unwarranted, but Dublin is a small place and Ireland at that time was enjoying the first fruits of freedom, and then as now a deep interest in the theatre was to be met with in every place.

So I confined myself to keeping my ear close to the ground and sending Sean all the news I could pick up. The letters had already appeared in *The Observer* and when a few days later they appeared in George Russell's *The Irish Statesman* (after Yeats threatening to sue both Russell and O'Casey if they appeared there) I sent him a number of copies. Macmillans were at this time handling the page proofs of the play but the Abbey's rejection caused no hold-up in publication though Sean gave the firm the option of withdrawal. Sean made much of the fact that Yeats's rejection—on account of the stature of the poet in literary circles—had done him considerable harm but I doubted this at that time and I still doubt it. After all, Bernard Shaw, then at the peak-point of fame, was strongly on his side. Shaw wrote a letter of protest to the Abbey's directors and asked Sean not to be too hard on them comparing them to 'to people who knew your uncle when you were a child (so to speak)' and 'always want to correct your exercises'. Writing in *The Irish Statesman* Sean summed up the rejection as follows: 'It was rejected because W. B. Yeats and Lennox Robinson couldn't see or wouldn't see, that the play was worthy of production by the Abbey Theatre; that was the ethical reason for its rejection.' Dismissing the Abbey's professed concern for his reputation as a dramatist Sean pointed out that this concern 'vanishes with its tail down when we remember that the replies to the Abbey's criticisms showed that O'Casey was prepared to risk his reputation, which was all his own business and none of theirs, to which they refused to respond by producing the play to show whether their opinions were right or wrong.'

Many theories have been advanced as to what might have happened had *The Silver Tassie* been accepted in the first instance. Some think that the dramatist would have returned to Ireland. It is difficult to say. Some contend that its acceptance would have allowed him to stabilise his position vis-à-vis 'expressionism'; though, there are others who stoutly maintain that he should never have abandoned 'naturalism'. My own belief is that the rejection was disastrous for both O'Casey and the Abbey Theatre. The Abbey's attitude by denying the dramatist's right to experiment with form bogged down the theatre in the rut of 'naturalism' and deprived up-and-coming dramatists of the right of being venturesome. Be that as it may it has always seemed strange to me that people who were prepared to accept the modern vocabulary, so to speak, in a Picasso, a Henry Moore or a Jack Yeats, were often those who were most determined that nineteenth century naturalism must not be allowed to pass from the theatre.

Had the acceptance of *The Silver Tassie* succeeded in bringing its author back to live in Ireland there is not a doubt that he would in the long run have been a far greater dramatist. In the first place he would have escaped that love-hatred which is bred in the bitterness of exile. In the second place it is now clear that his most inspirational material lay on this side of the Irish Sea. Time was when I used to reason that if one sends a good painter to another country he is just as likely to be as good a painter in that place as he was at home. Now I doubt this reasoning at least in so far as Sean O'Casey, dramatist, is concerned. Ploughing his native furrow he won, like Spain's Lorca and many others who did likewise, his international fame. Unlike others he never took kindly to his new surroundings. He spent too much of his time looking homewards. His most productive material was here. James Joyce succeeded in bringing his Dublin away with him; Sean O'Casey regrettably left his behind. He was troubled too by another spirit, by a hankering for material which he would like to make his own. In her introduction to her novel *Alexander's Bridge*, the American writer, the late Willa Cather, points out that a writer particularly in the beginning of his career is often more interested in his discoveries about his art than in the homely truths which have been about him from his cradle. Sean O'Casey's almost contemptuous rejection of his two early masterpieces in favour of his later experiments is a case in point. As Willa Cather puts it: 'When a writer once begins to work with his own material, he realises that, no matter what his literary excursions may have been, he has been working it from the beginning—by living it.' It is now my confirmed opinion that from *The Silver Tassie* onwards Sean O'Casey was no longer living his material in his plays. He was, by and large, going on literary excursions. But it was not of this I was thinking when, brimming over with enthusiasm for the rejected play, I at last accepted one of his many invitations to visit him in London and at the same time to see *The Silver Tassie* which was then running at the Apollo Theatre. How could I refuse him? A few weeks previously I had received from him a copy of the published text. Inscribed on its fly-leaf was the following: 'To Gaby Fallon, whose Friendship and Talent was and is a wonderful gift to his affectionate friend and buttie, Sean O'Casey.'

Nine

IF I harboured any suspicions (I didn't) that the Sean O'Casey I knew had suffered a sea-change in coming to London, if I thought (as many did) that he had, as we say, lost the run of himself as a result of fortune, fame and the friendship of the great, such suspicions and such thoughts would have been dispelled the very moment I crossed the threshold of 19 Woronzow Road, St. John's Wood. For here was a welcome that *was* a welcome, with Eileen, calmly radiant, helping him to reinforce it. 'We will make you as comfortable as love and circumstances will permit.' And both love and circumstances were generously steering them towards that end. Indeed, circumstances were greatly altered so far as Sean was concerned, at least to the extent of a comfortable and artistically furnished large double house with a housekeeper and a staff of three, including a Nannie for my now nine-months-old godson, Breon O'Casey. (His mother, Eileen, had at his baptism insisted on this spiritual relationship.)

Well, well, there was so much and so much to talk and talk and talk about. Inevitably *The Tassie* opened our conversations. It was still going well at the Apollo, he said: Laughton playing Harry Heegan with great strength and pathos. Shaw had been to it and said: 'It is the greatest play I have ever seen.' So much, then, for Mister-me-Friend William the-Abbey-Theatre Butler Yeats and his assistant Lennox Robinson. This was the mood but one could see that the wound had gone deep. The rejection had come at a difficult moment; Eileen and he were momentarily expecting the birth of Breon; a defective and old-fashioned bathroom boiler had burst almost taking with it the lives of mother and child. And on top of this Yeats's letter of rejection.

The Sean of Woronzow Road.

Sean in the 'belly of Bucks'.

'All the same' said Sean, 'it must have been a bit of a shock for the poet when he read my sentences hammering at the very door of his heart. I'm afraid that this outburst had been secretly seething in my heart for quite a long while; Yeats's cool impudence has only itself to blame in opening the thunderflow of resentment.' Why 'for a long while' I asked myself; I didn't ask him. Had he been feeling that the attitude of the Abbey Theatre directors had been much too condescending towards him? Was he resentful of the fact that the Senator in Yeats had used *The Plough* to provoke his political enemies? At all events he was convinced, though he offered me no foundation for this conviction, that Yeats and Robinson had between them made up their minds that if O'Casey's new play was a bad one they would accept it and that if it was a good one they would reject it. I was intrigued by his description of Yeats's attempt to work through Shaw to have *The Silver Tassie* re-submitted to the Abbey. The theatre had made a mistake, said Yeats; if Shaw could manage to induce Sean to re-submit the play all would be forgiven and forgotten. Sean told Shaw to tell the Abbey to write for the play. Armed with this letter Sean would be in a position to tell the world about a Poet and a Theatre that could both reject and accept a play, pronounce it bad and good in almost the same breath. But the Abbey never wrote. Yeats wasn't that kind of fool. 'As for the rest' said Sean, 'it would be bloody difficult to forgive, and impossible to forget.' And on that note at a quarter past three in the morning of the second day of my Woronzow Road visit Sean courteously conducted me to my bedroom in order to ensure that everything in that place was attuned to my ease and comfort.

I went twice to the Apollo Theatre; the first occasion with the author himself. I found the play in action to be as theatrically effective and as deeply moving as I found it in the reading. Raymond Massey's direction was sympathetically yet firmly understanding, though Sean himself was not wholly satisfied with it. There had been talk and correspondence a few months previously with a view to my going to London to direct the play. On my side this could not have been accomplished without my relinquishing the Civil Service and pledging the rest of my life (as well as those of my wife and two children) to the professional theatre. C. B. Cochran had been very impressed with all that Sean had told him about me but he was not in the theatre merely for the good of his health and had no intention of buying a pig in a poke. However, he expressed a wish to see me whenever I could come to London. Augustus John's design for the second act of the play was superb, and Laughton's performance as Harry Heegan could not have been bettered by the best of our Abbey Theatre actors even though it didn't completely satisfy Sean. I had heard sorry stories of the miscasting of this actor before I came to London. Lady Gregory had spoken of this 'big, fat, Englishman' who was spoiling Sean's play. But the fact remains that Laughton was essentially a great actor in any part; he was actually four minutes on the stage of the Apollo as Harry Heegan before I needed to remind myself that this was Laughton the English actor. Like all great actors Laughton could carry conviction with him in anything he appeared in.

Of course the Abbey Theatre was well represented in the cast at the Apollo. There was my old colleague Barry Fitzgerald who had finally left the Civil Service; and that fine actor of the Abbey's second great company, Sydney Morgan; as well as Eithne Magee and my theatrical godmother Una O'Connor, who, on the strength of my appearance in a Yeats play at the Irish Literary Society during my Civil Service days in London, believed she had found an actor and wrote to Lennox Robinson urging him to secure my services as soon as I returned to Dublin. Cochran's production, apart from the star-casting of the main roles (Beatrix Lehmann, Ian Hunter, Billy Barnes), was obviously a most expensive one. The play could have been effectively mounted at the Abbey Theatre for a minute fraction of the London cost. The result was that though the Apollo takings were considerable they were not satisfactorily chasing the overheads and it was obvious that the West End run could not be a prolonged one. So I went to see the play a second time, on this occasion with Augustus John and a young Welsh painter for whom John had high hopes, Evan Walters, a gentle kindly soul who died a few years later. I was just as impressed on this second visit. John kept tugging his beard and protesting in anything but a stage whisper that the play was tearing the heart out of him. At each interval he insisted on sweeping us out to the bar with him in order to lower quantities of heart tonic. The final curtain called for more medicinal aid but fortunately I had the good sense to consider that Sean would be waiting for me with fatherly care at Woronzow Road and so I courteously declined John's invitation to one of his many Chelsea haunts where the medicine would flow more freely than in the stalls bar of the

Apollo. Sean, as I expected, was waiting for me on my return and he courteously suggested that I had been drinking. I protested that we had been merely taking medicine to relieve the heart-ache that his play had caused us. He was relieved to learn that I had refused to go with John and he made it clear that John (who had refused a drink earlier in the evening at Woronzow Road) had been the victim of some of his (Sean's) most persuasive temperance lectures. Telling him that he was an old puritan and reminding him (who knew his Bible from cover to cover) that wine maketh the heart of man glad, we cracked jokes over a light supper and went early to bed.

In the few days at our disposal there was much to do and almost ten times as much to say. An early visit to the Tate Gallery was prompted by the remark that since he came to London he had been looking much and long at pictures and as a result he had pondered deeply 'on what had been lost to me, Gaby, when some Power decided I was not to paint'. His contact with Augustus John was, of course, part of this experience. I looked again at the portrait. John had painted him in sombre tones three-quarters-right-profile on, a strained questing puritanical figure, squared to his years of physical servitude. As we made our way towards Milbank by bus Sean showered his likes and dislikes upon me. He had no time for the half-tones and nuances of Corot; he couldn't see how anyone with good eyesight and right senses had. Now Picasso or Van Gogh. I had noticed a large reproduction of the latter's *Sunflowers* adorning the dining-room at Woronzow Road. Had I seen Picasso's *The Red Tablecloth*? I hadn't. Well, there was a picture for you! Or had I noted Van Gogh's flat zones of colour performing the symbolic functions of light and shade? Again, I hadn't. Or had I studied the work of Giotto who expressed his feeling for the divine in the common man? Again, I had to plead ignorance.

By this time we had reached the Gallery and had found common ground in front of the Epstein bronzes. These I loved. I reminded him of this sculptor's revealing head of Lady Gregory in our own Muncipal Gallery in Dublin and of the very fine handful of Johns we had there. He pulled me away from Epstein to see John's wall-stretching but unfinished cartoon entitled *Galway*. I agreed that it was a very fine piece of work. Suddenly he astonished me by saying: 'Look, I'd swap the whole bloody Lane Collection for that cartoon of John's.' Oh, Sean, what would Lady Gregory say? Perhaps my question found its mark, for many years after in *Inishfallen, Fare Thee Well* he saw fit to accuse the British authorities of 'the lousiest and meanest of robberies ever perpetrated by one country on another.' Declaring in the same context that the pictures were still exiled from their native land he went on to say: 'Though many in Ireland were blind to their beauty, so were others, better placed than the Irish to recognise their loveliness; for one of them, Renoir's *Umbrellas*, lay for a long time deep in the cellar of the National Gallery, too trivial, as the bigshots thought, for hanging on a respectable wall.' Incidentally Sean wasn't the only Irishman prepared to bargain the Lane Collection. A few years later Frank O'Connor, Irish short-story writer and a one-time director of the Abbey Theatre, declared that he would willingly swap the Lane Collection for the return to the Abbey of Hugh Hunt who had been a play director there for a number of years. It would seem that Frank believed himself to be an authority on art for when referring to Sean's autobiographical volumes in an article in *Holiday* in January 1956, he wrote: 'There he stands painted, as even Augustus John failed to paint, an international expert, insulted and oppressed by bowsies and gutties who wouldn't know a Giorgione from a hole in the wall.' I often wondered if Sean recalled that day in the Tate when he was writing the passage quoted above. As we walked through this interesting Gallery I discovered that he had no time for Turner. Constable, yes. As for the Pre-Raphaelite Brotherhood and their ilk he had nothing but curses both loud and deep. He was inclined to drag me away from Stanley Spencer whose work I was looking at for the first time. I gathered that he was not impressed. Back again, then, to worship at the shrine of John's *Madame Suggia*, and then on for Sean to wallow in Cezanne, Matisse and Picasso. Before we left I insisted on another look at the Epsteins. I found it difficult to catalogue Sean's taste in art. I'm afraid I belong to those much despised members of the human family who like what they like and on whom artists and their agents mainly depend for a livelihood. It occurred to me at the end of this visit to the Tate that Sean was hardly better than I was, though I felt he was a shade more biased.

We agreed that for the fun of the thing and for the experience too we would do a typical 'Tourist's Day' in London. Although I had worked as a Civil Servant at the Post Office Savings Bank in Blythe Road, Kensington, for twelve months following World

War I, I had never visited any of those places that visitors to London seem to find imperative adjuncts to their visit. So Sean and I 'did' Westminster Abbey and after it made for Regent's Park and the Zoo. Agreeing that the wonders of the aquarium at that place made the visit well worth while we caught a bus for Marylebone Road and the world-famous Madame Tussauds. Sean found the place utterly disgusting and professed to be horrified at the fact that Shaw allowed himself to be modelled in wax though he added that this was on a par with G.B.S's liking for that bastard art photography. I must confess that I was not particularly enamoured with the place either though I was taking it far less seriously than Sean seemed to be taking it. However, I did get one thrill there. There was still enough of the child in me when, with memories of Perrault thick upon me, I leaned over 'The Sleeping Beauty' and received what the French call a 'frisson' from the gentle rise and fall of the young lady's bosom. This didn't move Sean at all; 'Can't you see it's done by a bloody mechanical contrivance inside the thing?' Agreed, of course; but why spoil the illusion? After a hurried glance at the 'Chamber of Horrors' we left the building, Sean expatiating on the bloody morbidity of the English who revelled in such things as these.

The following day he proposed that we visit the Tower of London. Now this was one of the few London landmarks I had visited already. I did not like to remind Sean that when compared with Tussauds it involved a journey into grim reality. Did he remember his *Richard III* and Prince Edward's line:

I do not like the tower, of any place.

He did, of course; for he immediately came back with:

Did Julius Caesar build that place, my Lord?

I who had soaked myself in Harrison Ainsworth as a schoolboy had been well prepared for my former visit to the place. But how would Sean react? Well, he reacted as if someone were desperately trying to incarcerate him in the Tower. He was no sooner inside it than he wanted to get out again. I had to insist on seeing all those places I wanted to see, dragging a very reluctant Sean along with me. Finally after a grim reflection on those star-crossed ladies of the eighth Henry who lost their heads on Tower Green Sean vetoed a visit to the Chapel of St. Peter-ad-Vincula and, gripping me by the arm, bundled me out of the place declaring that it was even a damned sight worse than

Madame Tussauds. It looked as if this 'Tourist's day' experiment was doomed to failure. However, the following morning I suggested that we should spend a whole afternoon at the 'Speaker's Corner', Marble Arch. This expedition proved to be an uproarious success.

It was not so much on the formal platforms as in the small knots of off-stage disputants that Sean found those characters in action that lifted up the dramatist's heart in him. Once again, as in Dublin on many an occasion, it was a case of: 'Come over here; for God's sake listen to this fellow, Gaby!' or 'Wait, Sean, wait: this is too good to be missed!' All that we found here was listened to with delight, noted down, acted and re-enacted, until it finally made its appearance in *Within the Gates*, most of it falling into place in Scene IV. This sort of thing:

> *Man in Bowler Hat* (interrupting): Wait, hold on a second. Don't question me yet. Listen carefully; let your mind follow what I say, and you'll get the idea.
> *Man with the Stick* (from behind): Listen courtiously to wot the gentleman's a-saying; 'e knows wot 'e's torking abaht.

Now this was the sort of thing, these were the kind of characters, from which Sean had drawn some of the best material of his earlier plays. I felt that if he could make contact with London life at this level all would be well and that we would get a great play from him. Here were the colours best suited to the O'Casey palette. And London teemed with them. When in 1933 Sean sent me from Chalfont St. Giles a copy of *Within the Gates* he inscribed it to his 'dear friend Gaby Fallon, with the old affection that flamed around our journeyings through the life of London.' I'm afraid I was rather disappointed. I admired the attempted scope of the play and its form but I felt it marked the point-of-no-return between the 'naturalist' and the 'expressionist' in Sean O'Casey. It was as if with *The Silver Tassie* in mind Sean was saying to Yeats: 'You raised your hand and said to me: "Thus far, but no further". Well, I'll show you how far a dramatist can go.' It is undoubtedly O'Casey's first completely Expressionistic play and the most striking thing about it is its form. None of his other plays has the unity and the structure that this one has. I'm afraid I was not impressed by the fact that the pattern of the play closely follows that of the Breviary and the Missal; or that the four seasons are further reduced to the component parts of a single day—Morning, Noon, Evening and Night. I have no doubt whatever that the play has much religious significance.

What I find it lacking in is theatrical significance. It smoulders where it should burn; it burns where it should blaze. I find myself in agreement with the U.S. critic, Stark Young, who, writing about it in *The New Republic* following its New York production declared that 'its final sum, taken seriously, is likely to be adolescent'.

Two days before the play opened in New York (23rd October 1934)—its London production had been a failure—he discussed his attitude towards the theatre in an article in *The Sunday Times* in the course of which he said that dramatists '. . . have pilloried drama too long to the form of dead naturalism, and all fresh and imaginatively minded dramatists are out to release drama from the pillory of naturalism and to send her dancing through the streets . . .' Fair enough; dancing in the streets can be a most delectable pastime: unfortunately the poor girl is compelled to display her choreography behind that impenetrable 'fourth-wall' framed by a proscenium arch on a rectangle which is generally used to represent somebody's sitting-room with one wall down.

To say that I was depressed even while I was stirred to admiration by this 'Morality in Four Acts' is to put it mildly. *The New York Times* quoted him as saying during the rehearsals of the London production: 'I am out to destroy the accepted naturalistic presentation of character; to get back to the poetic significance of drama. We have a great heritage in the English language, and I feel that it is the theatre's mission to keep it alive. I do not want to appear egotistical but if I have any aim it is to link modern drama with the great main stream of English literature.'

Here was a big leap in ten years, from that March evening in 1924 when sitting at his *Juno and the Paycock* with Lady Gregory he turned and said to her: 'I owe a great deal to you and Mr. Yeats and Mr. Robinson, but to you above all. You gave me encouragement. And it was you who said to me upstairs in the office—I could show you the very spot where you stood—"Mr. Casey, your gift is characterisation", and so I threw over my theories and worked at characters and this (*Juno and the Paycock*) is the result.'

But there was nothing of this in our conversation that evening as we sat after dinner at his study fire in Woronzow Road and amused ourselves by playing the characters we had seen that afternoon, as London's traffic whirled around the Marble Arch and the leaves of autumn fluttered down on the speakers in

Hyde Park. 'Wait, hold on a second. Don't question me yet . . .'

In *The Silver Tassie* venture at the Apollo one of Charles B. Cochran's backers was Billie McElroy, a genial kindly generous soul of Scots-Irish origin. Billie's main interest was in coal but he gambled in almost everything. Indeed, during the run of the play he had a racehorse called *The Silver Tassie* which to judge by its form was as fine a dramatist as it was a racehorse. It was through Billie that Sean first made acquaintance with the stirring Scots ballad that gave the play its name. Sean's friends were Billie's friends and he and I had a long and interesting correspondence before I came on my London visit. He had been particularly anxious that I should direct the play, accepting without the slightest reservation Sean's assertion that there was no one better fitted for the task than I was.

In the middle of my visit Billie informed me that an appointment had been made for myself and Sean at Cochran's Bond Street Office. We duly went along and met Billie there. Cochran instructed his secretary, Miss Grimshaw, to cut off all phone calls for at least an hour, a fact which so impressed Billie that he almost took my foot off with the surreptitious kick he gave me. I had to sit there facing Cochran's baby grand piano, gazing at the photographs of some of his world-famous 'discoveries' as Sean sang my praises as an actor and as director of plays and Billie provided the purely faith-based 'Amens'. Cochran, a shrewd little man if ever there was one, listened intently and then calmly invited me to criticise the production at the Apollo. Having nothing to lose—though Sean and Billie believed I had much to gain—I calmly took the presentation to pieces and put it together again in a fashion nearer to my heart's desire. Amongst other things I criticised the expense of the production, making no bones about the fact that I believed I could secure at least five times the artistic effect for less than one third of the money. The whole performance was nothing if not brash, particularly in the face of a man of Cochran's wide theatrical experience. Behind it all I was nervous enough but was determined not to show it. At the end of this endeavour to live up to the reputation Sean and Billie had made for me Cochran courteously offered me a large expensive cigar, a fact which nervously made me feel rather like a fellow who has just knocked a coconut at a fair.

He then began to tell me something about his own experiences in the theatre and in particular the difficulties he had had with young 'geniuses' from Oxford and Cambridge who were thrust upon him from time to time as God's own gift to the theatre. The point was not lost on me. However, Cochran had a stage-manager, a first-class theatre-carpenter who had grown old in his service, to whom he put the 'geniuses' out to nurse. Sooner or later this good man would report to him that young Mr. A's designs were completely impracticable or that young Mr. B's production practices were getting him into trouble with some of Mr. Cochran's leading players; and that would be that. A polite note thanking them for their services would soon see them back at Oxford or Cambridge again dreaming of the time when the theatre would be really prepared to acclaim the new Gordon Craig or the far-greater-than Reinhardt. Cochran was a fascinating man to listen to and as he spoke of his experiences with some of his most memorable productions one sensed in him that rare combination of businessman plus artist which the theatre constantly needs. 'They call me a commercial showman' he said, 'and I suppose in a sense that is true. But consider this. I may believe that I have found the greatest artist in the world in finding Mr. A or Miss B but the world will never believe in the greatness of these artists until I compel it to do so.' Well, yes; there was something—indeed, there is a great deal—in this.

Miss Grimshaw popped in to say that it was past the hour. The three of us rose to go but before we left we discussed the possibility of producing *The Silver Tassie* at the Gaiety Theatre, Dublin. In this Cochran generously agreed to give all the assistance he possibly could. As we left Bond Street Billie was bubbling over with excitement. 'Ye see, I know Cochran, Gaby. Sean, did ye notice the way he half closed his eyes when Gaby told him that he would have used masks for the wounded in the second act? That's a sure sign he was keenly interested.' Sean was silent. He was thinking, as he told us later, that if Gaby could be induced to give up his Civil Service job, there might be more than a possibility that Cochran would take him on his production staff. This set Billie off; he would do nothing but talk of contracts, how Gaby should stick out for a short-term one and not a long-term contract which Cochran would assuredly want. I couldn't see the force of this until Billie explained that Cochran would want to get as much as he could for as little as he could even though that little might look enormous to me. 'In less than no time' said Billie, 'you would become dissatisfied, Gaby, by comparing the money you were making for Cochran with the money Cochran was giving you. A short contract then, with an option, Gaby.' It was all great fun this, but what would come of it? Billie was jubilant and certain; Sean was serious but not so sure. I knew that he honestly believed that I had a future in the theatre; I knew, too, that he would give much to have me near him in London. I knew as well that having given three hostages to fortune I would have to consider carefully any step that would lift me out of the little security I had. We talked late into the night about the whole project but had not reached a solution before we went to bed.

At long last the question came: 'What are you doing about your writing, Gaby?' He hoped I was not neglecting it. The correct answers were 'Nothing whatever' and 'I am'; but I replied evasively. I had plans, ideas, I said. I was promptly told that plans and ideas were not enough; I must practice, I must produce. 'Look' said Sean, 'I showed some of your letters to Shaw; and Shaw said "The man who wrote these letters certainly can write".' To Shaw? I squirmed at the thought of it. I felt that Sean with all his kindness was laying a responsibility upon me that I wasn't capable of shouldering. Heaven knows I was working hard enough at home but I was doing anything but writing. I was producing plays for amateur groups and at schools and convents for shamefully low fees. I was adjudicating at amateur drama festivals. I was standing week after week at Radio Eireann's microphones, on some occasions for forty-five minutes at a stretch (not counting rehearsal hours) for the munificent sum of one guinea. But I was not writing. From one point of view I couldn't afford to; my family was growing, my stature as a Civil Servant was staying put; there were bills and school fees to consider; and the cash though small had the advantage of being ready. Then there was another reason. Far too many young writers whom I knew at the time were, instead of living, taking life from books. The fact was only too evident in the books they were writing. Yet they had something which I lacked. I have watched one of them (not without a tinge of envy) go to his typewriter as a thirsty man goes to water and with seeming ease produce sentence after sentence after sentence. Writing to me has always been an affair of blood and sweat and tears. I could never convince myself that I was what they call a 'born' writer. And so, not to offend Sean's confidence in me, I gave him an evasive answer.

It was Eileen who said: 'Would you not write a book about Sean, Gaby?' But it was Sean who quickly interjected: 'Now it would be much better for Gaby to find his own subject.' So like Sean. Well, I dillied and dallied with the idea, said I would think it over; at which Sean generously offered to give all the help of which he was capable. Of course, it all came to nothing. I returned to the old grind and waited until opportunity came my way to become a drama critic. Yet Sean's faith in my creative ability never wavered. It even survived our big quarrel; a few years ago he was heard to speak with praise of my first contribution to *The Irish Statesman* and to say: 'What a bloody pity he didn't follow up this creative urge instead of going in for this critical stuff.' My visit was now nearing its end. The kindness and the hospitality of Sean and Eileen O'Casey had exceeded all bounds. I have never been given such a welcome elsewhere nor have I at any place felt so much at home from home as at 19 Woronzow Road. 'Tis true, and in the light of subsequent events, 'tis pity; and pity 'tis, 'tis true.

Towards the middle of the following year I began to make arrangements for an autumn production in Dublin of *The Silver Tassie*. In July I received the following letter from C. B. Cochran:

49 Old Bond Street,
London, W.1.
10th July 1930

My dear Mr. Fallon:
    I am delighted to think that there's a prospect of your producing *The Silver Tassie* in Dublin. From our conversation in London, I have great confidence that you will present Sean's masterpiece in a manner which will shame some of his fellow citizens who missed a great opportunity.

With all good wishes,
Yours very sincerely,
Charles B. Cochran

Before attempting to cast the play I approached a business manager, the late Lionel Cranfield, to negotiate on my behalf with Mr. David Telford, of the firm of Craig Gardner & Co., Chartered Accountants, who was then acting as manager of the Gaiety Theatre. At first the prospect of securing the Gaiety seemed favourable even though friends warned me of the danger which lay in the fact that Messrs. Craig Gardner & Co. were the then accountants of the Abbey Theatre. After some delay and some tentative discussions concerning the alleged 'offensiveness' of the play, I was informed that the Gaiety management couldn't see its way to book it. It was obvious that Abbey Theatre influence had prevailed and that the play's 'offensiveness' was merely an excuse. One cannot blame the Abbey for taking this step. After all, it had its prestige to consider. Besides, I had already produced *The Shadow of a Gunman* shortly after the Abbey's rejection of *The Silver Tassie* and it was strongly rumoured that the author had given me the production rights of all his plays. Since there was half a germ of truth in this matter it was up to the Abbey to be on its guard and to ensure that the O'Casey name should not pass from its repertoire. At the same time Sean was having his own very real difficulties with the theatre which was attempting by legal means to hold and extend its alleged sole rights of production over the plays it had already presented. Sean was obliged to engage a firm of Dublin solicitors to act on his behalf against this dog-in-the-manger attitude. The upshot of the matter was that the Abbey was granted a further twelve months extension while Arthur Sinclair (a former Abbey actor) and his company of Irish Players were allowed to proceed with their plans for presenting *The Plough* in Belfast and *Juno* in Cork. A few years later Yeats asked O'Casey to allow the Abbey to produce *Within the Gates*, declaring it to be 'a most successful achievement in your newer manner'. O'Casey suggested *The Silver Tassie* instead on the grounds that it would be a much easier play to put on the Abbey stage. At the same time he made it clear that while the Abbey would always be welcome to do any play of his they wished to do he would never again submit a play to its directorate. On the 12th August 1935, *The Silver Tassie* was presented at the Abbey Theatre and sparked off on moral grounds a controversy of such intensity that it is amazing that it didn't lead to another theatre riot. One of the theatre's then directors, Brinsley MacNamara, himself a dramatist, strongly protested against the play's presentation and then left the Board of Directors. Mr. MacNamara declared that he had been 'out-voted' by his fellow-directors in the matter of cutting 'objectionable' scenes, but that in any case he wanted 'Catholic cleanliness and wholesome entertainment in a theatre which our Catholic government is subsidising'.

Five years earlier, when I had been making preparations for the Gaiety Theatre presentation of the play, a Dominican priest mounted a large-scale attack in the then clerically managed weekly, *The Standard*, warning its readers in no uncertain manner that Dublin was about to be presented with a blasphemous draught from *The Silver Tassie*. Amongst other things His Reverence described the play as 'a vigorous medley of lust, hatred and vulgarity'.

When the Abbey presented the play the priest went into action again and a lecture given by him to the Catholic Young Men's Society of Galway was of such a nature that the Society felt impelled to pass the following resolution proposed by a Professor of University College, Galway:

> That we condemn vehemently the dramatic work of the Abbey Theatre in so far as it infringes the canons of Christian reverence or human decency and in so far as it injures the nation's prestige at home or abroad.
> That we commend the Galway Gaelic Theatre for its meticulous adherence both to Christian principles and to our national tradition.
> That copies of this resolution be sent to the President of the Executive Council, the Diplomatic Corps, the members of Dail Eireann, and the home and foreign Press.

This was the signal which many wanted. The play was attacked by the Catholic newspapers, *The Irish Rosary*, and the *Evening Herald*, *The Standard* and *The Irish Catholic*. It was attacked by the President of the Gaelic League who hadn't seen the play but who had seen *The Plough* and 'had to leave before the second act from a fit of nausea'.

The distinguished English actor, Robert W. Speaight, himself a Catholic, happened to be visiting Dublin during the week of *The Silver Tassie* and not having seen the play during its London run he went to the Abbey. He was appalled at the Irish reactions to the play and in his capacity as drama critic of the London *Catholic Herald* he wrote an article entitled 'In Defence of Sean O'Casey'. 'It is impossible' he wrote:

> to open the majority of (Irish) papers without being deafened by puritanical howls. The soul of the bourgeoisie has betrayed itself. And this surely is the essence of the bourgeois mind that it cannot look tragedy in the face. For O'Casey has seen into the heart of the horror of war and wrenched out its dreadful secret; that the co-heirs with Christ destroy one another in the sight of the Son of Man. Unless you nerve yourself to realise that the Crucifix occupied the background of Armageddon, that the agony of the world was played out before the elevated Host, that the words of the sacred Liturgy were mingled with the mutter of the guns, and the same prayers offered for mutually destructive causes—unless you grasp the appalling contradictions inherent in all this, not only have you failed to understand the tragedy of war, but you have not begun to grasp the elements of a Christian realism . . .

If there were any people in Ireland outside the literary coterie, lay or cleric, who agreed with Robert Speaight, they seemed to be keeping their mouths shut.

Not that Speaight's criticism lacked objectivity. 'I do not wish to exaggerate' he wrote, '*The Silver Tassie* is a statement and not a solution of suffering. It is the outcry of a passionate embittered mind. But it is much nearer to Christianity because it is nearer to life than the complacent criticisms levelled against it.' On September 3rd, in a letter to *The Irish Times* in which he reiterated his charges against O'Casey's Irish critics, Speaight described the dramatist as 'The most important new writer in the English language.' He then went on to say:

> Like many great writers, he boldly displays his errors, and I do not think he is capable of consistent or coherent thought. His genius is intuitive and emotional. Nor do I think *The Silver Tassie* a satisfactory play. It is spoiled by a mixture of convention and carelessness of form, which he has probably derived from what May Woolf calls 'The Elizabethan Lumber Room'. Mr. O'Casey should read his Racine. But it does seem to me, in its greater passages, a profoundly moving statement of the horror and the pity of war. For it lays bare the most dreadful aspect of warfare—that Christians kill one another in the sight of the Son of Man.

I need hardly point out that the attitude of Fr. Gaffney and his supporters did little to endear his Catholic fellow-Irishmen to Sean O'Casey or he to them. In particular the name of *The Standard*, from which weekly organ of Catholic opinion Fr. Gaffney had launched his attack on *The Tassie*, struck an ominous note in O'Casey's mind. This fact was to bear much ill fruit in our future relationship. Nor could Sean see in the attitude of his fellow-dramatist, Brinsley MacNamara, anything more than a fit of professional jealousy. The audience packed the Abbey for the run of the play. According to one who was there—I did not see this particular presentation—the play seemed to leave the audience 'stiff in their seats' and to have the effect of a sermon, which, of course, it is.

Sean wrote a defence of his play which he called 'A Stand on *The Silver Tassie*' and which he sent with a covering letter to W. B. Yeats on 23rd November 1935, telling him that he could do what he liked with the article 'print it whole or in parts, or ignore it altogether'.

This article was not published. It remained in the possession of Mrs. W. B. Yeats after her husband's death. However, it now appears in full in *Sean O'Casey: The Man Behind the Plays* by Saros Cowasjee. It is a defence of the play against the charges made by Fr. Gaffney and others on the grounds of its deliberate indecency, blasphemy 'and its mean mocking challenge to the Christian Faith'. Mr. Cowasjee sums up the situation as follows: 'O'Casey's purpose in writing *The Silver Tassie* was to awaken in the minds of men a feeling against the horror and indecency of war. To the London audiences he succeeded in conveying his passionate hatred of warfare, but to his own people and in his own country he failed to make himself understood.'

Most of this lack of understanding was due to a hopelessly retarded Catholic intellectuality. In his defence against indecency O'Casey quoted *inter alia* the words 'bastards', 'son-of-a-bitch' and 'arse' used in Paul Claudel's *The Satin Slipper* translated from the French by Fr. John O'Connor. But this would hardly convince people who cherish a Catholic literature that is wholly narrow and sectarian instead of fully and universally Christian, or as Romano Guardini puts it, one embracing 'the whole world spiritually as a vast kingdom of realities'. Such people as Mr. O'Casey's opponents in this issue have never hesitated to resort to ways unspiritual and rude and dubiously Catholic to uphold, as they believe, the name and dignity of the Church. It is a tribute to the salutary effect of *The Silver Tassie* that its Dublin audiences did not riot. But all this took place four years after Sean and his family had left Woronzow Road and settled in at 'Hillcrest', Chalfont St. Giles, a rural retreat 'deep in the belly of Bucks' as its latest and most distinguished resident elected to describe it.

Ten

❦

ONE of Sean O'Casey's biographers has suggested that the move from Woronzow Road was determined by financial stringency, that Sean O'Casey had hopes that *The Silver Tassie* would bring in enough to live on for one year, but that its eight weeks' run at the Apollo—it opened on the 11th October 1929, three weeks before the Wall Street crash—had brought nothing but 'extreme poverty'. There is undoubtedly an element of truth in this, but 'extreme poverty', particularly to someone like Sean who had deeply known the meaning of this term, is out of the question. In taking over Woronzow Road he had expressed the hope that U.S. dollars from the tour of *The Plough* would come to his aid. Some time before he had sold the film rights of *Juno and the Paycock* for a production which was directed by Alfred Hitchcock. He had had a quarrel with Hitchcock over the casting of this film. He wanted Barry Fitzgerald for his old Abbey Theatre part of Captain Boyle, but Hitchcock reported an unsatisfactory film-test on Barry's part and cast another actor, putting Barry in a minor role. In the light of Barry's highly successful Hollywood career one is inclined to doubt the efficacy of Hitchcock's film test. But if Hitchcock slipped up here he made no mistake with Sara Allgood in the part of Juno. He obviously considered that this was something he could, as they say, go to town on; and he did, extending the penultimate scene of the play in a long unforgettable sequence, a magnificent tribute to the greatness of the player and the part. Few seem to remember this film, but on the strength of this sequence alone it is a film which thoroughly deserves to be remembered.

Of course it is questionable if Sean received very much for the film rights, but even if he did, the Woronzow Road ménage

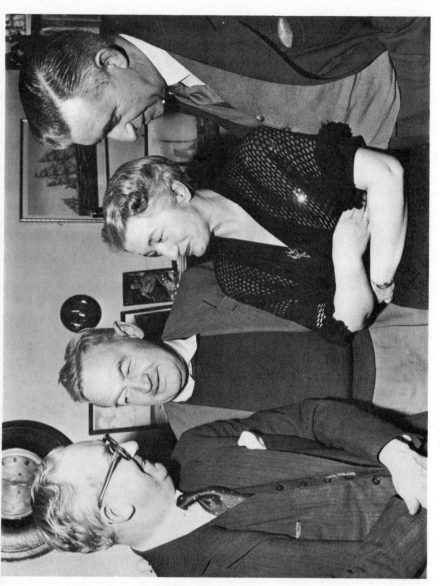

J. J. O'Leary, Barry Fitzgerald, Ria Mooney, the Author.

The Author as Seumas Shields in *The Shadow of a Gunman*.

would have made short work of it. It may have been in or around this time that he sold the amateur rights of *The Gunman, Juno* and *The Plough* to Messrs. French & Sons for £300. It hardly calls for an actuarial mind to consider how good a bargain this has proved to be for Messrs. French. Shaw advised him against doing this and I imagine that Shaw offered to lend him the money. But I have not the slightest doubt that Sean refused it. In matters of this kind he still has the pride of Lucifer. Any of his Irish friends could have raised the money for him. But the bond was signed, the deed was done, before any of us could even think of finding bail for him. I have not the slightest doubt that my good friend, and Barry Fitzgerald's 'buttie', J. J. O'Leary, a leading Irish businessman, and himself a publisher and theatre-lover, would have given Sean at least three times the money for a limited time-hold on the plays. But it was too late when we heard. I have often wondered to what extent the paucity of this deal reflected Sean's opinions of the plays themselves. Of recent years he has adopted the attitude that these were early works of little or no importance. Was he feeling this way about them even then?

But however much one may speak of hard times or straitened circumstances 'extreme poverty', as Sean had known it, was out of the question. Even in those days bungalows in Buckingham-shire were not to be had for nothing. In saying this I am not in any way minimising the strain and the uncertainty which arose from not knowing where one's next cheque was going to come from, or the labour involved in providing comfort and sustenance for his family. Despite his reputation he had a number of rejections from magazines and literary journals in or around this time and these 'no-thank-you's' hit hard; but his indomitable spirit had stood up to and survived circumstances far more pressing than these. He has always held that Yeats's rejection of *The Silver Tassie* had done him much harm in literary circles. This may well be so, though I could never accept the contention without adding the rider that the literary world must be a phony world. Busy at home on my own petty chores I felt that anyone who fairly weighed *The Silver Tassie* against Yeats's opinion of it must come out heavily on the side of Sean O'Casey.

Anyway, Sean seemed to be happy and content in Bucks. Working in the garden, using once again those glorious tools, the pick and the shovel, and coming in all new-springing muscles, as he put it, to a simple meal and a warm fire. Finding it curious as he sits there thinking that three friends should have scattered so, Gaby in Dublin, Sean in Bucks, and Barry Fitzgerald on the broad Atlantic bound for America. Old memories stir when he sees in a radio programme in an Irish newspaper that Gabriel Fallon and company will broadcast a play from the Dublin and Athlone stations on a certain date. Cursing fate that his five-valve Pye still refuses to stretch far enough to satisfy his longing to hear oul Dublin's (or even Cork's) voice again. Early in 1933 I found, much to my delight, that one of my chores involved going to London (expenses paid) to record a commentary in Wardour Street on a short Irish commercial film. What a surprise he got when, the task completed, I 'phoned from the studio to Chalfont St. Giles 154 and asked Sean if I could speak to Mr. O'Casey. Again the old courtesy; the kind, hospitable consideration. Could I spend the week-end with him? Eileen, he regretted, was not at home; but he would make me as comfortable as he could. I was coming? Spendid; now follow these instructions carefully: get a Green Line bus from the top of Regent's Street, and be sure to ask the conductor to let you off at Chalfont St. Giles, the first major stop after Gerrard's Cross. Got that? Right, Gaby: I will be waiting for you at the bus-stop. He was.

There followed two days of glorious weather through which we talked as we walked through the leafy ways of Bucks. This was more like the Dublin days than St. John's Wood had been. A neighbouring maid looked after Breon—now a sturdy youngster trotting around the extensive garden—and helped prepare the main meal. Sean did the rest. The inside of 'Hillcrest' like that of Woronzow Road reflected Eileen's good taste and sense of décor. I slept on the bed-settee in Sean's study. One morning about 8.30 a.m. — we had retired barely five hours before — I awoke to find him quietly tip-toeing into the room. I immediately pretended to be asleep. He stopped, looked towards the settee, seemed to be reassured. Then armed with the centre pages of the *Sunday Times* he quietly proceeded to clear out the grate and set and light the fire. This done, he replaced the hearth-brush, carefully folded his *Sunday Times* parcel of cinders, looked again towards the 'sleeping' figure on the settee and quietly moved from the room. This was the very essence of the man; a throw-back to his tenement days. I arose about nine-thirty. He hoped I had slept well. 'Like a log' I said: I never told him what I had seen.

The Abbey Theatre seemed far away now. At all events we had very little to say about it. One evening towards dusk, returning from a long walk we passed Milton's cottage on our way to 'Hillcrest'. Milton had been for both of us second only to Shakespeare in those evenings at '422'. Standing opposite the cottage I declaimed:

> Now came still Evening on, and Twilight gray
> Had in her sober Liverie all things clad;

declaring that I had always considered that 'Mantle' would be a more effective word than 'Liverie'. Ignoring my remark and looking fixedly at the cottage he declared that 'insanitary ould places like that ought to be pulled down; but, there you are, the English, who had no bloody interest whatsoever in Milton, insisted on maintaining the shanty'. And he would say as much for the Nicholas Breakspear shanty as well. I told him I couldn't care less so far as Breakspear was concerned. Wasn't he the bucko who as Adrian IV handed over Ireland to Henry II without as much as by your leave? He could throw a bomb into Breakspear's place if he felt like it but I begged him to spare Milton's. He barely smiled and we passed on. From all he had been telling me about his English neighbours it was clear that he had little more than peripheral contact with them. Most of them were, so to speak, getting under his skin, but Sean, in the dramatist's sense, was not getting under theirs. It was clear that he was observing what was evident, the external factors, but so far as their inherent patterns of feeling were concerned his guess was not even as good as mine. He was on the outside finding it difficult if not impossible to look in. Most likely he would remain that way.

'Hillcrest' had revived his love of flowers and growing things, a love he had inherited from his mother, a love which makes an early appearance in *The Gunman*. 'What's Mr. Shields doin' with the oul' weeds?' asks Minnie Powell. 'Those aren't Shields's; they're mine' replies Davoran. 'Wild flowers is a kindlier name for them, Minnie, than weeds. These are wild violets, this is an *Arum maculatum*, or Wake Robin, and these are Celandines, a very beautiful flower related to the buttercup.' In his auto-biographical volumes too, this love of flowers could move him from the tiresome convolutions of synthetic Joycean prose to such simple moving words as these:

> Outside, in a tiny garden, the few flowers have faded,
> or have been shoved from life by the sharp frost of the
> night before. The tall hollyhocks have toppled leaving
> a few lingering rose-like forms on one dismantled
> stalk nuzzling itself into the chilly clay . . .

137

Standing by a rose-bush in 'Hillcrest', it may have been a 'Lady Hillingdon' or even a 'Mdme. Edouard Herriot' (God knows, I didn't know, but Sean knoweth) a memory of the sentimental music-hall songs we used to sing at the fire in '422' came back to me; and, compelling Sean to join in, we launched into a chorus which went as follows:

> If my love you would treasure
> 'Twill give me great pleasure
> I fought by your side
> And defeated your foes.
> Then why should you slight me
> By cruel laws blight me?
> Said Ireland's green Shamrock
> To England's red Rose.

We didn't get as far as the verse in which the 'Unionist thorn' urges the Rose to ignore the Shamrock's plea, for Sean soared off into another ballad concerning that Irish dragoon who on the banks of the Nile read his mother's letter by the light of the moon, while:

> The tears rolled down his sun-burned cheeks
> And fell (we preferred 'dropped') on the letter
>   in his hand.
> Is it true? Too true.
> More trouble in our na-tive land.

And so we sang and talked and smoked and told old tales about the Dubliners we had known and seen, and I heard again that glorious unforgettable laugh of his, with its deep-down undertone of tears, a laugh inherited from his mother 'at the gate of the grave'. And then, suddenly, it is time to go and so I pack my things, walk with Sean to the bus, and waving 'Good-bye' make for that place which Oliver Gogarty used to call the first station on the Irishman's calvary—Euston.

Had Sean changed? Not to me, at all events; not essentially. Nevertheless, it was obvious that he could not commit himself to the society around him. Here he was bound to be an outsider. England, I felt, could never content him; like Dostoievsky before him he was bound to remain, so far as Ireland was concerned, a slice cut from the native loaf. Would his aloofness, his inability to merge give him a greater objectivity, make him a better dramatist? It was difficult to say. But I had my doubts. J. L. Hodson, who had visited him in Dublin, paid a visit to 'Hillcrest' and wrote about it in the News Chronicle of 21st December 1931. In Dublin when Hodson put it to him that he 'only wrote about what he knew of,' Sean had replied: 'What in Heaven should I write about? What did Euripides and Aristophanes write about? Born in a tenement house, I write about them.' Hodson reported that Sean at Chalfont St. Giles was 'writing a new play about London life. At first he thought he would write straight for the films, but he's changed his mind. He is half-way through a sort of autobiography; and has done a number of sketches—"weaving a pattern" he calls it.' Amongst the O'Casey 'assertions' recorded by Hodson are the following: 'That *Juno* was good enough for a man beginning to write—no more than that; that he can find Joxer Dalys (one of his great Irish characters) everywhere; that he'll never go back to Dublin except on a visit; that he's finished with that city as a play subject ("to be creative you must pass on to something fresh"); that he is not conceited, but proud; that his great ambition is that his next play may be a great play—and *not* to send his son to Oxford.'

Well, the play *Within the Gates* was presented at the Royalty Theatre, London, on 7th February 1934, in the presence of the author who sat in the stage box with George Bernard Shaw. Financially the play was not a success. Critical opinion varied. James Agate who had described the earlier plays as 'the greatest since the Elizabethans' summed up the new offering as 'pretentious rubbish' and in the course of a lengthy notice in the *Sunday Times* of 11th February 1934 declared that 'Grandeur of form may well go with vacuity of content, and it is the latter which makes the thing rubbish and the combination of the two which makes that rubbish pretentious'. On the other hand Florence Codman, writing in *The Nation* of 25th April 1934, declared that the play was 'a dramatisation of the Waste Land of the postwar world'. Gordon Beckles in the *Daily Express* challenged the author to tell the world what the play was *really* about, even while he declared that it wasn't a play at all but Mr. O'Casey's 'own ranting denunciation of the world's hypocrisy'. The author contemptuously refused to take up this challenge, pointing out that his mission in life was not 'to give Gordon Beckles a higher mind than he has, for I am not a worker of miracles'. In *Rose and Crown* he describes his play as a 'cry for courage, decency, and vitality in life'; so well it may be.

On reading the play I had written to Sean praising its form but summing up its content in the phrase 'These be your Israelites, O God'; and in this I sensed its adolescence. Could this be the effect of that expatriation which Yeats had sealed by his rejection of *The Silver Tassie*? One was inclined to think of Ibsen's lines in *Brand*, however villainous the translation:

> To a man's feet his native haunt
> Is as unto the tree the root.
> If there his labour fills no want,
> His deeds are doomed, his music mute.

Well, perhaps the situation wasn't as bad as all that. Time would tell.

It is the mark of a great playwright to fall in love with life as a spectacle. That's what Shakespeare did. That's what Sean O'Casey did up to and including *The Silver Tassie*. To tell me that *Within the Gates* is a morality play which is also a work of art does not help to rid me of the feeling that I would prefer more play and less morality, more work and much less art. There is more than a hint in this play that the author has become the slave of his 'poetic diction' and of 'ideas' as opposed to what Henry James called 'felt life'. But with all due respect to those who may be compelled to do so it is almost impossible to judge a work intended for the theatre outside the theatre itself.

If the London production of *Within the Gates* had been a success Ireland would have seen him for a short spell for he had intentions of coming over in the spring or early summer and was 'longing to have a look at Dublin again'. But by the summer America was calling out not only for the play but for the author himself. So here he was in the first place saying good-bye to Bucks. for a flat in Overstrand Mansions, Prince of Wales Road, and then suddenly leaving Overstrand Mansions for the sidewalks of New York. He was having a copy of *Windfalls* sent to me—it would be published during his absence—but here, with a fond farewell, was the inscription which I was to paste inside the cover: 'To my old Buttie, Gaby Fallon, with all the affection of old-time memories. When we forget thee, O Dublin, let our right hand forget its cunning. Dublin, forever changing, and ever remaining the same: from Sean O'Casey. With love and affection this copy of *Windfalls* Chalfont St. Giles 1934.' Well, little did Sean know—until I told him when he and Eileen visited Dublin on their return from the U.S. in the summer of 1935— that this copy of *Windfalls* was seized under our Censorship of Publications Act and instead of the book I received a copy of a circular from the Minister of Justice accusing me of attempting to import something which was in general tendency obscene or whatever the official wording of this rather terrorising charge may be. But such are the trials and tribulations of a conscientious Censorship Board that a friend coming from London brought me another copy within a week.

Sean and Eileen both looked well on their return from the U.S. They stayed in Dublin at the Standard Hotel for about ten days and visited the Fallon household twice. It was on the occasion of this stay in Dublin that Sean made his peace with Yeats and persuaded him to take *The Silver Tassie* for production at the Abbey rather than *Within the Gates*. The latter play had run for 101 nights at the National Theatre, New York; and Hollywood had closed a deal for the film rights of *The Plough and the Stars*. Sean had lectured at a number of Universities and Colleges and had controversy with a number of Roman Catholics (including the Rev. Terence Connolly S.J. of Boston College) over *Within the Gates*. Poor Father Terence! I came to know him very well in the years ahead. No matter who had written it, it wouldn't have been his kind of play. Unlike Stark Young he would not be content to conclude that 'its final sum, taken seriously, is likely to be adolescent'. Much more likely he believed it to be the work of a militant atheist. Sean and Eileen weren't long back in London before the Abbey Theatre mounted its production of *The Silver Tassie* and the trouble, mentioned in an earlier chapter, had begun. Sean was frankly puzzled by it and had every reason to be so for he honestly believed that *The Silver Tassie* and *Within the Gates* were sincerely religious plays from his point of view. He was trying, he said, to see if he could make any sober or sane thing out of the talk, the high talk and the low talk, the talk that says a little and means a lot and the talks that says a lot and means nothing.

The summer of 1936 found him holidaying in Wales with the family and being swept (temporarily) into the Welsh National Movement. Something like his old Gaelic League spirit moved him as he spoke at gatherings of Welsh nationalists, sang at their concerts, and found he had to restrain himself from roaring out the old cries of hatred against the Saxon. However, he managed to get a few words in for Communism. Strangely enough, this was a subject on which he and I never had very much to say. It rarely cropped up in his letters. In any case we had other things to talk about—wasn't there life and literature, brother, and what more could a man want. That he had Communist friends in Ireland and elsewhere I knew and had known. He had gone to

Russia early in the thirties to attend a meeting of the International Union of Revolutionary Writers at a time when the *Large Soviet Encyclopedia* was in course of publication. But he never once mentioned this visit to me. I often thought that it may have been out of deference to my Roman Catholicism that he kept Communist matters out of our discussions. It could hardly be that he was trying to hide one side of himself from me for he had sense enough to know that I was bound to find out. Later, of course, disguise was out of the question. Well, the Welsh holiday had one good effect—it found him well started on a new play. What this one would be like who could tell? In the meantime he wanted me to accept a cheque for ten shillings and sixpence being half royalties for two performances of *A Pound on Demand* which he had based on an incident that had taken place in a Dublin Post Office and which I had described to him. I was deeply touched by the kindness but I refused. Instead, knowing that he came on one side from Roman Catholic stock, and remembering the attraction which Catholicism once held for him, I asked him to work out my side of the bargain by wearing a small medal of the Virgin Mary, known as the Miraculous Medal. This, of course, was proselytism of a kind. Maritain was to teach me in the years ahead that love of one's neighbour in the fullest Christian sense must be innocent of an *arrière-pensée* of any kind, particularly one relating to conversion, and that a man is to be judged not by the explicit, conscious rational form of his belief or unbelief, but by the fundamental orientation of his intellect and will towards Truth and Goodness, which is ultimately known to God. Sean responded to the gesture in a courteous kindly way saying that while he couldn't promise to wear the medal he would certainly keep it near him.

In 1936 I was invited to join the staff of *The Irish Monthly* (edited by the Jesuit Fathers) as its theatre correspondent. Since early contributors to this literary review had included Oscar Wilde and William Butler Yeats I considered it something of an honour to be allowed to express my views on the theatre in its pages. Sean was pleased to know that I was writing again. 'I'm just as sure as ever I was that there is something in you besides Civil Service Sanctity.' At the same time I was contributing some articles to *The Capuchin Annual*, then edited by the Franciscan, Father Senan. When the latter was on a visit to London I asked him to call to Overstrand Mansions to see Sean, but he was rather shy of doing so. Sean was very disappointed that Senan did not call. 'He would have been most welcome', said Sean, 'and I would have been delighted to have shared a meal with him.' This set him off to reminisce about his friendship with a Catholic priest, a Discalced Carmelite from Gerrard's Cross, who used to visit him in his Chalfont St. Giles's days; and with a lay-brother of the same order, a Dublin man, like Sean himself. One very wet day the lay-brother arrived at 'Hillcrest' to have lunch with Sean, and while his coat was being dried had to be accommodated with one of Sean's famous jerseys. When he was leaving 'the two old Dublin boys, Carmelite and Communist, embraced and kissed each other'. Yes, Sean was indeed sorry that Father Senan had not called. There was no need for a son of St. Francis to be shy of a man who, if he had no share in the Saint's virtue, had at least shared in his poverty. And, besides, if one were to ask Sean, St. Francis was more of a Communist than he was a Bourgeois or a Conservative or a Fascist—and yet he was a gentleman for all that. Sean had no time for the timid prelates who out of their fear are always trying to close the Gates of the Church—it is the Saints who are always flinging them open. But there Sean goes again, my dear Gaby, blathering dogmatically, as usual, Sean, 'who should be the least dogmatic of men'. Yet he does this out of a desire that all men should be one in sympathy 'as we go blundering on through this life'.

Early in 1937 Sean took out Irish citizenship papers for himself, Eileen and their two sons. At the same time he sent me a copy of his newly published book of critical essays, aptly entitled *The Flying Wasp*. Sean's title seemed to have been prompted by a remark of James Agate's: 'There is a nest of wasps that must be smoked out, because it is doing the theatre infinite harm.' I doubt if Agate had Sean O'Casey in mind, or if indeed he recalled Robert Ashton's play *The Battle of Aughrim* (1727) in which a captured English colonel turns on his capturer, an Irish general, with the stinging remark: 'Thou proud Hibernian wasp!' However, Sean, turned wasp, proceeded to sting Mr. Agate in several places, and several other people in places as well. And Sean in full critical flight—as *The Silver Tassie* correspondence proves—can sting to the quick. In *The Flying Wasp* Sean administers his stings right, left, and centre, and seemingly without any regard for the fact that in pursuing this anything but gentle art he is steadily making enemies. With some of his criticism I found myself in agreement, but generally speaking, I considered that much of his thinking on the theatre was both woolly and unwise. That he wrote out of a strong *feeling* for theatre was very evident but for playwright turned critic *feeling* is not enough. At no point in his book did he explain what he meant, what he had in mind, when he used the word 'theatre'. Had he been compelled to define his terms it is possible that much of what he did say would be left unsaid. At all events there would have been less stinging, less personal prejudice, less mixed opinions. On the other hand by stinging sufficiently hard to make people think he possibly did the English theatre some service. But he did it at his own expense. It is possible, too, that some of those in the English theatre who were driven to thinking by Mr. O'Casey's waspish stings may have compelled him to pay for their thinking. Much was made in reviews at that time of his 'waspishness', of his tendency to talk at the top of his voice about the theatre. But this loud-speaking is a quality which calls for courage, particularly in a world which transacts so much of its business in a conspiracy of silence.

And speaking of silence, almost the whole of 1938 passed with but two letters from me to Sean and but one letter from Sean to me. It is difficult to pin down the reason. I may have said something which annoyed him. However, there was nothing of this in the lengthy and heart-warming letter which came in September 1938, in which he told his very dear Gaby of the O'Casey family's impending removal to a little place near Totnes, Devon. No, I wasn't the only one who had not heard from Sean. Even George Jean Nathan had written him asking the reason for such a long silence; and so, too, had our old friend, Dr. Joe Cummins. Well, one reason was that Sean's eyes easily tire and another was that he had been working on a volume for Macmillans, a biographical one 'which deals in stories with what I saw and heard and felt during the first eleven or twelve years of my life'. It is to be called *I Knock at the Door* and being rather behind time with it, it will miss the autumn list but will appear in the early spring; and, needless to say, Gaby is to have one of the first copies. No doubt I had upbraided him on his silence for he tells me that there is no such thing as silence between us, for if we don't write we think of each other and what could be better than that. He upbraids himself for what he calls 'flowering out into an Atheistical Pastoral' in which with a foresight which almost envisages John XXIII he declares that 'the man who limits the Catholic Faith (as I understand it) limits God'. It is his firm conviction that many who are defending 'The Faith' are doing the Faith a good deal of harm; and he fears that sometimes it isn't love of the Faith that gets them going, but a kink of personal conceit in themselves. With all of which, of course, I find myself in complete agreement. He sends us all his warmest regards but there must have been something in my letters to him to have warranted his warning to me not to question myself about him. This he finds a *little* unjust. I ought to know by now how he feels for me and mine. We differ from each other in a lot of ways but there should be no such thing as silence between us. He and his have thought of me and mine often and often and will continue to send such thought 'even though no postman carries it in his bag'. And so for the present he bids good-bye to his dear buttie.

I duly received my copy of *I Knock at the Door*. 'With deep affection' from my 'Dublin Buttie, Sean O'Casey'. By this time, early in 1939, he was well settled in at Tingrith, Station Road, Totnes, Devon. It was a big change after London. The usual amount of moving fuss with the addition of having to check the book proofs. And now one of the customary Abbey Theatre controversies is raging in the Dublin newspapers and he has been asked to join in. All the articles (by Frank O'Connor, Sean O'Faolain *et hoc genus omne*) have been sent on to him, but he is determined to keep out of it all. He feels that the Abbey should never have allowed me to walk out, banging the door after me. If he had had a high place in that institution he would have hung on to me like grim death and possibly have persuaded me to throw my job to hell! Still talking about the Abbey, he tells me he has forgiven Yeats and hopes that Yeats has forgiven him, though there wasn't anything to forgive really. It was the principle of the thing—'an', no matter how you may argue, ma, a principle's a principle'. And he thinks of how, had he, Sean, been given the opportunity to do so, he would have gathered around him in the Abbey the finest band of actors, producers and scenic designers the country was capable of supplying. And he is sorrowful; but his tears are idle tears, for the day (and the chance) is over forever.

But the Abbey Theatre was in a touchy mood at this period of its existence. And who would blame it with such an amount of criticism flying around its head? And so, when in the course of a lecture I made a perfectly innocent reference to the theatre's financial losses I found myself confronted with a severe threat of legal action. Sean was just as shocked as I was when I 'phoned him about it and generously wrote to the directors, pointing out that whatever I may have said about the theatre I was still in love with it. He also pointed out that the Abbey 'fighting as she has and is against all kinds of censorship should hesitate before she establishes a legal one herself'. The affair eventually passed off and the Abbey's honour was satisfied with a public admission of error on my part and the payment of costs which I could ill afford at the time. The affair had an interesting sequel exactly one year later when Lennox Robinson, writing on behalf of the directors, told me that they were planning to publish a copy of *The Arrow* in the middle of the spring. *The Arrow* was an occasional publication issued by the Abbey Theatre. (Most of its issues have now become collectors' pieces.) In the course of his letter Lennox said: 'You have often criticised our productions and our acting, and I wish you would do for us a thoughtful article of about 2,000 words, to which other people in *The Arrow* would reply. I know you feel very sincerely about this theatre and about what you think are our deficiencies in production and acting and this would give you an opportunity to express your opinions in a serious way.' I accepted the challenge immediately, making only the stipulation that I should be allowed a brief reply to the 'other people'. After all, there were five directors, including the Managing Director, and I expected that each of them would have something to say. This was agreed to and I sent Lennox my article which he acknowledged with thanks saying: 'I think it will be useful, the sort of criticism which is helpful.' That was in February 1940. By October of that year I had heard nothing and so I wrote to Lennox asking him what had happened *The Arrow* project. He made an appointment to see me and very courteously told me that the directors had decided to drop it.

In the meantime, Yours, as ever Sean, is trying to restore my confidence in myself by telling me once again that the Abbey directors' first mistake in my regard was to let me go, that they should have retained me in an advisory capacity. They were foolish to have recourse to law; what they should have done in Sean's opinion was to challenge me to public debate. (A year later, of course, they did so, and then funked it.) He is sorry that W.B. (Yeats) went so soon; he will be missed. The B.B.C asked Sean to do a talk on him; and down in Devon they wanted him to lecture on the poet. But he turned down both offers; he couldn't bring himself to talk about those who have just passed on. The Abbey has lost in Yeats both a fighter and a friend. They're all gone now—Lady Gregory, Yeats, George Russell. A new age and new men must carry the burden now. Well let's hope that they will be greater than those who bore it before them. He is very bucked at the fact that George Jean Nathan thinks so well of *I Knock at the Door*. 'A grandly beautiful job.' This takes the sting out of Sean O'Faoláin's slating in *The London Mercury* in which he protests that Sean is a genius at plays—but . . . And Sean remembers that the only time O'Faoláin criticised a play of Sean's was when George Russell got him to criticise *The Silver Tassie*. Some day, if Sean lives, he intends to criticise O'Faoláin's criticism. I must have given him some of my reactions to *I Knock at the Door*. I liked the book quite well but it was obvious to me that Sean's mature imagination had gone heavily into the making of it, with the strange result that it seemed to create a distance between the man portrayed and the man I knew, or thought I knew. I doubt very much if I told him this at the time, but I must have told him something, for he tells me that he thinks I am right about Rabelais, though he has never read him—'the indecency is all my own'. This reminds him that Yeats had once described him as the present-day Swift, but no thanks to Jonathan, for he had never read Swift either—'not even *Gulliver's Travels*'.

He is worried about this Censorship. He doesn't know where it's all going to end though he doesn't see why dirty and smutty things shouldn't be given the go-by. The Rabelaisian O'Casey, it appears, has often felt uncomfortable listening to things said in the Music Halls; aye, and even on the wireless. And Nathan too, far away in the U.S.A., often squirms in his seat when some dirty phrase, as often as not without meaning or wit, hits him in the eye. But, let that pass. He's had to bargain with the *Sunday Chronicle* for the serialisation rights of twenty-thousand words from his book and had he not been hard-up would not have accepted their final figure. He is having a lot of annoyance and much expense in a legal wrangle concerning an unfinished lease; and this—in half a sentence towards the end of the letter—the O'Casey family, it is expected, will be increased by one more member in four months' time. By that time, of course, our world was full of gas-masks and black-outs and in neutral Ireland we were glad that Sean and his family were in Totnes and not in London. He had finished the play he was working on, *The Star Turns Red*; a Communist play and not suitable for the Abbey; a

'Left Group' called Unity Theatre is arranging to do it. He expects the printed text to be available in February 1940, and when it comes he will let me have a copy. And, of course, the copy came. And, after that, a whole twelve months' silence. Of course there is a war on and even here, despite our neutrality, we are in a state of 'emergency'. But can there be any other reason for this silence? Towards the end of 1938 the clerical proprietors of the weekly *The Standard* sold out to a board of laymen. A new editor, Peter O'Curry, was appointed. Peter, who was a friend of mine, had often said to me: 'If ever I edit a paper you will be its drama critic.' He immediately offered me the post and I accepted it. It never occurred to me that the name of this paper held sinister undertones for Sean; or that he was under the impression that its contents were still rigidly controlled by clerical supervisors. On my part I was completely wrapped up in the fact that I intended, so long as the paper held me, to bring a more liberal approach to what had hitherto passed as 'Catholic' criticism. That I succeeded in doing so became only too apparent from the abusive letters which poured into the new drama critic's postbag, to say nothing of those which reached the desk of my much harassed editor, at least one of them from a member of the Irish Hierarchy urging him to tell his drama critic to take his liberal opinions elsewhere. Sean had other friends in Dublin who corresponded with him and I had no doubt he was aware of my appointment to *The Standard*. But if he was he didn't mention it.

When at length he wrote to his 'Very dear Gaby' he confessed that it seemed years and years since he had previously done so. He pointed out that he had sent me a long time ago a copy of *The Star Turns Red* and assumed that I liked it so little that I didn't bother to say I got it. He had also, he said, sent me through Macmillans a copy of *Purple Dust* and hoped it got through safely. The copy he sent to Dr. Joe Cummins got there all right. He couldn't send it direct with the usual inscription; the authorities wouldn't let it pass. If I liked he would tear out the inscription and send it on to me. I replied saying that I had reviewed *The Star Turns Red* in *The Irish Monthly* and assumed he had received a copy of the review in the usual way. Evidently he hadn't. But I seem to have repeated much of the review in my letter to him for he greeted it with: *Et tu Brute!* saying that he believed I was partly right about the play though he thought there were some good things in it. He found, for instance, that he liked the third act better than any act of any other play he had written with the exception of the second act of *The Silver Tassie*. Nathan, he tells me, agrees with my opinion of the play, holding it to be the feeblest Sean has yet written though it is 'peculiarly invested with a poet's prophetic vision'. Anyway, he himself holds that it isn't too well done; at least it's not as good as it might have been.

But he simply cannot agree with me about *Purple Dust*. Evidently I had attacked its overplus of symbolism. O'Gaby, and you subscribing to a religion which is packed skin-tight with symbolism! He protests that, tired of controversy about his plays, he determined to write at least one that wouldn't cause any comment, one that would be seen through bursts of laughter and that incidentally would bring him in a few quid which he badly needed. The play simply grew out of his first thoughts and it wasn't until it was finished in its rough form that he saw its implications. It looked as if he had builded better than he knew. Anyway, it was to be done in New York in the autumn. He has almost completed another volume to add to *I Knock at the Door*, one which he dares say will make people uncomfortable. It appears that in spite of his intentions to the contrary he is still writing things which make people feel uncomfortable. 'I always feel uncomfortable with O'Casey' said Sir Hugh Walpole— and thereby, said O'Casey, 'hangs a tail'. But Sean will go on doing what he is doing; not to make them uncomfortable out of malice or spite or pride, but because he feels uncomfortable himself in the midst of things as they are. No sensible man could possibly be satisfied. To take one thing alone: the civilisation that could let Joyce die in poverty, and crown with a Litt.D. a writer like Wodehouse, deserves fire and brimstone from heaven. What is more it is getting it. We are all at the bier of Finnegan's Wake. Well, my dear Sean, perhaps we are; but surely there is no need to be so bitter about it. It would, indeed, be a very narrow-minded heaven which would elect to bomb London on the head of poor Bertie Wooster receiving a Litt.D. If this is the kind of celestial judgment you elect to believe in you will find me its most confirmed atheist.

But Wodehouse and his Litt.D. wasn't Sean's only worry. Looking across the Irish Sea he had some bright things to say about Sean O'Faoláin and Frank O'Connor. A double harness team these. They seemed to Sean to be amusingly cocky, bestriding Ireland like a twin colossus—Castor and Pollocks: *literary* colossuses, of course. He notices, too, that Shelah

Richards is 'doing Gertrude Lawrence' in *Private Lives*. Now why on earth does she want to waste her time in this sort of thing? Someone has sent him a copy of *The Kerryman* of 19th April 1944. Now what do you think of this? A splendid night's entertainment was provided in the Carnegie Hall, Kenmare, on Easter Sunday night, when the Bernadette Players from Dublin staged the famous play *Night Must Fall*—a curious harmony to say the least of it. The Reds in Charlemont Lane, or wherever it is, couldn't do as bad as that. Mind you, Sean is not blaming Gaby for this, or the Church: it only shows you what we are all up against; Sean, Gaby, the Church and the Soviet Army fighting in front of Moscow. Sean thinks that if the Soviets can pull back their armies before the pressure, then Hitler's had it; if not, the war will last for years. But night wasn't the only thing that was falling in this poor distressful country. Some young men of the Luftwaffe had dropped several small bombs and one block-buster right in the middle of Sean O'Casey territory on the North Strand between the Five Lamps and Newcommen Bridge with considerable loss of life and damage to property. And Sean is stirred to ask if 422 North Circular Road was left standing. Are the Five Lamps still in it? And Newcommen Bridge? How often had Sean warmed his backside on its parapet on a fine fair sunny evening. Aye, and would again, please God, as a Dublin man would say were he standing by Sean's shoulder. Well the fine fair sunny evenings came again, but no Sean. The dead were buried, the rubble cleared away, the ruins re-built. Men still warm their backsides on Newcommen Bridge but he who looks for Sean O'Casey amongst them looks in vain.

Eleven

IT had often occurred to me that Sean believed that my opinion of a play was very likely motivated by an anti-Communist bias. This, of course, was utter nonsense. Art is still art no matter what philosophy inspires it. And although I had always maintained that while art is in itself a kind of propaganda, propaganda in itself is not art, yet I found instances of direct propaganda which were in themselves great art. Chiefly amongst them were the films of Vsevolod I. Pudovkin and Sergei Eisenstein. These I hailed, and still hail, as great art notwithstanding the fact that they are imbued with Communist propaganda. The films *End of St. Petersburg* and *Ten Days that Shook the World* are instances of what I mean. Indeed, so taken was I with Pudovkin's published lectures on *Film Technique* that I seriously considered the writing of film-scripts had we the opportunities we then needed in this country for the making of films. As for his indignation over the Kerry Easter Sunday presentation of *Night Must Fall* with its reference: 'The Reds in Charlemont Lane, or wherever it is, couldn't do as bad as that.' I had been regularly attending these 'Red' presentations, not at Charlemont Lane but in a converted stable at the rear of a house on Parnell Square. Here at all events I had the opportunity of making myself familiar with live 'engaged' theatre. It was well known to the directors of this little theatre (the first of many of our 'cellar' theatres) that I was on the staff of *The Standard*. For my part I didn't write about my experiences in that paper for the simple reason that it would have created another 'Red' scare and have given rise to a bout of witch-hunting to which pastime I had pugnacious aversion. Heaven knows, I had had difficulty enough in out-facing a riot when Orson Welles, labelled as a 'Red' by one of Dublin's 'religious' organisations, paid a wartime visit to the Gate Theatre where he had begun his meteoric career. Then one week some damn-fool of a journalist on the staff of *The Standard* turned in a scare article on *Reds at Play in Dublin*. I thought that this would put an end to my welcome at the little theatre behind Parnell Square. But it didn't; they knew I wasn't responsible for what had happened: and so I continued to attend. No anti-Communist prejudice moved me here. Nor did it disturb my judgment of Sean O'Casey's plays.

But my judgment of his plays was obviously disturbing Sean O'Casey. For in the middle of 1941 I find him gallantly defending *The Star Turns Red* and saying that he just tried to show in his own way the feelings of millions of workers to things as they are. There is really nothing noble in Communism as Communism, he went on to say, but there is something necessary in it. He may well be right here if by this he is prepared to agree that there is a great deal that is unnecessary in it. But I must have annoyed him with my views at this time for he tells me that we will have to leave it at that till we meet face to face, and then 'end it all or end each other'. But we can forget this at the moment as he rejoices at the presence of two Dubliners in Totnes—the Parish Priest, Father E. Russell, a grand chap who often spends an evening chatting with Sean and Eileen, and Dr. Varian—one of the Dublin, Talbot Street, Varians, a fine Bohemian who fits well and hearty into the O'Casey household. He (Sean) has quite a job on hand reducing the 100,000 words of his second volume to a more reasonable length to be entitled *Pictures in the Hallway*.

I find it necessary to mention these matters because Sean's emerging alliance with the Soviet Union and his growing suspicion towards those who refused to stand with him led in no uncertain fashion in the direction of the cross-roads at which he and I parted. I note that he has told his latest biographer that he was always a Communist. If he was he managed to conceal the fact from many of his early friends. So far as I was concerned his Communism began to thrust itself forward only towards the end of World War II when it was obvious that the Allies were likely to win and the Russian tanks were now pointing westwards.

Early in 1943 my former Abbey colleague Shelah Richards planned to present a season of plays at the Olympia Theatre, Dublin. She hoped to include *Red Roses for Me* and asked me to sound out Sean about the possibility. I was pleased at the idea since I felt that Sean needed all the royalties he could get at this stage in his career. Sean readily agreed to the production of his play. Shelah then asked me to cut the play to a length suitable for presentation. I told her that I wouldn't do this unless I had Sean's written permission to do it and I suggested that she should write to Sean and ask for this permission. She called to see me a few days afterwards and told me that Sean had written to say that he wouldn't allow me to cut the play, as I was writing for *The Standard* and that all my views were coloured by the biased ecclesiastical attitude of that paper.

The effect of this message was as if Sean in person had struck me a severe blow in the face. Had he himself written to me to tell me what he felt I might have borne the blow with less bitterness. I felt that what integrity I had had been unfairly impugned. I would not have cut the play without his permission, and, indeed, his acquiescence. All the super-sensitiveness in my nature bristled like a porcupine's quills. I knew now what it meant to have 'an ego like a raging tooth'. If I had hitherto criticised Sean's plays I had done so merely from the point of view of what I believed to be their viability in the theatre, and in comparison with his earlier masterpieces. His letter to Shelah was, to a person of my nature, nothing short of a challenge to combat. From now on, I reflected, I would meet him at every frontier—well armed.

Of course I wrote him a flaming letter. 'Woful' was what he called it, dropping a letter in his anxiety to forget what I had written. In the course of his reply he talked about many things and only incidentally of the thing that stood between us. Evidently I had told him of a passage in the play which I might have cut on the grounds that it would offend a Catholic audience with results which would hit his royalties at the box office. 'Between the two of us' he wrote, 'I'd love to be shown the passage that you think might be offensive. I haven't the slightest awareness of it . . .' As it happened, the passage in question caused no offence to the audiences who saw the play at the Olympia Theatre and a year or two later at the Gaiety Theatre; a fact which I attribute entirely to Sean O'Casey's overwhelming popularity with Irish audiences. The tone of Sean's letter was so reasonable and so placid compared with the burning indignation of mine that I felt rather ashamed of myself and after giving the whole affair some thought and discussing it with my wife I decided I would do my best to forget this blow to my integrity, and so Sean and I continued to correspond with each other. For the next two-and-a-half years letters passed between us but with nothing like their former regularity.

Then in June 1946 the thing happened which helped to snap the last link in our long-standing friendship. A young Irish poet, Val Iremonger, reviewing *Oak Leaves and Lavender* in the *Irish Times* wrote: 'I am still young enough to feel sorry—and a little angry—watching genius being squandered and frittered away upon ephemeral concepts such as Mr. O'Casey has elected to promulgate.' Now it so happened that I was about to review for *The Standard* the Gaiety Theatre presentation of *Red Roses for Me* directed by another Abbey Theatre colleague of mine, Ria Mooney. I opened my review by quoting Val Iremonger and saying that sorrow and anger in such circumstances are not solely the prerogatives of youth. 'Even middle-age may drown an eye unused to flow on being compelled to witness the incandescence of genius doused in an overflow of its own wilfulness.' I had found *Red Roses for Me* to be a mixture of modes, episodic, remotely autobiographical, and dripping over with sentimentality. And then in the middle of my notice this came:

> One of the author's conclusions about Dublin life has always made me pause—and take a deep breath. I refer to the conclusion which he attempts to enshrine in the hocus-pocus concerning his 'Our Lady of Eblana'. Faced with it, I find myself forced to recall the kindliness and the understanding of the personality I once knew in order to assure myself that this is not a piece of coldly-calculated bigotry. Protestant heroism does not necessarily postulate Catholic ignorance. Yet, for reasons best known to the author, the work is heavily weighted in this direction, despite the castigation administered in the interests of low comedy to an aspect of Orange intolerance.

I concluded the review with the following paragraph:

> Like it or leave it, Sean O'Casey is one of the world's greatest playwrights, a dramatic genius of the first order, but it is not on works like *Red Roses for Me* that posterity will establish its verdict. Unless there is a return to first principles, we shall be forced to join our young poet in his anger and tears.

I have often wondered to what extent my opinions of this play (which I see no reason to revise) were shared by others. Some English critics at that time saw the play as a magnificent piece of dramatic poetry, beautifully conceived and written, 'with an Irishman's passion and poet's fervour' (as one put it). However, when the play was presented in New York in December 1955 the critics saw it otherwise, John Chapman of the *Daily News*

saying that it belongs more to a page than to a stage, while Walter
Kerr of the *New York Herald Tribune* wrote 'the fog licked
steadily at the beautiful settings but the fog gets into the bones of
the play too. Indeed, this rhetorical exercise is seen to have no
bones.' Robert Coleman of the *Daily Mirror* doubted if the play
'would have better than a limited appeal, because it is controversial, and may prove highly objectionable to the truly devout
. . .' It was interesting to find that I was not alone in sensing an
element of offence to religious suceptibilities.

Sean's immediate reaction to my notice was to write a letter to
the editor asking what 'your critic Mr. Fallon' meant by certain
passages in his criticism. The editor (as editors will) replied to
Sean saying he would like a public discussion on the matter,
assuring him that he would put as much space as he required at
his disposal. Sean's reply was as follows:

> Sir—There is neither time nor reason for what you call 'a public
> discussion'. I am not concerned with the criticism of the play as a play.
> Your critic is as likely to be right there as he is likely to be wrong. I am
> only concerned with the charges made during the course of the
> criticism. So I shall be very glad if Mr. Fallon tells me the reason he
> had for giving the name 'hocus pocus' to the episode of 'Our Lady of
> Eblana'; and why he thinks the treatment of this an instance of 'cold
> calculated bigotry'. Less than a quarter of a column will, I'm sure,
> serve the purpose. It is but just, that, since the charge appeared in your
> journal the reason for it should be given there.

Sean's letter was published in *The Standard* of the 9th August
1946, along with a two-column open letter from *The Standard's*
drama critic to Sean. In the course of it I wrote: 'Your play *Red
Roses for Me* was first produced here some years ago (March 1943,
in fact). On that occasion I said as much about it as I said last
month. Possibly more. Yet you found no reason then to write to
"Mr. The Editor" about it. I wonder why; and why you should
do so now?' I found it impossible to believe that Sean had not
seen my review of the first production; Shelah Richards, if not
one of his many friends in Dublin, was bound to have sent it to
him. And yet he had never referred to it in any of his letters to
me in the years between.

Having described the whole of the 'Our Lady of Eblana'
sequence, from its beginning in Act 1—when a group of women
and men enter carrying a statue of the Blessed Virgin 'more than
two feet high' and the first woman's speech to the Protestant
Mrs. Braydon is: 'Could you spare a pinch of your Hudson's
soap to give the Blessed Virgin a bit of a wash?'—right up to the

chorus of hymn-singing men and women who hail the return of the statue (new painted by the Protestant Brennan Moore who had taken it away for this purpose) as a miracle. After the hymn singing, three of the women speak. Eeada tells us:

> She came back; of Her own accord.

Dympna declares that:

> From her window little Ursula looked, and saw Her come; in the moonlight along the street. She came stately. Blinded by the coloured light that shone around Her, the child fell back, in a swoon she fell full on the floor beneath her.

This is followed by the First Man's speech:

> My eyes caught a glimpse of Her too, glidin' back to where she came from. Regal and proud she was, an' wondrous, so that my eyes failed; me knees thrimbled an' bent low, an' me heart whispered a silent prayer to itself as th' Vision passed me by, an' I fancied I saw a smile on Her Holy face.

I then went on to say:

> Now, what can anyone with eyes to see, ears to hear, and common-sense to reason with make of this scene? What do *you* want us to make of it, Sean O'Casey? Are these liars and hypocrites and fools, your chosen representatives of the Catholics living in the poor working-class districts of Dublin? You asked me why I called this scene a scene of hocus-pocus, why I feared the possibility of a cold-blooded bigotry? Knowing me as you do, knowing that I know (and that you know) a great deal about the Catholics in the poor working-class districts of Dublin—I am amazed you should ask me! You will hasten to point out, of course, that you dealt far from tenderly in Act 3 with Orange ignorance and bigotry in the persons of your Dowzard and Foster. But you took care, did you not, to provide throughout your play a carefully dramatised corrective in the dignified bearing and the dignified words of the Rev. Protestant Rector and in the characterisations of Ayamonn and Mrs. Braydon? What corrective did you provide for the lying and the hypocrisy and the folly of your representative working-class Catholics? In your first letter to this paper you said that you felt sure that 'Catholics want to rid their city of things *ugly and common and mean as much as Protestants do.*' Will you allow me to tell you in return that I defy anyone to see and hear or read your *Red Roses for Me* and detect even a jot or tittle of that feeling of yours. We may take your letter's word for it, Sean O'Casey, but in deference to our understanding, we must reject your play's. Make no mistake about this. I am not so foolish as to expect that you ought to write plays to suit a pattern of thought other than your own. But, for integrity's sake, do stand by that pattern and do not assume amazement if some other—even an old friend turned critic—should elect to stand against it. Let us be faithful to the light that we have . . .

The conclusion of the letter read as follows:

Sitting here in the cool of an August twilight I am thinking of our long and valued friendship, of the fundamental differences of opinion which that friendship has so far survived, of your many public and private kindnesses to me, and of that deeply-rooted affection for our native city which we in common share. But how could I honour that truth and frankness which you have always respected in friend and foe, how could I face you again, or my good friends and neighbours again (of every description, without any exception of persons) if I did not boldly deliver myself of the opinions that are in me. These opinions may be right or they may be wrong, but . . . such as they are, take them. With every good wish and all the old affection.

There was no reply.

Looking back on this affair I could see that it had little to do with Sean's 'Communism' but much to do with that 'anti-Catholicism' which Alan Simpson some years later (in *Beckett and Behan and a Theatre in Dublin*) was to sense when comparing O'Casey with Behan. He found that this 'anti-Catholicism' was 'tinged slightly and I am sure subconsciously with Orangeism . . . his anti-clerical jeerings have a Protestant rather than an atheist slant . . . His atheism, in fact, strikes me as being of a super-ficial nature; one might almost say adopted for the sake of annoying the Irish clergy.' In subsequent plays, *Cock-a-Doodle-Dandy* for instance, and in one of his essays *Merrical of Miracles* (particularly in this) Lourdes and Fatima are sneered at with all the invective he can so readily bring to his command. To me, of course, this is merely a logical extension of what moved him in *Red Roses for Me*, to *invent* a 'miracle' based on the ignorance and hypocrisy of Dublin's working-class Catholics. I may be out-rageously old-fashioned in my attitude towards these things but I know that I respect the traditions and beliefs of my Jewish friends and neighbours, as well as those of my separated Christian brethren. I can admire the Indian concept of the Atma no less than the Chinese idea of the Tao. I would not consider it beneath my dignity to remove my shoes before entering a mosque and I would be extremely offended at anyone who sneered at this custom.

From this point on the one time 'friend and buttie, Gaby' became 'Mr. Fallon' and then 'Fallon'. Yet the break was not quite complete. A few frayed strands of the tow-rope held on my side, at least. One cannot shake off a long-standing friendship with a man of pervasive personality as easily as all that. In the spring of 1947 the Abbey Theatre's great actor, F. J. McCormick (Peter Judge), died at the comparatively early age of 56. He had been Sean's first friend amongst the actors of the Abbey Theatre. He was married to the Abbey actress, Eileen Crowe. He had created the roles of Seumas Shields in *The Gunman* and Joxer Daly in *Juno and the Paycock*. His death was a national shock and created a national mourning. Later that year a memorial gathering was held and its organisers were anxious that Sean should supply a few words in praise of the dead actor. They approached me in the matter but I tried to point out to them that I was now *persona non grata* with the dramatist. However, my wife 'phoned Eileen O'Casey and having exchanged pleasantries about the families on each side she broached the subject of the tribute to McCormick. Eileen immediately protested that Sean was ill and she changed the conversation. After the 'phone call my wife wrote to Eileen pointing out that nothing more than a sentence was required—Sean's signature would do the rest. There was no reply to that letter.

Then out of the blue in an edition of *Irish Writing* of June 1947 came a thunderbolt entitled: *Tender Tears for Poor O'Casey* launched by the great Jove himself. In it he collected all his Irish critics together, amongst them Valentin Iremonger, T. C. Murray, the Abbey dramatist, Fallon, Liam O'Flaherty, F. R. Higgins, poet and Abbey director, the poet Austin Clarke, Professor Daniel Corkery, R. M. Fox, who wrote about O'Casey in *The Irish Statesman*, Brinsley MacNamara, another Abbey dramatist, and the then dead A. E. Malone (a former drama critic on *The Irish Times*). Like the valiant little tailor in the story *Seven at a Blow* be belaboured the lot of us good and hard and each according to kind. None of us seemed disposed to answer him. Anyway, *Irish Writing* was a very occasional publication and Heaven knows when its next issue would see the light. However, there was one reference in Sean's defence of himself and his plays which caught most of us on the raw. It ran as follows: 'Here's what A. E. Malone (then considered an authority on the theatre), Malone with his pert moustache on his little, frightened face; here's what he said: "*The Plough and the Stars* isn't as good a play as *Juno*. It is a series of *tableaux vivants*. O'Casey is a photographic artist . . .".'

'With his pert moustache on his little, frightened face'! A. E. Malone was not a friend of mine. I occasionally bumped into him in the theatre. I disagreed completely with his assessment of Sean O'Casey's plays. But the fact remained that he was no longer in the land of the living and could not defend himself. I had asked Valentin Iremonger if he intended to reply on his own behalf and he said he might do so in the next issue of *Irish Writing*, provided there *was* a next issue of that periodical. Then one day a woman called to see me in my office. It so happened that she was the widow of A. E. Malone. She wanted to discuss the article and in particular its reference to her late husband. Tears were shed during that interview and they were not for Mr. O'Casey.

'Never destroy anything you've written' said Sean to me on one occasion, 'for you never know when it will come in handy.' And he instanced this by pointing out that much of the dialogue in his rejected script of *The Crimson and the Tri-Colour* had found its way into *The Plough and the Stars*. True to precept he saw to it that most of the material in *Irish Writing* appeared many years later in *The Green Crow*, the contents of which were aptly summarised in the opening paragraph of a review in *Time* of 26th March 1956. The paragraph is as follows:

> Like most men, Sean O'Casey is a hero to his mirror. Yet he has reason above vanity for some of his pride; he climbed out of the Dublin slums to the fame-upholstered penthouse of playwriting leaving at least two masterpieces to mark the trail, i.e. *The Plough and the Stars* and *Juno and the Paycock*. Along the way he has also taken on a habit of piling chips on his shoulders and wearing them like epaulettes. *The Green Crow* is largely a dress parade of pet peeves, mostly in the form of journalistic pieces on the theatre, actors, critics, fellow-playwrights, and Lord have mercy on their souls, the benighted detractors of Sean O'Casey.

From time to time onwards it fell to my lot to review Sean's autobiographical works either in the pages of *The Irish Monthly* or at the microphones of Radio Eireann. It was a task I did not particularly relish for the simple reason that the broken friendship added, no doubt, a touch of bitterness to my general dislike of the books themselves. Though they have won for him much esteem in the U.S.A., particularly amongst the Joyceolators, and have helped many a sabbattical student to an easily earned Ph.D. I could not help thinking of the energy content which, had things been otherwise, might have gone to the making of great plays. This created a situation comparable, no doubt, to that which brought a memorable reply from Oscar Wilde when told he would be cross-examined by Edward Carson: 'No doubt he will perform his task with all the added bitterness of an old friend.'

My basic dislike of the autobiographies was to be found mainly in three directions; first of all, the narcissism of the style which the use of the third person gave the writing as well as the attempts to out-sing Synge or to out-jump Joyce in the manufacture of 'portmanteau' words—'playing Jeff to Joyce's Mutt' was how Padraic Colum put it. Then the unreliability of the content, the total absence of dates; indeed, the absence of what even the common reader would describe as material evidence. Finally, his unaccountable bitterness. I was not alone in expressing such dissatisfaction. Reviewing *Rose and Crown* in *The Observer* of 12th July 1952, Louis MacNeice refers to the author's 'mythopoeic talent' to which, he held, neither London nor New York gave such openings as Dublin did. And he went on to say:

> And while no reader could do other than sympathise with the struggles and sufferings of O'Casey many will be bored by these pages upon pages of complaints about the directors of the Abbey Theatre and the dramatic critics in London.

Many were; and I was amongst their number. MacNeice found that some of the O'Casey prose reminded him of the work of the ineffable Amanda Ros, a conclusion to which I (being a devotee of that lady's genius) had already come.

Another poet, Austin Clarke, reviewing *Sunset and Evening Star* in *The Irish Times* of 6th November 1954, found nothing in it of the serenity implied by its title. 'Vigorous and unbowed despite his years' he wrote, 'Mr. O'Casey remains a mighty literary assailant, a ferocious fighter—from a safe distance.' Of the author's style he wrote: 'He alternates the vernacular of dear dirty Dorset Street with the "aesthetic prose" which he has fashioned for himself in recent years.' Much earlier, George Orwell, reviewing *Drums Under the Window* in *The Observer* of 28th October 1945, complained of the 'masses of pretentious style' and the effect of narcissism produced by the use of the third person. He also wrote this:

> Considering the story of Anglo-Irish relations, it isn't surprising that there should be Irishmen whose life-work is abusing England: what does call for remark is that they should be able to look for support to the English people, and in some cases should even, like Mr. O'Casey himself, prefer to live in the country which is the object of their hatred.

Orwell in the grave, Sean was to remember this.

On the grounds of the reliability of content of these auto-biographical books, it must be said for Sean that he insisted that he was writing 'a story' of his life. Indeed his publishers had on hesitation whatever in quoting in a blurb an English novelist who described the first volume of autobiography as 'a gorgeous farce'. His latest biographer, Mr. Saros Cowasjee, acknowledging this 'story' aspect (in *Sean O'Casey: The Man Behind the Plays*) writes: 'A student who uses the autobiographies for a critical study of the man faces one serious difficulty. O'Casey rarely gives dates and seldom tells us his age or gives the time of a particular incident. Thus it becomes hard to relate events to their surroundings.' A little further on he writes: 'Another problem, and a minor one, is that some of the accounts are not very factual.' However, some of the *dramatis personnae* concerned in the accounts did not consider the problem to be such a minor one. Sean's work of hacking and hewing at his life until it reached the meaningfulness he considered necessary led on at least one occasion to a complaint being lodged with his publisher, the author himself agreeing to make amends in the next volume. The complainant was the distinguished Dublin art critic, Mr. Cornelius Curran, who in that intemperate chapter on the poet AE (George Russell) in *Inishfallen, Fare Thee Well* found that certain sentences not of his authorship were interpolated into a passage purporting to come from the critic himself. This, of course, may not have been an act of deliberate malice on Sean's part.

In an article in *Irish Writing No. 6* Padraic Colum, dealing with the three volumes which preceded *Inishfallen, Fare Thee Well*, accuses the author of manifest injustice to his contemporaries. 'He does partial justice to James Connolly' he wrote. 'He does injustice to AE, Arthur Griffith, Douglas Hyde, Eoin MacNeill, Countess Markiewicz. Thomas MacDonagh and Joseph Plunkett are mentioned once, and that with a jibe at their poetry. But each wrote beautiful poems and each went to their death knowingly.' But if there is something beyond injustice Sean administers it to AE in *Inishfallen, Fare Thee Well*. His treatment of T. P. O'Connor and Joseph Holloway (the well-known Dublin theatre note-taker whose many manuscript volumes are now in the National Library of Ireland) is unnecessarily virulent. Holloway's crime was, of course, that he disliked O'Casey's plays and took exception to the character of Rosie Redmond in *The Plough and the Stars*.

However, it was for the dead George Orwell that, in *Sunset and Evening Star*, Sean reserved his bitterest words. His defence was to the effect that Orwell's publishers asked for O'Casey's blessing on some early Orwell work. O'Casey refused. Some time after the refusal Orwell reviewed *Drums Under the Window* in which amongst other things he spoke (in that passage quoted above) about Irishmen being content to live in and on a country which is the object of their hatred. If Sean answered Orwell when that review was written the answer has escaped my attention; nor can I recall its being referred to in any of the other volumes. But in *Sunset and Evening Star* a whole rambling chapter is devoted to 'Rebel Orwell'. Challenging Koestler's statement that the dead Orwell's life 'was a consistent series of rebellions against the condition of society in general and his own predicament'— which seems to be a reasonably just appraisal of the man—Sean has this to say: 'Rebel indeed! Rather a yielding blob that buried itself away from the problems of living that all life has to face and overcome. No fight in him; always a-running away and a-yielding. What did he rebel against... ?' Most Irish reviewers resisted the obvious temptation to ask the author what Sean was doing when rebellion blazed in the streets of Dublin in 1916 and guerrilla fighting ran through the years that followed. Readers of *Feathers from a Green Crow* will in that collection of early writing learn of a young man who wanted 'please the God of the Gael' no less, to be in the van of the Irish people, to 'write with a sword, an epitaph to Emmet on the hearts of their foe'. Only the God of the Gael and Sean O'Casey know why that sword should fall from the young man's nerveless hand. So far as the world is concerned Orwell fought for 'the Reds' in Spain and never complained that he hadn't met Sean O'Casey there. However, Orwell's crime was apparently that of accusing Sean O'Casey of abusing England. (If there were other crimes—and I suspect there were—they didn't come to the surface.) Sean's answer to the dead Orwell came like a thundering broadside from Nelson's *Victory*—'an uncle of Sean's had fought and was wounded at Balaclava, a brother had fought in the Boer War, another in the first World War, a nephew in a submarine, a son of his had served in the Royal Artillery, and another was serving in the Artillery now.' But Sean—oh, where was he? In face of that reply to Orwell there was little that Irish reviewers could say to the man who had written so scathingly in his anti-recruiting ballad about *The Grand Oul Dame Britannia*, the man who in such lines as these pointed to others where freedom lay:

Beneath thy flag fresh hopes we feel,
     Ireland, dear Ireland
We'll gild its folds with glint of steel,
     And rifle's flame, dear Ireland.
In garish day, 'neath night's damp dew
It's green and white and orange hue
Shall signal death to England's crew
     And hope to thee, dear Ireland.

Laughter, holding both its sides, since Sean had forbidden tears, seemed to be the only way of greeting such amazing acrobatics. Was it possible that despite the hacking and hewing (or, indeed, because of it) Sean was actually building better than he knew, that a portrait of the man complete in every contradictory aspect of his character was inexorably emerging? At all events this is what seemed to me to be happening. There is a particularly revealing chapter in *Sunset and Evening Star* entitled 'The Dree Dames'. In it Sean dramatises with the convincing faithfulness of video-tape the visit to him of three women, one of whom bitterly attacks the Soviet Union for the alleged arrest of her husband 'By the Ogpu!' The ever reasonable Sean tries to be patient with the lady and her supporting companions but all to no avail. On the departure of the unpacified, still-excitable ladies, Sean communes with himself:

What an arrogant mind, what a blustering manner, that woman had! The truth is mine. Some seem to think that truth comes banging at everybody's door. A mind that flushes into a rage whenever another ventures to disagree with it. Out for free thought, yet dragging compulsion into every word she uttered! Only what I say, only in what I believe, is the Truth. An individual authoritarian. Only her truth contained divinity. The way some hurl the truth about: down a man with it!

O, Sean, Sean, would that we had the gift of seeing ourselves in the beam of the blinding searchlight we turn upon others.

And yet, Iago, the pity of it! Sean O'Casey, the man I knew, was by no means lacking in courage. His early struggles against near-blindness and grinding poverty bear testimony to that. Padraic Colum has praised him for his treatment of the environment of the poor in the early years of this century in Ireland's capital city—'their proximity to filth, the indecently crowded rooms where men and women and children slept'. 'He might' wrote Colum, 'have written of this environment complainingly, protestingly. Instead he has written of it defiantly.'

163

The psychologist, now considered a necessary adjunct to both divine and physician, will soon need to companion the literary historian. Such a man reading the volumes of this informative autobiography will find much to explain in the quirks of character it reveals. Fame came to Sean O'Casey much too late to ensure that a reasonable balance would be kept throughout his literary pilgrimage. Then fate struck hard in Yeats's rejection of *The Silver Tassie,* a savage blow which marked the point of no return both to the theatre-workshop which Sean's developing genius needed and to the country which he loved so well. His repeated insistence in recent years that Yeats was the only worthwhile critic Ireland ever produced is part of that psychological inversion which in a similar fashion overtips his love-hatred of his country into bombastic criticism of almost everything she does. He has never to my knowledge said with his much-loved Whitman: 'Do I contradict myself? Very well, then, I contradict myself (I am large, I contain multitudes).' Such an acknowledgment might have helped the world to understand him better. Instead, he has always adopted the attitude: 'I am right because I was always right.' There is one short sad sentence in *Inishfallen, Fare Thee Well* which as a piece of self-revelation might stand as a fifteen-word epitaph for this remarkable man:

'He had to submit to many humiliations that ground rage and bitterness into his soul.'

Chesterton, whose rhetoric Sean secretly admired, even while he publicly hated all that that writer stood for, once rightly said of the Irish that all their wars were merry while all their songs were sad. One of my difficulties from our quarrel onwards was to persuade Sean O'Casey's friends and mine that despite what had passed between us I still retained a great affection for the man. Perhaps it was that, more than another, I had known—and felt I still knew—an O'Casey whose characteristics did not tally with the public image drawn by the man himself. This Sean was a kindly, generous, hospitable man, having little in common with the man of the autobiographies, whose ire is deepened by the Old King Cole jollity which the volubility is made to assume. One of my Abbey Theatre colleagues, our distinguished actress and producer Ria Mooney (the creator of Rosie Redmond in *The Plough and the Stars*) told me that when she visited Sean in exile on one occasion she taxed him with this bitterness and contrasted his literary pugnacity with (to his intimates) his well-known kindness and hospitality. She said that he told her that he didn't know what happened to him whenever he sat down to write, that things just seemed to come out that way and that there was nothing he could do about it.

After our break in friendship I found myself with some one hundred and sixty O'Casey letters on my hands. I felt I ought to do something about them. I told some of my friends that I would write to Sean and ask permission to edit them under his supervision. Some of them were astonished that I should think of doing this. I must confess that I do not understand such people. I can violently disagree with a man and still retain a great affection for him; and most of my race can do the same. I have watched the Leader of the Opposition in Dail Eireann meet our Taoiseach (Prime Minister) on a most amicable social footing each knowing that they, as we say, 'were going to knock the daylights out of each other' in verbal conflict in Dail Eireann the following afternoon. I felt it would be just like that between myself and Sean O'Casey. It wasn't; not exactly, that is. I wrote him a warm friendly letter. I got a cold, though not unfriendly, reply. The letters 'were not written for publication no more than your own as you should know'. Well, that was that. Four years later, with in between many hard critical words on my side, I sent him, in an outburst of the old affection, a copy of the first edition of *Purple Dust* (I had two) on learning through a mutual friend that he had none. It was returned with a polite, courteous, though oh, so cold, letter, that I have seldom been able to bring myself to look at it. Yet, what had I a right to expect? I had criticised him up to the top of my bent. I would, if I deemed it necessary, continue to criticise him. Sean knew that, and I knew Sean knew it. I had criticised him with severity. This was to a great extent a product of his own training. The disparity in ages had brought about a kind of father–son relationship. Perhaps I should have been kinder, more considerate in my criticism. Perhaps he should have been more considerate in his. It was a problem which even the writing of this book may not be competent to solve.

Twelve

I HAVE read and studied many analyses of the plays of Sean O'Casey, but for clear perception of form and content in relation to the theatre, none to equal the analysis made by Richard Findlater in his book *The Unholy Trade*. Findlater is neither an Irishman nor a Roman Catholic and must therefore be deemed free of that bias which the dramatist and his supporters hold to be the main approach of Irish and Catholic critics to his plays.

It is Findlater's contention that it is on the earlier plays written between 1923 and 1929 when the dramatist still lived in Ireland that his reputation rests. He sees the later plays as only partially successful works 'morality plays in Limbo, ambitious monuments in which the creator has not had the capacity to realise his intention'. According to Findlater, O'Casey, a master of urban realism, failed to transplant himself in exile and so failed to find a tradition in which to work or a speech or a form in which to clothe his vision. 'The story of Mr. O'Casey's later evolution" he writes, 'is the story of a dramatist in search of an audience.' Perhaps the most penetrative of Findlater's comments is that concerning Sean's anti-clericalism which he considers to be 'the unresolved personal problem whose intrusion has helped to thwart the development of his later style'. To my knowledge Findlater is the only critic who has succeeded in deducing this 'unresolved personal problem' from the plays themselves. Indeed, on this score the words used by Hamlet in another context might well be applied to Sean in this one: 'In my heart there was a kind of fighting that would not let me sleep.'

In an article in the *New York Times* of 8th January 1964, entitled 'O'Casey Explains Ban of His Plays' (of which more later) Sean points out that his first three plays *Juno, The Plough and the Stars* and *The Shadow of a Gunman* 'always hailed in Ireland as O'Casey's great plays, when they appeared on the Abbey stage were received by poet, critic, playwright and novelist with biting scorn and decided condemnation'. Poet, playwright and novelist consisted at most of three people, Higgins, Clarke, and O'Flaherty. As for the critics. The *Irish Independent* critic wrote of *Juno and the Paycock*: 'This play stands as one of the greatest things done by the Abbey Players. It is a distinct advance on *The Shadow of a Gunman* and is a courageous play, providing entertainment for the many. Better still, it stimulates thought and exercises the imagination.' And the scholarly W. J. Lawrence, though strangely blind to the searing irony of the play's final scene, wrote in *The Irish Statesman*: 'I doff my hat to Mr. Sean O'Casey. He is the realisation of one of my long cherished hopes. There are moments in *Juno* that transcend all mere theatricality and thrill one to the marrow.' And there were other equally favourable notices.

Sean's memory is more selective than most. The fact that life wasn't roses, roses all the way has seemingly forced him to believe that it was nothing but thorns and has led him into (to quote his own words in the *New York Times*) 'fighting what I thought to be aggression where none was meant'. Richard Findlater's picture of him, living on in England 'nursing his anger—a man in perpetual opposition, a real genius who was always the only one in step' is one which has been largely painted by the thoughts, words and deeds of Sean himself. In his early plays, as Findlater points out, it was not with dramatic form but with human content that Sean was concerned. 'He was busy with the urgency of what he had to say, not with the problem of how to say it.' The problem of dramatic form made its entrance with *The Silver Tassie* but the human content was there as well. To dramatise the horrors of war he instinctively broke the bonds of naturalism and experimented with a form derived from his experience of German expressionism. Had Yeats accepted the play either of two things might have happened. Sean might have mastered the form completely, or reverted, before it was too late, to that naturalism from which his earlier masterpieces were hewn. Unfortunately, he felt he had a mission to restore colour and life and poetry to the English theatre. This delusion of grandeur led him away completely from the ground on which his earlier battles had been fought and won. As Findlater points out 'the holy fire abated in O'Casey's work' with his departure from Dublin,

> and his subsequent plays—whatever their streaks of genius—are ultimately unsuccessful. For he was trying to create a new drama in an alien country out of his own head, and he had the imagination but not the intellect to do it. He turned away from the naturalist play completely, experimented in the symbolic drama, and in his recent work has attempted to resolve an uneasy amalgam of the two, with a copious admission of song and dance. There is a mixture of prose and verse, of naturalistic characters and symbolic figures, of rhetoric and cross-talk, and he has consistently failed to organise the diverse elements of his material on the same level of intensity and to find a suitable form in which to house his experience.

This analysis of Findlater's is one with which any Irish critic who knows the theatre would wholeheartedly agree, but had such a critic as many heads as Hydra, O'Casey's retort of 'Irish and Roman Catholic bigotry' would stop them all. Sean is a first-class propagandist so far as O'Casey the dramatist is concerned and he has seen to it that most of his American friends firmly believe that the Irish under the domination of the Roman Catholic Hierarchy have cast out a great dramatist from their midst. In this the dramatist is mistaken, as I propose to show when dealing with *The Drums of Father Ned*, and its alleged banning by the Roman Catholic Archbishop of Dublin. Most of Mr. O'Casey's American friends seem to subscribe to the doctrine that their favourite dramatist is much too outspoken for what they call a 'priest-ridden Ireland'. It is seemingly futile to point out that 'priest-ridden' Ireland has but one priest for every five-hundred Roman Catholics, that there is one Church of Ireland, Presbyterian, or Methodist clergyman for every 200 of our separated brethren, or that in respect of the total flock in each case, our separated brethren have close on three clergymen to every one Roman Catholic priest.

At the end of August 1954 I left the staff of *The Standard* to take up an appointment as drama critic on the newly launched *Evening Press*. Shortly before my departure the editor of *The Standard*, Peter O'Curry, resigned his post and had been replaced by a man whose views were rather less liberal than Peter's. Early in 1955 it was announced that Cyril Cusack (formerly of the Abbey Theatre) proposed to present a new play by Sean O'Casey at the Gaiety Theatre, Dublin, on February 28th. It was entitled *The Bishop's Bonfire*. The news created much interest for two reasons. The first, amongst O'Casey fans who were looking forward with interest to what would be the first new O'Casey play to be presented in Dublin since *Red Roses for Me*; the second with a small section of the unco' guid who saw—or thought they saw—in the new play's title an 'atheist's' challenge to Ireland's orthodoxy. Two weeks before the play opened an attack was launched on its author in the pages of *The Standard*: 'Mr. O'Casey's name is now in the public eye' it warned, 'His bishop's bonfire is shortly to be ignited. Is it inflammable material?' A week later the same paper said: 'It is rather an understatement to write that the article on Sean O'Casey which appeared in last week's *Standard* aroused considerable interest. It goes without saying that people were shocked by the full realisation of the bitter venom with which O'Casey regards the Faith and its ministers.' The article then went on to say: 'It is one of the contradictions of modern life that he should be offered a stage in the capital city of the country most steadfastly ranged against the enemies who are his friends.' And in conclusion the article asked: 'Where is the nation's self-respect?'

Now this was not only unjust but it amounted almost to an incitement of a breach of the peace. It was an attitude which, of course, had a strong appeal for a section—a very small section—of the community. It appealed in particular to a McCarthy-like 'religious' organisation called *Maria Duce*—with anti-Communism and anti-semitism as main planks in its platform—an organisation which I had fought against in the columns of this very paper *The Standard* until the authorities took notice and the organisation was officially suppressed. Conor Cruise O'Brien (the 'Donat O'Donnell' author of *Maria Cross*) wrote a strong letter of protest to *The Standard* which *The Standard* published. Yet Sean O'Casey himself was in a great measure to blame for the attitude which this paper took towards his coming play. In the *Daily Worker* of 23rd March 1944 he had written an article entitled *Shadow of the Vatican* which began 'Everywhere there is a Vatican Community, there is the shadow . . .' and ended with a criticism of a pastoral issued by Cardinal MacRory of Armagh, who in Sean's view could choose between being dubbed ignorant or a liar. 'Is it any wonder' concluded Sean, 'that Marx thought religion to be the dope of the workers?' In March 1948 he had been asked by *The Irish Democrat* what he thought of the future prospects for Labour and Republicanism in Ireland.

His reply was as follows: 'I have no views on the next step Labour or Republicanism in Eire should take, except to found a new order under the guardianship of Matt Talbot. I'm far more interested in the political and military conditions of China—it means far more to the world than Dev. or Dillon or Sean McBride.' Again in 1948 when interviewed by an *Irish Press* correspondent (the late Terry Ward) he told that paper: 'All the good men in Ireland are dead. I take no further interest in the Dail until there are 50 Communists there.' So that the new editor of *The Standard* had plenty of fuel obligingly supplied by Mr. O'Casey himself for this attempted pre-*Bonfire* bonfire.

On the opening night of *The Bishop's Bonfire* my wife Rose was recovering from an attack of influenza and felt that a visit to the Gaiety Theatre would be hardly likely to speed recovery. Under the circumstances I invited the editor of *The Evening Press*, Douglas Gageby, a non-Catholic and a distinguished scholar of Trinity College, to come with me. Douglas gladly accepted. On my part I was pleased to have an unbiased witness in my company. When we got to North King Street a mob, consisting mostly of students who failed to secure admission to the theatre, was milling outside the Gaiety. Here and there were members of the *Maria Duce* organisation, acting presumably as anti-Communist pickets. I would not have been aware of their presence had not one of them shouted out: 'There he goes, Fallon the pervert!' the young man quite obviously being unaware of the fact that the word has two possible meanings. Douglas and I made our way without much difficulty to the theatre vestibule. From there we watched through the glass doors the milling students being kept on the move by a dozen stalwart Civic Guards. I mention this fact for the simple reason that Sir Tyrone Guthrie in his memory of that evening declares that he saw a squadron of mounted police charging the mob in King Street at three in the afternoon. Unfortunately for Sir Tyrone's memory mounted police had not been seen on the streets of Dublin or indeed in any part of the twenty-six counties for well over thirty years.

Mrs. O'Casey had arrived in Dublin in time for the dress rehearsal and in an interview had said that she felt confident that Dublin people would like this play. In this, so far as box-office returns are concerned, she was perfectly right. I reminded Douglas Gageby of her presence in the Gaiety and of the inevitability of meeting her but I was totally unprepared for the nature of that meeting. As we went to take our seats in an already crowded dress-circle I suddenly heard an unmistakable voice call out: 'Gaby! Gaby Fallon!' To say that I felt embarrassed is to put it mildly. However, I walked over to where Eileen was in the centre of the dress-circle and accepted an introduction to Sean's shy yet attractive daughter Shivaun whom I had heard about but had not met. As the orchestra were tuning up I excused myself and began to move towards my seat. As I did so Eileen in a voice loud enough to be heard over several rows of seats said 'Don't be too hard on the old man!' Even while I could have hugged her for this loyalty I choked on a stupid reply to the effect that I knew nothing about the play, and what I was likely to think about it must wait.

The curtain rose and the first two acts were received by an audience that, so to speak, had its thumbs crossed for the success of the author. It laughed whenever there was an obvious cause for laughter (and there were many such causes) and it tried to laugh even when the playwright's occasion clearly pointed in the opposite direction. During the intervals I had time to examine my programme. It contained a pretentious note by Cyril Cusack which described Sean as

fiercely *engagé*, provocative and controversial; the same O'Casey who, long ago swaddled in the sulky swirl of Anna Livia Plurabelle, long ago mother-propelled madly out of doors, now angrily clowns round the closed-in arena of the world, at the end of a crooked wand spinning his globe into a green map of Ireland. And Ireland—happily grappled in grips with this latest *saeva indignatio*, an indignation also betimes both sad and gay is here liberated into the battlefield of European theatre.

There was also a note from the 'fiercely *engagé*, provocative and controversial' playwright. And this is what it said:

Here's what's called a play by what is called a playwright. O'Casey's the name, and here he is trying once more to dance a polka on the stage. See him dance the polka. He hopes you'll like it, and he hopes you'll laugh. We writers are inclined to be a cocky crowd, thinking so often that what we say should be, not written down on paper, but graven deep down in marble so that newcomers to life won't miss the great news; when, in reality, most of what is written by us are but plumes of smoke getting into the eyes to make them water, and into the nose to make us sneeze. Apart from the great geniuses like Shakespeare, Tolstoy, or Shaw, we writers are, in our artistry, of no more importance than the artistry in the energy of the farmer, the miner, the builder,

and the housewife in keeping the home and bringing a family safely
through the earlier years of life.
Well, here's another plume of smoke which I hope may have a little
flame in it to light up life for a moment or two; to make us think again
of some of the problems Ireland has to face in the midst of the sound
from the singer's song and the politician's shout.
So with the gallant orchestral help from the Producer and the Actors,
here's O'Casey trying out another polka-play on an Irish stage. He
hopes you'll like it and he hopes you'll laugh.

How gentle this introduction seems in the light of the author's
statement in *Time* (14th March 1955) just a few weeks after the
play's stormy reception by those whom he described as Ireland's
'bum critics'. *The Bishop's Bonfire*, he told that journal, 'is a
play about the ferocious chastity of the Irish, a lament for the
condition of Ireland, which is an apathetic country now, losing
all her energy, enthusiasm and resolution.' Nothing here of the
old man dancing a polka which he hopes you'll like enough to
laugh at.

Towards the end of the third act there was a certain amount of
hissing and an equal amount of shush-ing the hissers to behave
themselves. The final curtain fell to a mixture of applause and
protests, the applause predominating. When the curtain rose
again on Cyril Cusack and the entire cast the applause was
clearly in the ascendant. Then Mr. Cusack stepped forward to
make a speech and this was where the trouble started. Mr.
Cusack's approach was described by me at the time as being
rather like that of Aquinas saying: 'This will settle the Manichees!'
Donat O'Donnell, writing in *The New Statesman and Nation* of
5th March 1955, saw it as 'Ajax defending a damp Monday
evening'. Cusack began his speech in Irish and then went on to
refer to the 'heretical hisses', a reference which immediately lost
him some supporters on the O'Casey side. He then went on:
'We may not produce our Claudels or Bernanos but Dublin
has in Sean O'Casey a playwright of deeply religious feeling.
There seemingly are some with us tonight, self-appointed
defenders of God in the manger. But I think that their attitude
is rather that of dog in the manger!' This, very naturally, was
the signal for a vociferous outburst of booing and hissing.
However, Mr. Cusack continued to defend his author as best he
could before an audience which in the upper regions of the
theatre was becoming increasingly angry. At one point be began
to tell us of something that happened when he (Mr. Cusack)

went on penitential pilgrimage twelve months previously to St. Patrick's island purgatory, Lough Derg. Suddenly a voice roared out: 'You should bring Sean there!' and this helped in a great measure to restore good humour to an audience that, thanks to Mr. Cusack, might at any moment attempt to riot. At this point, thinking of the notice I would have to write for delivery on my way to the office at nine-thirty in the morning, I rose to go. Douglas Gageby rose with me and we left the theatre with most of the audience still in the mood for a gala occasion.

Richard Findlater writing about *Within the Gates* states the essence of that play's message 'thrust home at every turn, is that life must be lived and enjoyed to the utmost, but that it is thwarted by the hypocrites, the pious and the Puritans. It is a somewhat self-conscious apothesis of sexual indulgence and youth, the invalid's glorification of health'. Now *Within the Gates*, unlike *The Bishop's Bonfire,* was not written about Ireland; but by a remarkable coincidence the message of each play is exactly the same. Perhaps the coincidence is not so remarkable after all for the message is to be found in most of Sean's later plays. In *The Bishop's Bonfire*, however, the message is sharpened by attacks on the Irish clergy and on the Roman Catholic veneration of saints. Cecil Wilson in the *Daily Mail* of 1st March 1955, said of O'Casey's chief target, one Canon Boheroe: 'He makes the priest such an unctuous villain . . . that the play positively cries out for trouble.' *The Daily Telegraph,* 1st March 1955, describing the play as 'anti-clerical' went on to say: 'In earlier years it is certain that this play would have given such offence to the devout that it could not have reached the Dublin stage.' Robert B. Considine, columnist for the International News Service, New York, described the play as 'interestingly blasphemous'. Sean's latest biographer, Saros Cowasjee, commenting on this statement says: 'O'Casey does not blaspheme. He has given the saints fictitious names, so that his mockery of them may not hurt the feelings of those who have reverence for saints.' A defence which is surely enough to make the two home-canonised specimens of Mr. O'Casey's hagiography, St. Tremolo —the Boy with the Buckinino—and St. Casablanca of Ballyronagh laugh their haloes off.

I wrote of the play: 'Dramatically, it is a series of not too bright music-hall sketch situations strung on an outlandish story and laced with the extraordinary encyclical pronouncements of Mr. O'Casey himself.' Even at this remove I see no reason to retract that analysis. I went on to say that I found the dénouement 'in which a six-shooter is used to hasten the final curtain' to be dramatically embarrassing. 'I set it down with regret' I continued, 'that however much the Bishop's Bonfire blazed in the imagination of Mr. O'Casey, the dramatic fire that burned *Juno* and *The Plough* into an incandescence of greatness is now a handful of grey ash. Let Mr. O'Casey read again the so-rightful letter of Yeats that accompanied the so-wrongful rejection of *The Silver Tassie.*'

Most of the Irish critics wrote in the same strain. Strangely enough *The Standard* selected an Abbey Theatre dramatist to review the play for them—Seumas Byrne, whose play *Design for a Headstone* had almost precipitated a theatre riot on the head of its 'Anti-clericalism'. In this at all events *The Standard* could not be accused of a pro-clerical bias. According to Seumas Byrne the play opened

> to an audience as receptive and as anxious to be pleased as one could reasonably demand. But *The Bonfire* failed to burst into flame; it sputtered promise, flickered awhile, and expired like a damp squib. These are cruel words to write of any play, more especially of the work of a dramatist of Mr. O'Casey's stature, whose earlier work resuscitated the reputation of Irish theatre thirty years ago: yet I cannot see that his latest play *The Bishop's Bonfire,* can do anything but diminish the repute of our greatest playwright.

Byrne found the play to contain

> a plethora of characters, some amusing, pathetic, frustrated, or harsh, but none fully drawn or with adequate motivation; and mostly without function. We met no spontaneity, and no homogeneous structure, nothing to lift our interest or raise our expectations. There were long static passages in which the play nearly met its doom . . . The author himself seems to have been aware of the defectiveness of the work; for, in the third act, he makes a desperate effort to retrieve the situation by an incredible piece of melodrama . . .

It was this piece of melodrama which led Donat O'Donnell to say in his *New Statesman* review that the action of the play consisted of a revolver shot in the third act.

The attitudes taken by London's leading Sunday critics, Harold Hobson and Kenneth Tynan, to the play and its reception were such that I found it necessary to comment upon them in a special article in the *Evening Press,* 12th March 1955. Writing in *The Theatre Now* Mr. Hobson had stated that 'A Sunday critic generally has the opportunity for careful thought, if, that is, we suppose him capable of such a thing.' Both these

gentlemen provided us with such specimens of 'careful thought'
that I went on to say:

> Last Sunday we had the privilege of reading the views of two English
> Sunday critics, Mr. Kenneth Tynan of *The Observer* and Mr. Harold
> Hobson of the *Sunday Times*, views which strayed well beyond the
> bounds of their immediate task, views in which both these drama
> critics (with an arrogance hardly surpassed since Queen Victoria elected
> to autograph *The Book of Kells*) proceeded to tell their readers what
> they thought of the Irish people. It was, perhaps, only natural to
> expect that both should reserve the right not only to criticise Sean
> O'Casey, but to criticise the Irish for criticising him.

I went on to say that one never expected that men, who ought to
be familiar with their Shaw, would so outrageously out-
Broadbent his Broadbent. I wrote,

> Dublin, according to Mr. Hobson, is living in a past world under the
> delusion that it is vigorously contemporary. Some of our reactions
> to O'Casey's play he compares to 'the astronomical views of palaeo-
> lithic man being taught in the Science Sixth'. He accuses us of being
> unaware—he will not say of modern literature—but even of modern
> Catholic literature. On the credit side he likes the 'squalid loveliness'
> of Dublin, and he likes our taxi-drivers, 'men of intelligence and
> charm, having only a single topic of conversation—what happened at
> Easter thirty-nine years ago'!
>
> Mr. Tynan opens his article with the pompous declaration that
> 'Truly the Irish never forgive those they have insulted.' And then he
> steps down from his imperialistic pedestal to explain that 'Back
> from long exile came Sean to Dublin and his compatriots hissed his
> play at curtain-fall.' He concludes that 'there were more stage Irish-
> men in the house than in the cast' and he assures us that 'by the first
> interval venomous tongues were already lamenting the play's failure.'

Now of the play itself Mr. Hobson found that in the first act
'the master's salt has lost its savour and his hand its cunning'.
Then after declaring that the play made what he described as 'an
amazing recovery' in its second act he concluded that the third
act 'despite some fine moments' fell away. In short it was Mr.
Hobson's opinion that *The Bishop's Bonfire* was not so hot. Mr.
Tynan found that Mr. O'Casey's genius was now 'manic-
depressive' and that his hand had lost its sureness of shifting from
mood to mood. He summed up the dramatist's work by saying:
'Mr. O'Casey was never a great thinker; he is no longer a great
craftsman: but he remains a great singer.' It was obvious that
both of these distinguished critics considered that *The Bishop's
Bonfire* was anything but a 'blazing masterpiece'. Yet they
seemingly resented their Irish counterparts coming to the same
conclusion.

175

Mr. Hobson's accusing the Irish of being unaware of modern literature and in particular of Catholic literature was simply laughable when one considered that ignoring Shaw, George Moore, Russell, Stephens and the rest, this city of 'squalid loveliness' had supplied a not inconsiderable part of modern literature in the works of William Butler Yeats and James Joyce.

As for our knowledge of 'modern Catholic literature' one of the few worth-while studies of this subject was to be found in the then recently published *Maria Cross* by Dubliner Donat O'Donnell whose unequivocal opinion of *The Bishop's Bonfire* Mr. Hobson could read in the unprejudiced columns of *The New Statesman and Nation*. As for Mr. Tynan's vision of 'stage Irishmen' it was not so long before he saw them in the Gaiety Theatre that in a fit of heroic pique at the condition of the British theatre he declared that, since Shakespeare, English drama had consisted of a procession of glittering Irishmen. Stage Irishmen, no doubt. A few years ago Richard Findlater had said the same thing of course in greater detail in *The Unholy Trade*. It was my considered opinion (just as it was that of my colleagues) that *The Bishop's Bonfire* was dramaturgically a failure. It was difficult to believe in the face of what they had written about it that Messrs. Hobson or Tynan thought otherwise.

On Tuesday evening of that week shortly after my criticism of the play had appeared in the city edition of *The Evening Press* my wife and I were discussing the possibility of inviting Eileen and Shivaun O'Casey to share a meal with us on Thursday. The 'phone rang and my wife answered it. She returned almost immediately saying: 'Mrs. O'Casey wants to speak to you.' Thinking it strange that the ladies evidently had nothing to say to each other, I took up the receiver and was told by Eileen that she had just read my criticism in *The Evening Press* and was astonished at it. I asked her why. She said: 'I heard you laughing at the Gaiety last night!' I said that was perfectly true; I did laugh but my laughter had nothing whatever to do with the general impression which the play made upon me. This didn't seem to satisfy her. She again insisted that she had heard me laugh. I told her that Rose and I would like herself and Shivaun to come up on Thursday evening, or, indeed, on any evening it suited them to come. She said they couldn't accept the invitation. I then asked her not to tell Sean that she had 'phoned me about the criticism. I felt that Sean would consider that she had demeaned herself by doing so. She said she would most certainly tell Sean she had 'phoned me. Finally, I told her that what appeared in *The Evening Press* represented my opinion of the play—it might be right; it could be wrong—but that being my opinion I was sticking to it. I was certain, I said, that Sean felt the same way about his opinions. I told her I was sorry that she could not see her way to come and see us; I was sorry too, to have to disagree with Sean but there was nothing I could do about it. On this note the conversation ended.

Eileen returned to Devon at the end of the week. By this time the play had settled into what promised to be a long run, proving, if proof were needed, the affection of Dublin audiences for Sean O'Casey. The reaction of the average play-goer to the play's anti-clericalism and to its social criticism of things Irish was summed up in the attitude of one of them who said to me. 'Ah, well, sure we can take it. Anyway, even the worst of his criticism is good for a laugh, even his caricature of a Canon singing: "When Irish eyes are smiling".' And so it was. The foundations of affection which he had so solidly laid with Dublin audiences in *Juno* and *The Plough* now stood him in good stead; and there is not a doubt that some time later had he taken the dynamic Sam Wannamaker's advice and allowed him to open his production of *Purple Dust* in Dublin instead of Brighton, it would, thanks to Dublin audiences, have lived ever so much longer than its half-week on the stage in that salubrious place.

When Sean read what his 'bum Irish critics' had to say he at once was in high rage. He immediately opened a campaign of letters to their newspapers. It was obvious from the amount of fiddle-faddle in his protests that he was thoroughly enjoying himself. He hit out all round with one exception only—the critic of *The Evening Press*. This exception could have had its origin in only one of two reasons—the memory of an old affection; most unlikely, I thought: or the possibility that I might give him as good as I got. Most of his vehemence was directed against the critic of *The Standard*, Seumas Byrne, the dramatist; and against the critic of *The Irish Press*, Niall Carroll, a brother of the dramatist, Paul Vincent Carroll. Something of Sean's mood and style may be gleaned from this letter written to *The Irish Press* (15th March 1955):

Dear Sir: I am very interested in Archaeology; in the Sumerian, the Minoan civilisations, the astonishing graves found in the Egyptian sands, the prehistoric pictures brightening the dark walls of French caverns, the ruins of the temple of Mithras, recently dug into view in London, the unveiling of the River-dwellings from under the waters of the Irish lakes.

Now, Ireland is a fascinating study of this subject, for there are many examples of living archaeological remains there as well as a few dead mains. Among the archaeological specimens of what are jovially called 'drama-critics' there is one that is most astonishing and ancient—the one establishing his stone head on the columns of the paper calling itself the royal Standard of God Almighty.

Who is, what is this fascinating figure? Where was he found? Is he one of the earlier or later stone-age? On the columns where the figure stands are odd and eerie ogham scratchings which would be a delight to interpret: such as 'Whose earlier work resuscitated', 'The healthier proclivity,' 'former fiance', 'the general factotum', 'adequate motification and without function', 'no homogeneous structure', 'looked for a moment as if his entry heralded plot development', 'exacted the maximum value but still no plot development', 'author injected harshness into the concept', 'difficult job in the part in that it lacked matter'. What do these passages mean? Are they slogans, clichés, coronachs, catch-cries? Is there ne'er a scholar in the Colleges of Dublin, Galway, Cork or Belfast with wit enough to decipher them? What's coming over Ireland? The saints are there right enough—but where are the scholars? Is the ogham writing so esoteric to explain? Or are these but the careless scratching(s) in an idle moment of some poor wandering Irish R.I.P. Van Winkle? Couldn't the neighbour who sent me the paper persuade the School for Advanced Studies to prove the problem.   Yours sincerely,
                                                       Sean O'Casey.

But the heartiness of the jollity failed to disguise the soreness of the critical rejection. Almost a week later in a letter to the *Irish Press* he defended himself in a rather more serious vein from the Irish critics and pointed out that he intended to write a book about them. 'I venture to say' he wrote, 'that I amn't in the least put out by their cries of music-hall humour, farce, or even a snatch of slap-stick. Shakespeare had all of these scattered amongst his plays, and didn't shy at a touch of melodrama, and Aristophanes didn't hesitate to love a little slap-stick.' He went on to castigate the dramatist St. John Ervine for saying, fifteen years previously, that O'Casey was mostly superb music-hall. To down Ervine completely he quoted a long passage from George Jean Nathan in which in his preface to *Five Great Modern Irish Plays* the U.S. critic defends O'Casey from the music-hall charge. This letter had a P.S. which read as follows:

Just received a letter from G. J. Nathan which says: 'It is very gratifying to hear about the excitement stirred up in Dublin by

The Bishop's Bonfire, but sad to read of the stillborn blindness of the Irish dramatic critics.' Blindness? Maybe he's right.

There were other letters from the dramatist to the Irish newspapers, all of them increasingly sharper in tone. However, I found the P.S. quotation particularly intriguing. Who spoke of blindness? For the same George Jean Nathan despite his subsequent praise of Sean O'Casey had on his first contact with *Juno and the Paycock* written this (in his *Art of the Night*): 'His second act is almost entirely in the low comedy vein and his third act, cut off from the other as with a meat axe, piles tragedy upon tragedy so exaggeratedly that it would take a professional pall-bearer to profess any show of sympathy over his characters, plight. The impression is of a man stopping suddenly short in the midst of a comic story to tell the plot of *Oedipus Rex.*' Few Irish critics were ever as blind as that.

Happening to meet the editor of the *Irish Press* (at that time Mr. Jim McGuinness) when all this letter-writing abounded, I asked him to allow me to write an open letter to Sean. He agreed. I suppose I felt, as many an Irishman feels, that if there was a good fight knocking around I wanted to be in it. I began by asking Sean what in the name of good fortune was the matter with him. Beginning with George Jean Nathan, who had described him as the only great Irish living dramatist, I quoted all the current favourable opinions of *The Bishop's Bonfire* and asked him why he should be so upset by the unfavourable reactions of an insignificant handful of Dublin critics. I contrasted the dancing Dervish of the letters with the gentle old man who came upon the Dublin stage to dance the polka ('See him dance the polka' you said). Then I ventured an answer as to why he was so evidently upset by the opinions of an insignificant few. 'In the first place' I wrote, 'your overweening vanity is severely hurt. You don't like criticism, Sean O'Casey; you only like praise.'
I then went on:

You are making a great fuss now out of the fact that the critics are Irish critics. But you made an even greater fuss when the critics were English critics. You remember Jimmy Agate, don't you? You know what you did to him? You haven't forgotten George Orwell, have you? You took him out of the grave to pulverise him. And there were other, many other, English critics. But you, the great *Flying Wasp*, buzzed them all. When you launched your first massed attack on the Irish critics (in *Irish Writing*—don't you remember?) you told them a thing or two. One of the things you told them was that there hadn't been a critic in

179

the country since William Butler Yeats. But did you think they had forgotten what the critic Yeats had said about *The Silver Tassie* or what you had said about Yeats's qualification as a critic? Pull yourself together, man; try to order your memory with some of the efficiency you devote to that black book in which you record the misdeeds of modern Ireland. But, vanity apart, there is another reason why the unfavourable opinions of these Irish critics have so upset you. Like them you are Irish. For all your long wilful exile, you are a slice cut from the loaf. Deep down in you nags the possibility that the Irish critics may be right. Time was when you acknowledged one of them as your 'first friend in literature and the drama' when you claimed that 'his friendship was, and is, a wonderful gift to his friend and buttie, Sean O'Casey'. Isn't there an awful possibility that such a fellow may not have lost his wits completely and that with a spark of that talent left he may, like his colleagues, be visionary enough to see what pride and wilfulness can do to a greatly gifted writer?

I concluded as follows:

Have a tither o' sense, man! The critical 'buckineeno boys' of Dublin wish you well. They hope time will spare you to return to your former dramatic greatness. They hate to see you eating your heart out because praise has been denied you by those you are pleased to describe as 'knaves and fools'. Never mind the book about them; more than one can play at that game; and the long view of posterity may turn out to be a poor one. Forget *The Bonfire* and get on with the next play; and this time, who knows, it may be the buckineenos turn to cheer.'

Now, if Sean wanted a Donnybrook Fair—and his letters seemed to indicate that he did—here it was for him. I had twirled my shillelagh in the best faction-fighting manner and I awaited his onslaught. A week went by and this was the result from Devon:

(5.4.55)
Dear Sirs—I see that a Certain Party has given vent to a terrible blast from his Buckineeno. Oh! Me vears, me vears!

But the blast ends with a pathetic twittering aria. When the Certain Party tremulously says: 'Isn't there an awful possibility that such a fellow may not have lost his wits completely' the Certain Party seems to forget that there still remains the more awful possibility that such a fellow has.   O'Casey.

My feelings on reading the above are best expressed by a remark overheard in a Dublin pub the evening the letter appeared, incidentally a remark which many years before might have become a piece of O'Casey dialogue: 'Now, what could yeh do with a fella like that. Yeh wouldn't know whether to kick him or kiss him.' No, you wouldn't.

Most of us knew, of course, that Dublin owed the presentation of *The Bishop's Bonfire* to Cyril Cusack; but until the publication of *Sean O'Casey: The Man Behind the Plays* by Saros Cowasjee in October 1963, we were ignorant of the circumstances leading up to its presentation. It now appears that Cyril Cusack, having heard that Sean had completed a new play, wrote and asked to see it. On reading it he wrote to Sean in such laudatory terms that the dramatist was impelled to reply: 'If it be three-quarter as good as you both (Mr. and Mrs. Cusack) think it to be, I shall be well pleased.' Cyril then passed the play to Tyrone Guthrie who wrote 'The more I read the play the more I am impressed by its quality.' Under these circumstances Sean had every reason for entertaining high hopes of the outcome. In the meantime Cyril sent the play to 'a Catholic prelate' in London for his opinion. This prelate's letter and Cyril's reply to it are given on pp. 226 and 227 of Mr. Cowasjee's book. In the course of his letter the prelate said:

> My immediate reaction is one of regret that you have decided to put it on. Of course it is good theatre; anything of Sean O'Casey would be that. But the bitterness that runs through all his plays and his scorn of the Church and of religious practice vitiate his art. ... Is it only drunkards and n'er-do-wells that have the vision of the truth? Is all prayer to be sneered at and the intercession of the Saints a thing for mockery? ... I hate hypocrisy, as I know you do. I gladly see it exposed, as I know you do. But in this play there is not a hint of the existence of anything else in the Church or in Catholic life ...

Cyril replied to the prelate, stating that he was committed to presenting the play. He conceded that the play's viewpoint 'comprehends only one unhappy aspect of the country which the playwright from a too distant pinnacle perhaps sees as a whole view rather than as a single facet'. Cyril concluded his letter by saying:

> On my visit with Maureen (Mrs. Cusack) to Sean O'Casey recently I formed the impression of an idealist—however misdirected his idealism may be, which history indicates to be a dangerous thing—whose one obsession was Ireland. If he is a tormented soul may not this be an encouraging sign? May he not hate what he believes to be evil? I sometimes think that O'Casey's egomania—which, may I add, is better vented than sequestered, left lurking in the secret places of the soul—comes from an identification of himself with Ireland. I had the impression that he was possessed with the thought of Ireland and that his passion was a strange compound of love and hate.

The two letters furnish an intriguing analysis of their subject. That Sean's passion for Ireland was a strange compound of love and hate is right on the mark. But the Ireland Sean loved was an Ireland that existed in Sean's imagination, an Ireland as he would have her, free from the trammels of the Catholic Church, from the shadow of the Vatican, from the superstitious practices that he associated with Catholicism; an Ireland which would tally at every point with his own particular brand of sentimental Communism. Cyril's admission that the playwright was failing to see Ireland either steadily or whole was strangely at variance with his vehement defence of the play in his curtain speech at the opening performance.

One cannot help thinking that what the psychologists call 'rationalisation' had been for a long time at work in the dramatist. Beginning with an excessive love of an imaginary Ireland he ends with an excessive hatred of the existing one. Strongly attracted in his early days towards Roman Catholicism he ends by hating all that that Church stands for. There is much in *The Bishop's Bonfire* to suggest that this was the Ireland which expelled Sean O'Casey, the Ireland from which he cheerfully accepted expulsion, an Ireland of bigoted oppression, which, as any sensible person might see from the play, was an island in which no self-respecting artist could choose to live. This was not the Ireland of which he had written:

> Dost hear the tale the traitors tell
> Ireland, dear Ireland?
> In whisper low or joyous yell
> Of thee, of thee, dear Ireland?
> That thou dost eat the Saxon bread;
> That all the hopes thy soul hath wed,
> Now prostrate lie with all thy dead,
> Ireland, dear Ireland!
>
> They lie, they lie—the cowards—they lie,
> Ireland, dear Ireland.
> Nor blazing guns, nor measures sly,
> Can conquer thee, dear Ireland.
> Our blood may tinge our rivers' tide,
> Our bodies lie our homes beside—
> We stand where stood all those who died,
> For Ireland, for Ireland.

No, the Ireland of *The Bishop's Bonfire* was Sean O'Casey's *other* island, the island to which he was determined never to return. And who in the face of it, could blame him for that?

Thirteen

For almost three-and-a-half years things were reasonably quiet on the O'Casey–Ireland front though it had not escaped the notice of both his friends and foes that in October 1957, with the memory of Hungary still lingering in men's minds, Sean had elected to 'raise his Irish hand to his Irish forehead' in a salute to the U.S.S.R. and all its works and pomps. In or around 1956 a friend of mine in Hollywood, Dan O'Herlihy the screen actor, wrote to say that some friends of his out there, hearing that Sean O'Casey was living in Devon in a state bordering on penury, proposed to arrange some readings from his works and to send the proceeds, which would be fairly considerable, to the dramatist. Knowing that Sean was a particularly sensitive creature about such matters Dan wanted to know how he ought to open up the project. I replied saying that—although I did not know for certain—I didn't think that the dramatist's financial situation was as bad as the Hollywood people thought. However I warned Dan that Sean was as proud as Lucifer, particularly where financial assistance was concerned. I advised him to make his approaches through Sean's wife, Eileen. Better still, I said, do the thing whatever it is, and send on the money.

It must have been in 1957 that I had my second meeting with Shivaun O'Casey. It took place at a theatre garden-party held in the grounds of an hotel at Dun Laoghaire. The garden-party was the closing event in what was known as a Tostal Festival. The Tostal Festival, like its current counterpart the Dublin Theatre Festival, was planned as a tourist-catching event. For the first two years of its existence its theatrical contribution consisted of an historical pageant held in Croke Park. The garden-party was intended to wind up the general festivities which moved around musical, sporting and theatrical events. This particular garden-party opened in sunshine but before long the inevitable soft Irish rain drove everyone indoors. I caught sight of Shivaun at the far end of an overcrowded lounge and ploughing my way towards her through local and visiting theatricals I managed to get near enough to her to say: 'I don't think you know who I am.' To my astonishment she replied, 'I do; you are my daddy's friend, Gaby Fallon.' It was as much as I could manage to say in reply: '*Was*; Shivaun, *was* your daddy's friend.' I told her how shocked and sorry Mrs. Fallon and I were on hearing of the death of her brother, Niall; and how frustrated we felt that the gulf which seemingly stretched between Sean and myself prohibited our writing to offer our condolences. She replied stoically to the effect that what had happened had happened. I asked her if she would like to meet Harold Hobson. She said she would like very much to meet him. When leading her away after a short chat with H.H. I said to her—using her father's richly emphatic intonations—'Now, Shivaun, you can tell your daddy that you met one of England's "gorgeous" critics.' The child was too fascinated by the faithfulness of the mimicry to laugh. Before I left her I asked her as diplomatically as I could if her father had at any time recently received a royalty cheque from a group of people in Hollywood. She said: 'He did; and he sent it back.' Well, Sean was still Sean; so that was that.

Early in 1958 the Dublin Tostal Council announced that its 'International Theatre Festival'—as it now began to call its theatrical adjunct—would include a new play by Sean O'Casey, and a dramatisation of James Joyce's *Ulysses* by a young Belfast actor, Alan McClelland. The echoes of this announcement had barely died away when Dubliners became aware of a 'situation', sparked off by the appearance of a letter in the daily press. The letter was from the Secretary of His Grace, the Most Rev. John C. McQuaid, D.D., Archbishop of Dublin and Primate of Ireland, to Mr. John Dunne, Secretary of the Dublin Congress of Irish Trade Unions. 'The Secretary of the Dublin Tostal Council' the letter read, 'requested permission for a solemn Votive Mass to inaugurate the Tostal. His Grace gave permission to approach the Very Rev. Administrator of the Pro-Cathedral to have celebrated a Low Mass, as on previous occasions. Then, having learned from the Dublin Tostal Council that it had sanctioned the production in Dublin of a presentation of Joyce's *Ulysses* and of a play by Sean O'Casey, His Grace, the

Archbishop, withdrew permission for any religious ceremony, more especially for the celebration of the Holy Sacrifice of the Mass in connection with the Dublin Tostal of 1958.'

Now there can be no doubt, whatsoever, of the effect which the publication of this letter had on the atmosphere surrounding the forthcoming Theatre Festival. Dublin seethed with rumour and bristled with opinions, some publicly expressed but most of them whispered under the counter. Some wanted to know why the Votive Mass had been requested in the first place; others wondered how it was that the first public knowledge of the refusal should come through such an unlikely source as the Secretary of a Trade Union Congress. Had His Grace the Archbishop read O'Casey's play? This seemed most unlikely; but it was probable that he had read Joyce's *Ulysses*. There was not the slightest doubt, of course, that he had not forgotten, amongst other things, Sean's flamboyant gestures of camaraderie to Communism and its leaders; and it is possible that he was aware that Sean was at this time a fairly regular contributor to Soviet journals. As for *Ulysses*, Irish opinion was divided on the merits of James Joyce, and while there are many in this country who are broadminded to the extent that their sympathy with and appreciation of literature is well in advance of the unreading bulk of the Catholic population, it is possible that it was the bulk which, from a protective point of view, His Grace had in mind. These, of course, are merely guesses; for no explanation of His Grace's action was ever offered, possibly on the grounds that none was necessary.

Sean on his side had some interesting facts to disclose. He had been asked for a play by the Chairman of the Tostal Council but was reluctant to give one. Perhaps he had the critical reaction to *The Bonfire* in mind. At all events he said that he did not want to stand in the way of younger and promising dramatists. Give these lads a chance. However, the Council Chairman insisted that it was an O'Casey work which was required, and rather reluctantly Sean sent on a script entitled *The Drums of Father Ned*. According to Sean, the Chairman, having read the script, wrote to say he liked it immensely and eagerly requested that it be allowed to have its première during the Festival. But all this took place before the storm broke in the form of the Archbishop's letter. The question was, what would the Council do? There was the usual amount of muddling indecision and a great deal of publicity, pro and con. The *Irish Times* in a leader (15th February

1958) pointed a finger at the Archbishop of Dublin as the censorious villain of the piece. Hilton Edwards, who was to have directed *Bloomsday* the *Ulysses* dramatisation, declared in a letter that there had always been in Ireland 'a rigid censorship of plays as well as everything else'. He then accused an unspecified 'they' of having been so timid as to 'come to their conclusions without having read the play'. He then went on— rather inconsequently—to say: 'Whether or not it is a good play aesthetically I am not prepared to say. It is an exceedingly moot point whether it is a play at all in the accepted sense of the word or whether you can make a play out of a book like that.'

Mr. McClelland spoke his mind by saying that he was 'certain that His Grace has not read the script' (of *Bloomsday*). 'I know that' went on Mr. McClelland, 'because I had the play vetted by an authority on moral dogma and I was advised on any blasphemous passages which I naturally agreed to cut. I did not harm the play in any way by taking out such passages. In actual fact Joyce never intended them as actual blasphemy. They highlight the effect of the book, but were not intended as blasphemy. No serious reader would ever look upon them as such.' If Mr. McClelland expected that this explanation would bring an all-clear signal if not an *imprimatur* from Archbishop's House he was doomed to disappointment. After the original letter from that place there was nothing but ominous silence. This Sean broke by saying that the Archbishop's 'objections were against the authors, not the plays'. Sean may well have been right. In the meantime an announcement was made to the effect that the Dublin Theatre Festival Council had decided to postpone the Festival. In his *Irish Press* theatre column (24th February 1958) Niall Carroll, commenting on this decision, let slip the fact that responsible people had informed him that certain 'competent theatre personages' who had read Sean's script carefully 'have made no secret of their disappointment. In brief, and without mincing words, they have informed me that it is "very mediocre stuff".' Sean jumped in immediately and challenged Carroll to publish the names of these 'important people and competent theatre personages' in the columns of the *Irish Press*. Carroll defended himself by pleading the 'first law' of the newsman's trade 'namely, that he does not disclose the source of his information'.

Announcing the postponement of its Festival the Council had declared that it intended to present the O'Casey play. There was some talk of returning the script to the author for amendments. This prompted Sean to say that while he would not describe *The Drums of Father Ned* as 'a good play'—'I would never for a moment allow a play of mine to be tampered with'. No doubt he overlooked the fact that he had allowed his first tragic master-piece, *Juno and the Paycock*, to be 'tampered' into a (frightful, as it happened) off-Broadway musical. By this time, of course, everyone in Dublin was jumping into the controversy so that it became increasingly difficult to disentangle fact from opinion. However, when the Festival at last got under way it was announced that the O'Casey play had been given to the Dublin Globe Theatre to produce. We then heard that the Managing Director of that organisation, the actor Godfrey Quigley, had sent his producer, Jim Fitzgerald, to Devon to discuss certain aspects of the script with the author. What happened at that interview is known only to God, Fitzgerald and O'Casey. Author and producer had each his own story to tell. Shortly after Fitzgerald's return Quigley wrote to Sean saying that one of the conditions of presentation would have to be that the Dublin Globe Theatre reserved the right to make what alterations it pleased in the script. Sean immediately and publicly withdrew his play. Who could blame him? It will always be a matter of doubt as to whether Godfrey Quigley (who knew, of course, that Sean had no option under the circumstances but to withdraw his script) took the step he did as the result of the atmosphere created by the Archbishop's letter or because he sincerely believed that *The Drums of Father Ned* was not worth doing. There is not the slightest doubt that, whatever the play's quality, the Gate Theatre, which at that time was the headquarters of the Dublin Globe organisation, would have been packed to the doors for a long run.

Then Sean struck hard, and in his own name and the name of the dead Joyce forbade the professional production of any of his plays in Ireland, making no secret of the fact that had he the power to do so he would have banned amateur production as well. (He had sold the amateur rights to Messrs. French many years before.) Samuel Beckett, who had a play listed for produc-tion at the Festival, joined Sean to the extent that he forbade its presentation. Now Sean's action—and well Sean must have known this fact—struck at one organisation only—the Abbey Theatre, an entirely innocent party in the whole affair. The Abbey down the years had been consistently producing Sean's first three plays—*The Gunman, Juno,* and *The Plough*. Since the rejection of *The Silver Tassie* he had never submitted a play to that theatre and had permitted the belated production of the latter play only because Yeats had requested it. Public sympathy —which had little time for the Festival schemozzle—immediately ranged itself on the side of the Abbey Theatre. Only a year or two previously the Abbey had won much fame for Ireland by its presentation at the Paris International Festival of Dramatic Art of *The Plough and the Stars*. The whole French press, from the right-wing *L'Aurore* to the Communist *L'Humanité* joined in praise of the production and the players. The representative of the *New York Times* in complimenting M. Julian, the Festival's Director, on his choice, said 'Here is modern drama at its best.' It is for the psychologist to say whether or not Sean, in thus attacking the innocent party, was motivated by his deep-down resentment of Yeats's original rejection of *The Silver Tassie*.

Sean had said that the dropping of the plays by the Festival would be 'a subject of ridicule all over the world'. He was not wrong. His status as a dramatist of international repute saw to it that the story of the Festival fracas was carried far and wide and soon *The Drums of Father Ned* came to be known, particularly in the U.S.A., as the play which 'had been banned by the Catholic Archbishop of Dublin'. However, time was to bring in one of its customary revenges. Came in 1961 Dublin's Fourth International Theatre Festival (by this time the name 'Tostal' had been dropped). The programme, geared to cover three weeks, included plays by Shakespeare, Shaw, Ibsen, Brecht, Strindberg, Kafka, Molière, Feydeau, Williams, Ionesco, Genet, Wilde, Yeats and Joyce. The Joyce offering was *The Voices of Shem*, a dramatisation based on *Finnegan's Wake*. A semi-professional group of players called the Civil Defence Theatre Group, obviously intent on defying the so-called archiepiscopal ban, decided to present *The Drums of Father Ned*. They wrote to Sean asking for production rights. Sean refused. An English theatrical friend of mine commenting on this situation said: 'It's only in Ireland and amongst Irishmen such things could happen.' I felt he was right.

In August 1958 I resigned from the Civil Service. Within four months I was invited to join the Board of the Abbey Theatre to fill the vacancy caused by the death of Lennox Robinson. I hesitated before accepting. In the first place I considered that my old friend, Micheál MacLiammóir, who had devoted so many years of his life to the arts of the theatre, would have been a more suitable candidate. In the second, I felt that my position vis-à-vis Sean O'Casey might hamper the Abbey's chances to retrieve his plays. Even before my retirement I had had a couple of offers to lecture in the U.S. but I wasn't very keen on accepting these engagements, particularly in the light of what I had read of Kathleen Ferrier and Dylan Thomas. Eventually I made up my mind; or rather had it made up for me by my wife who held that the invitation was an honour crowning a life of interest and activity in the theatre. So I accepted; and on becoming a director of the Abbey Theatre, relinquished my position as a drama critic. I decided to write to Sean. I had come to this decision for a number of reasons. First of all, his friends and acquaintances were mine in the sense that most of them, particularly his U.S. biographers, had developed the habit of calling on me after calling on him—David Krause, Robert Hogan, Robert Ginna, Ron Ayling amongst others. French, German and Swedish students writing theses on Sean always made it their business to spend some time in my company discussing his Dublin background and his initial steps as a dramatist. So in July 1959 I sat down and wrote him a letter.

In the course of it I pointed out that I had been urged to do so by that passage in Kierkegaard's journal in which he looks back on his life and, seeing everything as a whole, 'was strengthened to understand things differently, to admit how often I had blundered, and to forgive others'. I saw, as Kierkegaard saw, 'that pettiness which is so often the cause of numerous misunderstandings separating minds which if they properly understood one another would be bound together by indissoluble ties'. I went on to say that I still retained '(as even in the midst of my most bitter disagreement with your views or with your work, I never failed to retain) a deep and warm affection for you and yours. How could it be otherwise? You were an integral part of what were, perhaps, the most exciting years of my life. You were the greatest personality I ever met, or am likely to meet. Our friendship, while it lasted, was deep and enduring on my part. I believe it to have been so on yours.'

'The world, which understands so little' I continued, 'will think it strange that under these circumstances I should have acted as I did, criticised your work and your opinions with all the severity I was capable of. But you, I should imagine, know human nature better than the world knows it, and you must know that even while protesting my lasting affection for you, I would not retract one iota of the opinions I have expressed.' I went on to say that if at times I seemed to have criticised him with unnecessary bitterness or caused him more hurt than the occasion called for I asked his pardon. I told him how keenly my wife and I felt the tragedy of the early death of his son Niall and how much we longed to send him and Eileen our sympathy, but 'my cursed pride whispered that your cursed pride would be certain to misunderstand the gesture'. I emphasised that I had never failed 'to praise the real manner of man you are, your courtesy, your hidden kindness, your inherent hospitality'. I got no answer to that letter.

His biographer, David Krause, had asked me a number of times to give him, for use in his book, two drawings by Sean from my collection of O'Casey letters. I eventually agreed to let him have them. I had them enlarged in photostat and sent them to Sean to give to Krause. They did not appear in Krause's book though he thanked me for them and said his publishers proposed to use them on the dust jacket. That was the last I heard of them. Robert Hogan, author of *The Experiments of Sean O'Casey*, then called to see me. He was making a collection of Sean's early writings from 1905–1925 which he subsequently published as *Feathers from the Green Crow*. He was particularly anxious to secure for this collection the scripts of two forgotten plays, *Kathleen Listens In* and *Nannie's Night Out*, which happened to be in my possession and so had escaped the Abbey Theatre fire. Now it had so happened that the editor of the *Tulane Drama Review*, learning from a friend of mine, Professor Stephen Ryan of New Orleans, that these scripts were in my possession, told Stephen that he would be prepared to pay 100 dollars for the single printing of each script. I replied saying that this request could not be met, that the scripts were the property of Sean O'Casey, that the fee offered was a ridiculously low one, that if the Editor decided to raise his fee to about four times that figure and Sean agreed to the release of the scripts at this price, I would send them on. All this I told Sean in a letter which I sent him in October 1959. I got no reply.

When Hogan called on me—he had just been in Torquay with Sean—I told him about the Tulane offer. He pointed out that he was anxious to get both scripts for his *Feathers from a Green Crow*. He was aware that I had written to Sean and that I had received no reply to my letter. He ventured the opinion, based on his conversations with Sean, that there could be no question of a rapprochement between the dramatist and myself unless I was prepared to withdraw every contrary opinion I had expressed of Sean and his plays. I found this difficult to believe. If it were true, then Sean had changed out of all knowledge. However, I gave Hogan the scripts of the plays to give to Sean and not very long after (certainly before the publication of Hogan's book) both appeared in the *Tulane Drama Review*. I had noticed with Hogan and indeed with most of Sean's friends, Krause, Ayling, and the rest, that they were not prepared to listen patiently to any objective criticism of the dramatist and his work. This I attributed to their contact with Sean's warm pervasive personality and to his seemingly now ingrained habit of posing as a man more sinned against than sinning.

Early in 1960 a handful of young Irish writers thought it would be a good idea to honour Sean's 80th birthday. They approached me for a subscription which I gladly gave. I raised the matter at a Board meeting of the Abbey's directors and they voted a very generous sum on the understanding that the presentation would be suitably generous and not merely a hole-and-corner affair. Sean's birthday was now close at hand—I had warned the young men that Sean wasn't very keen on celebrations of any kind—but the young men had not made much progress. Ernest Blythe, the Abbey's Managing Director, asked them for the list of subscriptions. When he saw that even with my subscription thrown in the total was under twenty pounds, he advised the young men to drop the idea and said that the Abbey's subscription (which was about double the available total) would be withheld. Nevertheless, the young men decided to go ahead. They managed to get a silver tankard for the money they had. They then decided to have their names engraved on this 'Silver Tassie'. One of them 'phoned me and said that there was a certain difficulty. 'It's like this' he said, 'if your name appears on the tankard it will raise questions about the Abbey's other directors.' 'Well' I replied, 'don't put my name on it; put "The Nameless One"—the title of a poem by James Clarence Mangan—on it instead.' This seemed to satisfy the young man. I heard later that Sean didn't want to accept the gift but that Eileen persuaded him to do so. At all events I was told he wrote a letter to the chief organiser of the presentation thanking each of those whose names appeared on the tankard and 'also "The Nameless One"—Gaby Fallon'. The young men assured me that they hadn't as much as breathed who 'The Nameless One' was.

Something of the view taken by others of this extraordinary man at this time may be gleaned from Micheál MacLiammóir's birthday tribute which appeared in the *Irish Times* of 30th March 1960. It was headed—'Always the Giant':

> Sean O'Casey is a giant, not always bad and not always good, and he has ridden and stridden and howled and growled and taught and fought and strived and contrived and incited and indicted, and he has muttered and spluttered and finally uttered. All that was at the time when he was a young giant and it was then, after his uttering, he saved the life of a theatre. And then one day the theatre turned down a play he was after writing with passion and love, and the turn-down dam near killed Sean and everyone else who happened to be within a couple of leagues reach of him, because the green flames of fire that came rushing down out of his nostrils and the bitter black clouds of bloody invective that lept beelze-bubbing up out of his gullet was that desperate that a lot of people began to realise that Sean, like all the giants were ever born on the green globe of the world, was not only a darling man but a dangerous one. And he went away then from his own darling, darkling Rosaleen or Cathaleen or whatever name she called herself, and the plays he commenced to write weren't so good for a while, because he wanted to forget all about Rosaleen or Cathaleen and he wasn't able rightly to forget or to forgive her, and he turned himself into a green crow; and he began to write the story of the days when he was a poor lad, and he sneaking around the streets of the ford of the hurdles. And then, because his head was full of all those old things again and the sounds and sights and the smells of them all came back to him, he found he could still write, and he wrote better than ever before, better than any man in Ireland that wrote in the Tongue of the Stranger that was no longer a stranger's tongue at all, my thousand griefs on fellons like myself and Ernest Blythe, but only had the appearance of strangeness on it to the strangers themselves, the people had it off that well.
>
> And that, of course, was not all that happened, but it must serve for those that never understood the greatness and the crankiness of Sean the Crow, or the glory and the bitterness of the gatherings-up of his memory that was at once his triumph and his curse.

Surely a portrait which is as typical of Micheál as it is true of that Sean O'Casey painted by no less an artist than Sean himself.

I wrote a few more letters to Sean in 1960, one in which I gave him the result of an enquiry made on his behalf—though not at his request—to the literary executor of Lennox Robinson concerning the missing typescript of *The Crimson and the Tricolour*. In this letter I attempted to clear his mind of the suspicion—mentioned to me by Ron Ayling—that I had sent

Ernest Blythe to visit him to ask for a return of his early plays to the Abbey. Ernest had been on holidays in Devon and suddenly made up his mind to visit Sean at Torquay. At Abbey Board level my policy had been that the theatre too had its pride and that if Sean insisted on withholding his plays that was his own affair. I now pointed this by telling him that I would sooner cut my throat than call on him with a view to securing his plays. To none of these letters did I receive a reply. Finally David Krause arrived from the U.S. and having visited Sean came to Dublin armed with an authority from Sean to see the hundred-and-sixty letters in my possession. Krause was returning to London (and Torquay) to begin his work there. By this time I was thoroughly riled with these comings and goings, fetchings and carryings. I wrote to Sean and reminded him that in October 1946 he had written: 'I'm afraid I cannot consent to the publication of my letters. They were not written for publication, no more than your own, as you should know.' And, again, in September 1958, he had written: 'Mr. Krause can examine the letters to the fullest possible extent to your own particular convenience. He does not want to publish them, but to get an impression from them about me and add this to whatever he may write.' And now here was Krause asking for the letters to publish them. There is not the slightest doubt that had Sean made even a tiny gesture when I wrote him in July 1959, I would have handed over the letters to David Krause without question. Now I would hold on to them. I would do more than this. I would never write to the dramatist again:

For, you see, Sean:
    The white moon is setting behind the white wave
    And Time is setting with me, O!
Besides, I have grown tired of talking to a man who isn't there.

What a marvellous title for a book on Sean O'Casey, said a graduate of Uppsala University who was doing a doctorate thesis on the dramatist—*The Man who Wasn't There*. It could be.

By this time the public mind was so confused about the O'Casey v. Abbey Theatre controversy that some people actually believed that the Abbey had done an injury to Sean and not Sean to the Abbey. This confusion was particularly widespread in the U.S.A. where for long enough the ghost of Yeats rejecting *The Silver Tassie* continued to drift across any mention of Sean O'Casey. The impression that the Abbey Theatre had done him some further injury was reinforced by Sean himself and by his U.S. friends, who either unwittingly or deliberately had established a kind of 'Establishment' opposition to the man—The Archbishop of Dublin, ergo the Irish Government, ergo the Abbey Theatre. Nothing could be further from the truth. In a leading article (26th August 1962) the *Irish Times* declared that the time was long overdue for ending the quarrel between Sean O'Casey and his countrymen. Since I felt that the leader-writer was less than fair to Mr. O'Casey's countrymen I wrote a letter to the Editor in the course of which I pointed out that it was not correct to say that apart from the three plays 'which have become an integral part of the literature of the land' the rest of Mr. O'Casey's work had been poorly treated. I drew attention to the two major productions of *Red Roses for Me*, one by Shelah Richards, one by Ria Mooney; and also to Cyril Cusack's long-running production of *The Bishop's Bonfire*. I pointed out that since *The Silver Tassie* Sean O'Casey had discontinued the practice of submitting plays to the Abbey Theatre. Since I felt that the real cause of the quarrel might be lost in pointless recrimination on both sides I re-capitulated the events which led up to Sean's withdrawal of his plays from the Abbey and then drew attention to his forbidding the Civil Defence Group to produce *The Drums of Father Ned* at the 1961 Dublin Theatre Festival. Here was a group of players willing to defy the so-called archiepiscopal ban and the only barrier in the way was Mr. O'Casey himself. It was obvious that Sean was trying to adopt the attitude that there was no audience for his plays in this country.

My letter went on to say:

The truth is, of course, that there is a large audience in this country willing and anxious to accept Mr. O'Casey's work in the theatre despite Mr. O'Casey's opinions, and the opinions of his critics, both lay and cleric. I suspect that Mr. O'Casey knows that this fact does not fit into that picture of Ireland which he has elected to paint for the world at large, and which even the world at large is beginning to suspect may be a figment of Mr. O'Casey's imagination. Your point that disagreement with a dramatist's views may possibly stand between that dramatist and an Irish audience, has, I think, been successfully exploded by those large audiences, both lay and cleric, that I saw engaged in interested acceptance of J.-P. Sartre's *Les Mouches* at Galway and Athlone in the spring of this year. Again, this is a picture which does not fit in with Mr. O'Casey's picture of Ireland. Mr. O'Casey is undoubtedly Ireland's greatest dramatist but he is, I suspect, a dramatist who feels that his greatness is above criticism. This of course is to claim a privilege which was denied even to Shakespeare. Mr. O'Casey rejoices in seizing upon the clamour of a vocal few—myself included—in order to build up the pretence that his work is not acceptable in the land of his birth. This, of course, is utter nonsense. It may be true, as you point out, that most of O'Casey's opinions are at variance with those of the vast majority of his countrymen—though I think there is an element of exaggeration in this statement. But are J.-P. Sartre's opinions, for instance, any more acceptable?

My letter concluded:

No one is standing in the way of presentation of Mr. O'Casey's plays so much as Mr. O'Casey. His attitude to the Civil Defence Theatre Group has made this only too clear. I have no doubt whatever that, should Mr. O'Casey, by lifting his ban, give the Abbey Theatre permission to embark upon a season embracing every play in the canon in the order in which they were written, Pearse Street wouldn't be long enough to hold the booking queues. So it's up to Mr. O'Casey.

Sean, though a regular reader of the *Irish Times*, made no reply to this letter. I wonder why. Was it because he believed that the Abbey Theatre would keep this promise? There are times when I think it was. In March of the following year I was invited to take part in an I.T.V. programme entitled 'The Irish and the Arts'. In the course of an interview I was asked why the Abbey Theatre couldn't settle its differences with Sean O'Casey. Pointing out that the 'differences' were all on O'Casey's side, I said that speaking on my own behalf—and, indeed, on the part of my fellow-directors—I would like to see the breach repaired and we would do much to help repair it. Asked to send a direct message to Sean in Devon I made a plea that he ought to 'let bygones be bygones' and renew his link with the Abbey. The following day the London Correspondent of the *Evening Press* 'phoned Sean and asked him to comment. Rejecting the plea flatly, Sean said: 'I told them I will not give my plays to Ireland. Why can't they leave me alone? If I happen to change my mind in the future I will let them know and that should be enough.' Again I felt that the Abbey Theatre had its own pride to consider and that it was about time we stopped considering Sean O'Casey's. If the Abbey Theatre was in debt to Sean O'Casey, Sean was very much in debt to the Abbey Theatre. I swore I would never again ask him to withdraw his ban.

In the summer of 1961 I was asked by the Editor of the *Kilkenny Magazine* to review three newly published plays by Sean—*Behind the Green Curtains*; *Figuro in the Night*; *The Moon Shines on Kylenamoe*. On the appearance of the volume a Dublin publisher had written to Messrs. Macmillan asking if the 'blurb' on the book's jacket was theirs or Mr. O'Casey's. In this 'blurb' it was stated that the 'curtains' of the first play's title 'symbolise the obscurantism and humbug of Irish Catholicism which the author attacks with his still glorious use of language'. In reply to the Dublin publisher's letter Messrs. Macmillan wrote that 'the blurb for Sean O'Casey's *Behind the Green Curtains,* which does not, of course, necessarily represent our own views, was as usual prepared by ourselves after a careful reading of the title-play and submitted to the author for his approval'. Opening my review with this intriguing information I suggested that Messrs. Macmillan, by disassociating themselves from this 'blurb' even while using it, were, so to speak, having it both ways. On second thoughts it seems to me that Messrs. Macmillan had no option but to describe Mr. O'Casey's play in these terms. I would fault them only on the 'glorious use of language' part. Much depends on what one means by the word 'glorious'.

I found the plays to be experiments in a medium in which Sean's ability shone less and less. Their content was tragically the mixture as before. Irish Catholics are an ignorant, super-stitious lot. One of the plays in this volume, *Figuro in the Night,* a priapic extravaganza in two scenes, understandably ran into difficulties with the British Lord Chamberlain's office when Alan Simpson planned to produce it in London in 1963. It was a pity it did for its presentation would have enabled audiences and critics to measure the decline in Sean's genius. In his days of power the dramatist might have written a pointed and moving morality on his subject. It is merely a dramatised presentation of what, apropos *Cock-a-doodle-Dandy,* Richard Findlater called the 'Phallus v. Cross' theme. There is a very illuminating para-graph in the Foreword to this play which he tells us is 'prayerfully and solemnly dedicated to what is known as The Ferocious Chastity of Ireland'. Suddenly he breaks off in the middle of a serio-comic vein in order to refer on a note of deadly seriousness to 'those decent and law-abiding members of that section of the Irish community who live, work and worship within a religion and political belief contrary to, and at enmity with, the life, worship and political activities within what is regarded as the twenty-six counties of Southern Ireland'. Here was something which I first detected in *Red Roses for Me,* part of that 'unresolved problem . . . the symptoms of a displaced religious appetite' which Richard Findlater had assessed in his analysis of the dramatist in *The Unholy Trade,* the tinge of Orange bigotry which Alan Simpson had noted in making his comparison between O'Casey and Behan.

When the review appeared under the title *How Green are our Curtains*? (in the Autumn–Winter 1961 issue of the magazine) it happened that Robert Hogan, author of *The Experiments of Sean O'Casey,* had arrived in Ireland to enjoy the fruits of a Guggenheim foundation scholarship for which, knowing the cachet of an Abbey Theatre directorship, he had asked me to recommend him. I had done so with the result that he had written to me in March of that year: 'A hasty and doubtless incoherent note to tell you that I've gotten a Guggenheim and to heap thanks on you for your good words to the Foundation.' Beyond two 'phone calls I had not heard from him since his arrival, with his family, in Ireland. Then without a word of warning he attacked my review of the O'Casey plays, and me as a critic.

The first reaction of the editor of *The Kilkenny Magazine* was to send the stuff back to him since he felt that much of it was libellous. I pointed out that if he took this step Mr. Hogan would be in a position to say he had not been allowed to express himself freely in this country. Eventually the editor agreed to publish the less libellous part of it with my reply attached. I contented myself with pointing out the kindnesses Mr. Hogan had received (and acknowledged) at my hands since he had come to Ireland to pick up all he could about Sean O'Casey. In correspondence in the *Irish Times,* which followed this contretemps between myself and Robert Hogan, Sean O'Casey thrust forward the information that he had instructed his publishers, in this case Messrs. Macmillans, not to send any copies of his books to Ireland for review. He deplored the fact that Messrs. Macmillan had disobeyed this instruction.

In the spring of 1962 I was invited by Telefis Eireann to interview Bernard Miles who was preparing a season of O'Casey plays for presentation at the Mermaid Theatre, London. I gladly accepted the invitation for Bernard Miles is an interesting and charming fellow and his theatre, the Mermaid, is my favourite London theatre, mainly for the rich potential it offers the imaginative play director. My fellow interviewer that evening was Seumas Kelly, drama critic of the *Irish Times,* who is by no means well disposed towards the Abbey or its directors. However Seumas and I found common ground in asking Bernard if he considered it quite wise to open his season with *Purple Dust*. Why not *The Plough*, we said, or even *Red Roses*? Bernard disagreed, said he found a great deal of rich comedy in *Purple Dust* and believed that London audiences would find it too. His plan was to present this season of plays at the Mermaid and then—he had Sean's approval for this—bring them to Dublin and Belfast. To what theatre in Dublin we asked? Bernard wasn't certain, perhaps the Gaiety or if that wasn't available, the Olympia. Why not the Abbey, I asked? Bernard side-tracked this by saying that it was a great pity that we couldn't resolve our quarrel with Sean O'Casey. Whereupon Seumas and I joined forces in pointing out that it wasn't our quarrel with Sean, it was Sean's quarrel with us.

But Bernard's visit to Dublin never materialised for the O'Casey season at the Mermaid was not a success. The *Daily Herald* described it as 'A sad, fumbling attempt to do honour to O'Casey'. The *Daily Mail* said (of *Purple Dust*) 'There is precious little evidence on the Mermaid stage that anyone is conscious of the fact that this play is a comic masterpiece.' It described the production as 'a shambles'. The *Evening Standard* said 'Sean O'Casey without a cast of Irish actors is like staging opera without singers'; and the *Financial Times* agreeing said: 'The proper way to have celebrated O'Casey was to have gathered an all-Irish cast.' This was something which my former colleague, John Finnegan of the *Evening Herald*, another of Ireland's 'bum critics', had consistently maintained. 'If ever proof were needed' he wrote, 'that Sean O'Casey should end his squabble with the Abbey in particular, and the Irish professional theatre in general, it was starkly provided this week by the London drama critics, almost to a man.' Since I had contributed a piece about the dramatist which appeared in the Mermaid's programme I felt it incumbent on me to see if the season was as bad as the critics made it out to be. It was obvious that if this rot continued Sean O'Casey's stock, which was falling rapidly, would be well below par. I got to London in time to see one of the last performances of *Red Roses for Me*. The following morning I attended a rehearsal of *The Plough and the Stars*. It was my opinion that here was a failure to utilise the Mermaid stage potential, to match it imaginatively with the spirit of the play. I did not agree with the critics who held that an all-Irish cast was absolutely essential. But I clearly saw the damage to Sean's reputation that this season of plays was bringing about. I even met people who were beginning to express doubts about 'the blazing masterpieces' the 'greatest since the Elizabethans'. However there was nothing that I, or the Abbey Theatre, could do about this.

On the last evening of my stay I received a 'phone call from Sean's biographer, David Krause, who had got my 'phone number from Elizabeth Coxhead. He told me that he was 'phoning on behalf of Eileen O'Casey who was anxious that I should have supper with herself and David 'to have a chat about Dublin and all its doings'. They were going to a performance of *Madame Butterfly* but if I couldn't conveniently call on them after the show they would pick me up at the club where I was staying. I explained that I was having dinner with a daughter of mine who lived in London and whom I saw only occasionally and that I was leaving for Dublin the following day. David said that under these circumstances Eileen and he would call for me. He would ring back later. When I put the 'phone down I did some quick thinking. I made up my mind that if I did meet Eileen I would try to meet Sean. So many people had said to me: 'Why don't you go to Devon to see him?' I discussed the matter with my daughter and arranged with her, in the event of my meeting Eileen, to 'phone Dublin and tell them at home that I was going on to Devon. But the necessity did not arise. About ten-thirty the 'phone rang again and a thoroughly disappointed David informed me that Eileen had changed her mind. So that was that.

Towards the end of 1963 the Abbey Theatre received an invitation to take part along with the Comédie Française, the Moscow Art Theatre and other famous theatres in honouring the quatro-centenary of Shakespeare's birth by presenting some plays at the Aldwych Theatre, London, in April 1964. Since the Abbey's presentations would be in the English language the privilege of covering the actual birthday would be given to that theatre. When this invitation reached the Board of Directors it was agreed that the only possible presentation would be one selected from either of the two great peak-points of Irish drama-turgy—Synge or O'Casey. But what about the ban? Personally I felt that a first-class presentation of *The Playboy of the Western World* would suffice. In the meantime the Managing Director, Ernest Blythe, wrote to Sean and explained about the invitation. He got an immediate reply giving the Abbey Theatre permission to do either *Juno* or *The Plough*, or both, in London. Now it would be a very arduous task for the Abbey's players to rehearse these plays and at the same time have to rehearse and present their current repertoire. So Ernest wrote to Sean a second time explaining this position. Permission was immediately granted by Sean for the presentation of the plays in Dublin as well as London. Immediately people began to see in this gesture on Sean's part a thawing of the ice, the beginning of the end of the quarrel with the Abbey. There were others, however, who saw it as a shrewd step on Sean's part to retrieve his reputation with London audiences.

But Sean, as usual, had the last word. In the *New York Times* (8th March 1964) in the course of a long and rather rambling article he attempted to explain his reason for this about-turn. Admitting that he himself withdrew the play *The Drums of Father Ned* reputedly banned by the Catholic Archbishop of Dublin, he went on to say that O'Casey had lifted his ban 'only for a special reason and a particular period of time lasting no more than five or six weeks'. He then outlined the purpose of the Aldwych season and continued: 'None of the Abbey actors had had experience in acting in my plays, so the Abbey appealed to me to allow them to have this experience by public performances before they faced a London audience.' Since the cast of *The Plough and the Stars* planned for the Aldwych is basically the same as that which won such renown for the Abbey at the Paris International Festival of Dramatic Art in the late fifties, since at least three members of the company to appear at the Aldwych played in the twenties in the first productions of *Juno* and *The Plough*, Sean's explanation would appear to be a very lame one.

As I come towards the end of my story of Sean O'Casey, as I knew him, I find that a leader-writer in the *Irish Times* (29th January 1964) has summed up the current situation in a manner with which I find myself in complete agreement. Here is what he says of 'The O'Casey Truce':

> It would be a happy ending to a long and rough story if peace could be made between the Abbey and O'Casey. The theatre owed a great deal to him. He gave it new life such as it had not known since the death of Synge. But the Abbey deserves well of O'Casey. Without it, and Lady Gregory, in particular, he might never have launched himself. He was not one for whom the way was easy. He had to learn by trial and error; and there was no lack of help for his prentice hand. The Abbey that fought with him was the Abbey of Yeats. The decision to refuse *The Silver Tassie* was a psychological blunder of the first water. O'Casey had come out of leading strings, and the persistence of his

artistic governors would have tried a more temperate man. Since then there have been other troubles. The ineptness that led to the squabble over *The Bishop's Bonfire* reflected no credit on the good sense of O'Casey's supporters. It will be of perennial critical interest how much O'Casey's talent suffered from transplantation in late middle age. All that is of the past. Before the London season, we are to see the plays at the Abbey. It is a special permission, a truce in the war between O'Casey and the Abbey. How fitting if that truce should be a prelude to permanent peace and if the new Abbey should open with O'Casey. He can never be interpreted by actors who do not know their Dublin.

Ah, yes, as Sean himself put it in the fly-leaf of my copy of *Windfalls*:

> When we forget thee, O Dublin, let our right
> hand forget its cunning . . .

Fourteen

❦

EXPERIENCE has taught me, and has taught others, that any attempt to set forth an objective view of Sean O'Casey has invariably met with an attack from three sides. First of all, from those friends and admirers who worship the man and his work this side idolatry. Many of these are to be found in the U.S. where as a visiting Irish writer to that place put it: 'the Joyce–O'Casey image of the "rejected" Irishman has been bought big (see Owen Dudley Edwards in *Irish Times*, 11th January 1963) and Americans are getting their money back in degrees for dissertations which in the view of some should have won penitentiary sentences.' (I need hardly point out that this is not true of U.S. scholarship in general.) The second attack comes from those who see nothing in the man and his work but a blasphemous atheist peddling a distorted picture of his country and countrymen for American dollars and British gold; an enemy of religion, a Communist dedicated to the ultimate destruction of the Catholic Church. The third attack invariably comes from the man himself, who standing in front of his self-painted portrait, and using his shillelagh as a pointer, attempts to teach the world a lesson in the virtues of justice and charity. In face of all this confusion truth tends to hide her face like a frightened girl and quit this place of frienzied disputation.

Sean O'Casey is a deeply religious man, his admirers say. Well, the dramatist who made Juno say to her daughter Mary when that distraught girl cried out . . . 'There isn't a God, there isn't a God; if there was He wouldn't let these things happen!' . . . 'Mary, Mary, you mustn't say them things. We'll want all the help we can get from God an' His Blessed Mother now. These things have nothin' to do with the Will o' God! Ah, what can

God do agen the stupidity o' men!' . . . that man was a deeply religious man. So, too, the man who made his great-hearted, good Samaritan, Bessie Burgess, about to dash through bullet-splattered streets to get help for her neighbour say: 'Oh, God be Thou my help in time o' throuble. An' shelter me safely in the shadow of Thy wings!'; the man who makes the same Bessie, one act later, when laying down her life for her neighbour say:

> I do believe, I will believe
> That Jesus died for me;
> That on th' Cross he shed His blood,
> From sin to set me free.

So, too, the man who makes his war-weary soldiers in the second act of *The Silver Tassie* chant in unison:

> Each sparrow, hopping, irresponsible,
> Is indentur'd in God's mighty memory;
> And we, more than they all, shall not be lost
> In the forgetfulness of the Lord of Hosts.

Yes, that man was a deeply religious man. Unfortunately, he suffered, through no fault of his own but rather through a fault of heritage, from what our friends the psycho-analysts call 'ambivalence' and which they describe as a simultaneous operation in the mind of two irreconcilable wishes. This is the symptom that Richard Findlater detected in Sean's anti-clericalism, that 'unresolved personal problem whose intrusion has helped to thwart the development of his later style'. It was this unresolved problem intensified by the loneliness of exile which led him to tear and rend, in an ecstasy of love-hatred, his people, his country, and their most cherished beliefs, even while he protested that he did nothing of the kind. It was the deep consciousness of this problem, acting as a kind of guilt-complex, which led to his believing that he was a man more sinned against than sinning. It was this too which drove him on to repudiate his earlier plays and to speak highly of his later ones, to sell, so to speak, his birthright for a pot of message.

In an interview with W. J. Weatherby (*The Guardian*, 10th September 1959) he said: 'I can't stand the early stuff like *Juno* and *The Plough* as a matter of fact.' It was at this point that Eileen O'Casey, with a woman's sure instinct, put her finger on the one thing that was then hampering Sean's dramaturgy: 'It's a pity' she said, 'that Sean hasn't a theatre or a group in which to try out his plays before they were presented to the public.' This, indeed, was getting close to the heart of the matter.

The Abbey had been a theatre-workshop for him. Sean probably remembered this fact when he capped her suggestion with the placid remark: 'I would have liked that.'

A man of mixed feelings, a man of contradictions, 'a mixed-up genius' someone once called him. In a later interview with Weatherby (*Irish Times*, 15th August 1962) they talked about the recently dead Marylyn Monroe: 'I never knew she had such a hard upbringing' said Sean, '—all those foster homes, never a real home.' Someone then said: 'It was incredible that it didn't make her hard and bitter.' 'Oh' said Sean, 'bitterness is no good to you. You only lose if you're bitter.' Ah, yes, Sean, you only lose if you're bitter; you only lose. Towards the end of the interview he asked suddenly: 'Do you believe in life after death? I can't. I would like to because I have so many loved ones that are gone and I would like to meet them again.'

Good God, the pity of it, when one thinks of this man's great love for his mother, when one thinks of his essay on the death of his son Niall, *He died under a greenwood tree*, surely one of the most poignant pieces of literature in the English language:

> Weep with me all you that read
> This little story
> And know for whom a tear you shed
> Death's self is sorry.

One wonders if Sean numbered amongst his loved ones his faithful friend, George Jean Nathan, hedonist and agnostic, who a year or so previously had been received into the Roman Catholic Church shortly before death launched him into that bourne from which no traveller returns. This must have caused Sean some deep soul-searching; but if it did, he didn't speak about it.

Sean O'Casey is a greatly courageous man, his admirers say. And so he was; the man who, handicapped with near-blindness, pulled himself out of grinding poverty by his own bootstraps and using the theatre as a sounding-board set the whole world talking about him. But not the man who fought with shadows, the man who had no time for those who risked their lives in the cause of freedom. Again the ambivalence, again the rationalisation of the fierce patriot who suffered the Great Disillusionment; the man who in the early years of this century taught the Irish language, the man who after a day at Wolfe Tone's grave in Bodenstown could find it in his heart to cry out: 'Talk of peace is nonsense, and deep down they know that this talk of peace is nonsense.' One would give much to know on what Damascan road, and how, this transition from sword-and-rifle patriotism suddenly changed to pacifism.

Sean O'Casey is a much misunderstood man, his admirers say. But much of the misunderstanding is fathered by the man himself. If Sean wants us to understand him he must speak more clearly. His words will need to be fewer and more effectual. Much of his autobiographical writing, which was obviously a refuge from the difficulty of his later playwriting, is confused by his contradictory opinions no less than his acquired habit of thinking of himself as another Joyce. In the *New York Times* (10th November 1958) he wrote 'Like Joyce, it is only through an Irish scene that my imagination can weave a way, within the Irish shadows or out in the Irish sunshine if it is to have a full, or at least a fair, chance to play.' Now Joyce and O'Casey did have one thing in common—Dublin. As Joyce's son said of his father (*Irish Times*, 5th February 1949) when talking to Donald Giltinan: 'No man could possibly have been more attached to his native city than my father was. He was avid for news of Dublin and for the Dublin newspapers. In all his writing did he ever write a line about any other place?' He never did; but he was content to write about the Dublin he knew, the Dublin he took away with him. He went backward into that Dublin, but did not presume to write about the Dublin that had gone forward in his absence. And Joyce's style was the man; he never wrote in a borrowed overcoat.

Am I presuming to write objectively of Sean O'Casey? I am not; simply because I couldn't. When I speak of 'the man I knew' the emphasis must be placed on the personal pronoun. Our friendship until it was broken off at his end was a kind of father–son relationship. And such a relationship has all the faults of its virtues. One aspect of it disturbs me and it is that most people think that you cannot disagree with a man and be friends with him at the same time. When Niall O'Casey disagreed with his father on the horror of Stalin's tanks ploughing down the Hungarian freedom-fighters I feel certain that he loved him no less even while he disagreed. Probably more. I feel that Sean too on his side loved the boy despite this rift in their opinions.

We Irish, believe it or not, can fight without destroying friendship. That good Irishman and brave freedom fighter, Piaras Beasli, could write (*Irish Independent*, 8th January 1964) of a dead comrade, Liam Pedlar, in this revealing fashion:

My association with Liam resulted in my forming a high opinion of
his character—and capability. I renewed my acquaintance with him in
New York when Michael Collins sent me on a mission to the United
States in 1922. Liam was openly opposed to the Treaty but we remained
good friends. In fact I had so much confidence in his integrity that I
gave him my revolver and ammunition to keep safely for me when I
was starting on a tour of the States. My confidence was not misplaced.
I received them safely on my return.

Even Sean's hostile attitude towards such men, even his
lampooning of them in his over-publicised play *The Drums of
Father Ned*, cannot keep me from still thinking with much affection of the man I once knew, the kindly, generous, though
sensitively proud resident of 422 North Circular Road, the man
whose success and failure can be attributed in great measure to
that 'kind of fighting in his heart' that would not let him sleep.
He would still be one of the world's greatest dramatists had he
never written anything beyond *The Silver Tassie*. When posterity
makes its final assessment I feel that the genius of the early plays
will far outweigh the later experiments and that the faults of
the autobiographies will be forgiven in the light of Sean's mercy-
pleading and epitaph-like sentence (in *Inishfallen, Fare Thee
Well*): 'He had to submit to many humiliations that ground rage
and bitterness into his soul.'

De Mortuis—An Addendum

⚯

AT 3 a.m. on the morning of Saturday, September 19th the telephone rang incessantly. Though ordinarily a light sleeper, I did not hear it ringing. My wife woke me saying: 'Listen: it has been like this for the past five minutes. I'm afraid it can only mean a death in the family.'

When I returned to the bedroom my face must have suggested that her guess had been right if one were to judge by the look on hers. After a pause I said: 'That was the *Irish Times* to tell me that Sean O'Casey died last night in a Torquay nursing home following a second heart attack.' Neither of us spoke for some moments.

The news had shocked us profoundly, even though a few weeks previously Shivaun O'Casey had warned me that her father who had already suffered a first heart attack was, indeed, far from well. Yet the old warrior had been on his feet since then, in good fighting trim, telling the world that he felt in the best of form and was about to start another book.

He had been unable to travel to London to see the Abbey Theatre's productions of his two 'blazing masterpieces' at the World Theatre Festival at the Aldwych, though his wife and daughter saw the plays on that occasion. The London notices of the presentations were, on the whole, as denigrating as the Paris notices were loud in praise. There was an ominous note sounded by some London critics who suggested that the plays, as plays, were by no means as great as they were said to be.

Shortly after the Abbey Theatre Company's return from Paris some mischief-making journalist assured the dramatist that the presentations themselves had been at fault and the trumpets sounded for battle. 'Everybody was agog with these presentations' said Sean O'Casey, the world's headlines echoing him. 'It

207

was a glorious artistic opportunity for Ireland. The houses were filled, but the Company failed lamentably . . . What a blasted waste, what a glorious opportunity lost. There is only one thing for the Abbey Theatre. The whole board of directors will have to be cleared out and the whole thing re-started again if they want to have any proper theatre in Ireland . . . It's the dead hand again. No direction, no illumination, no training. What a great pity it was that the productions here were not good. Obviously the people loved them and gave the players a warm friendly reception. But that is not enough. We should have had proper productions . . .'

The directors of the Abbey replied with a statement saying that since Mr. O'Casey had not been present at any performance of his plays at the Aldwych Theatre he was not therefore in a position to form a personal opinion on the merits or demerits of the performances or the players. The statement went on to say that since Mr. O'Casey had not been in Dublin for twenty-nine years he was not at all in a position to pronounce a general judgment on the work of the Abbey Theatre. 'The directors' said the statement, 'gladly acknowledge the indebtedness of the Abbey to Mr. O'Casey, but submit that the artistic benefits have not been entirely on one side.'

The directors expressed their complete satisfaction with the work of the Abbey's players and producer and pointed out that this satisfaction had been endorsed by the London and Paris audiences and by the Paris critics. The directors added that, strangely enough, after the return of the Company to Dublin, Mr. O'Casey had, through his agents, acceded to the request of the Abbey for permission not only to give some additional performances of the plays presented at the Aldwych, but also to present *The Shadow of a Gunman.*

But this charge of inconsistency did not stand in the way of Sean's declaring that the directors of the Abbey Theatre were all dead. And when these gentlemen assured him that, as in some other notable instances, this report was greatly exaggerated, he immediately yielded to their request to extend the run of *The Shadow of a Gunman.* It was becoming obvious that in this typically Irish contretemps a good time was being had by all. Naturally the Abbey Theatre's habitual enemies took full advantage of the situation and before long our Hercules found a wilderness of pygmies rushing to his support.

Towards the end of August the Abbey Theatre received a

request from a Catholic priest in Derry to bring their production of *Juno and the Paycock* to that city. At the request of the same priest the theatre had gone there about a year ago bringing with them Brian Friel's play *The Enemy Within*, a very fine dramatisation based on the life of St. Columbkille. In the light of the situation existing between Sean and the Abbey the Managing Director thought it well to address his request for *Juno* to Mrs. O'Casey. In his letter he mentioned the success of the Friel play in Derry and pointed out that the Protestant Bishop and some of his clergy had come to see it on the second night, this being perhaps the first occasion on which a Protestant Bishop had ever attended an entertainment in a Catholic hall in Derry. To the surprise of all concerned, a reply—hand-written—came from the dramatist himself. It was one of the last letters, if not the last, that Sean O'Casey wrote. Here it is:

Flat 3, 40 Trumlands Road, St. Marychurch, Torquay, Devon.
Tel: Torquay 87766.
1 Sept. 1964.

Ernest Blythe, Esq.
Dear Mr. Blythe,
    Yes, yes; go ahead with your proposed visit to Derry. Let League of Dramatists know that I have agreed to it.
    Glad to hear the Protestant Bishop came to see a play in a Catholic Hall. Is this the beginning of the end of the stupid religious Apartheid in Ireland? I hope so, for Derry is as Irish as Cork or Cahirciveen.
    Let the Orange and Green flags fly over the Hall while the play is on, for we are flesh of each others' flesh, and bone of each others' bone, and there's no blottin' it out!

All good wishes,
Sean O'Casey.

Had Sean's long contention with the Abbey ceased? Was this to be the beginning of the end of the stupid quarrel which began with the rejection of *The Silver Tassie*? Had the occasion helped, too, towards resolving that personal problem of religious apartheid which, like a kind of fighting in his heart, would not let him sleep? We shall never know.

On the morning of the 19th sleep for me was out of the question. In any case the telephone rang at ever decreasing intervals. About 8 a.m. Francis MacManus of Radio Eireann, who many years before had dined here with Sean and Eileen O'Casey, 'phoned to know if I would speak about the dead dramatist on the 1 o'clock news. I agreed, realising that it would be difficult to do so under the circumstances. How compress into a four-minute talk the memory of a man who had by his overwhelming personality made his life an integral part of mine? What eventually I did say was halting, yet sincerely meant:

It is difficult to believe that Sean O'Casey is—dead. He was such an intense, vibrant personality—meeting every moment of life with a challenge—and answering it with a defiance, grave or gay—just as the spirit moved him. It was typical of him that he was moved more often to laughter than tears, though he was a man who had room for both.

For many years of our lives he and I were inseparable companions. I knew him better than most—and when, on my devaluation of his later work—that close intimate friendship was painfully broken, I knew that he felt the wrench just as keenly as I did.

His was the richest personality I knew, or am ever likely to know. He was a man of indomitable courage—meeting the obstacles of poverty, hunger, near-blindness and frustration, and turning them into weapons of success.

We were together during his formative years as a dramatist—when those two great plays *Juno* and *The Plough* were being painfully fingered out letter by letter, and line by line, on his second-hand typewriter, in the front drawing-room of 422 North Circular Road. Was he or Synge Ireland's greatest playwright? I have long since come to the conclusion that on the strength of these 'blazing masterpieces' alone, Sean O'Casey can claim the peak-point in Irish drama.

He loved his country and his countrymen with an intensity which can be measured by his constant criticism of what he believed to be their follies. He should never have left Ireland—for his most productive material was here in his native city. He might have returned had not Yeats's scornful rejection of *The Silver Tassie* pinned him irrevocably in exile.

He professed to be an atheist. He was not one when I knew him. On the contrary his constant searching after God helped to deepen and sustain the faith in others. He openly declared himself to be a Communist, and exultantly on the side of Stalin's red battalions. But it is questionable, had he gone to live in Russia, if he would have tolerated Stalin, if Stalin would have tolerated him.

He would have loved Pope John, even while believing that John was on the wrong side. And John would have loved him, finding him much nearer to the Kingdom of Heaven than most of us.

When I was roused from my sleep in the small hours of this morning to be told of his death, lines from Browning's *Prospice* began to dance in my mind:

I was ever a fighter, so—one fight more
The best and the last.

I felt that it had to be that way with Sean. His young son Niall—whom he loved with a great love—had made the dark journey before him. And I felt that Sean O'Casey, who had suffered much, who had loved and hated greatly, who had faced life valiantly had at last come to know that

        . . . peace out of pain
        Then a light, then thy breast
        O thou soul of my soul.
        I shall clasp thee again
        And with God—be the rest.

By the time I had reached the Broadcasting Station I learned that
messages of condolence from all over the world were pouring into
Torquay. Notable amongst them were one from the President of
Ireland, Eamonn de Valera, and one from his Prime Minister,
Sean F. Lemass.

   That evening towards sunset I stood on the steps of 422 North
Circular Road facing the cameras of Telefis Eireann. The house,
derelict and condemned, was empty now, its door grimly pad-
locked, a problem for the planners. The granite steps were
cracked and weeds—but Sean would have had a kindlier name
for them—were thrusting themselves boldly up between the
broken flag-stones. Only the sycamore tree flourished, determined, it seemed, despite constant lopping, to outface the house
itself. A misty intermittent rain fought with the sunset as I
attempted to recall those evenings spent at the blazing fire in the
front drawing-room, discussing literature and life and the
theatre, and the multitudinous ways of God to men. Several times
the cameras had to stop running as the caretaker's dog, temporarily deserted by its owner, bayed its solitary protest from
behind the locked door. Eventually the task was completed and
we moved away, not unwillingly, in the now softly falling rain.

Over the week-end Dublin's newspapers paid their tribute. In
the course of a lengthy editorial the *Irish Times* pin-pointed what
was the turning point in the whole O'Casey story:

W. B. Yeats was in charge of the theatre when *The Silver Tassie* was
sent back to its author. The blame, if blame there is, lies on a more
august shade than any in the precincts of the national theatre now.
The rejection infuriated and further embittered the sensitive soul
that O'Casey, for all his thunderings, essentially was. But he had gone
to England before he wrote that play. Unlike Yeats, who bound his
genius firmly to his native rock, and Joyce, who lived in a state of
perpetual somnambulistic communion with Dublin, O'Casey seems to
have been written out as a dramatist when he went away. He was no
longer a young man. His impressionable years were behind him. The
only vivid writing that came from his pen after *The Plough and the
Stars* was in prose volumes of autobiography as wayward, uneven, and
as surely lit by flashes of genius as the plays which were founded on
the Dublin of those terrible and thrilling years of revolution. O'Casey

owed not a little to the Abbey. His genius required nursing, and Lady Gregory gave him the help she never withheld from talent worthy of it. One could wish that she had prevailed on Yeats to allow O'Casey to submit his last Abbey play to the judgment of the public.

The *Irish Independent* found itself in complete agreement with the *Irish Times* about the falling off in the O'Casey dramaturgy after his departure from Dublin:

With cruel truth it can be claimed that the playwright, Sean O'Casey, has been dead these thirty years. The controversialist, the anti-clerical, perhaps even the artist in occasional autobiographical flights, lived on. But not the dramatist. It is the dramatist we mourn, and none the less sincerely because he turned his back to the country and the city which alone could spur his mighty talents. What other *Gunman*, or *Juno*, or *Plough* was smothered in Devon's stifling orderliness we shall never know, but O'Casey's exile, beyond doubt, was a tragedy as great as any he put on the stage. That turbulent anarchic mind, craving after justice, needed Dublin's seething streets and alley-ways for context. Without them the humanity was lost, and the magnanimity which saw not only the weaknesses in good men but the virtues in all. The man of the people became the arid ideologist; and the once-twinkling eye could see its native land only through a veil woven of bitterness and introspection.

Yet who are we to judge? Genius carries its own pains. To be rejected, abused, misunderstood, is enough to shatter the spirit of any man who has given all that is in him; only the truly talented can know what it means to suffer so after the emotions have been drained in the composition of a masterpiece. Perhaps after all O'Casey was right and we did drive him from our shores. Perhaps, too, we are in some degree responsible for the venom; unless we share feelings of the same intensity we cannot tell how we would ourselves react. If that be so then Ireland also is part of the tragedy and is rightly excluded from tomorrow's sad commitment at Torquay. Yet, let us keep our sense of proportion. What nation or city has ever conformed to an artist's ideal? Or could live in such conformity? We are only human, as O'Casey once knew. And that humanity remains crystallised in a splendid trilogy on which Dublin will surely never ring a final curtain.

There were many other laudable tributes and only one discordant note, sounded in a leader in *The Irish Catholic* of September 24th under the heading 'Tragic Artist'. But Sean would have expected this, for it summed up the opinions of that narrow-minded and ungenerous few who had dogged him all his life-time.

Yet this small shrill protest was quickly forgotten in the unprecedented tribute of our Department of External Affairs which devoted its entire Bulletin of September 22nd to the

'Death of Sean O'Casey'. Following a well-balanced biography of the man it dealt with his years of exile as follows—

> In his years of exile Ireland and Dublin were never far from his thoughts. The many controversies and the attacks on public figures, critics and clerics were a reflection of his intense pre-occupation with the country. The dialogue was not one-sided ... It must be remembered, however, that in 1944 when, for historical reasons, this island needed all the friends it had, O'Casey in an essay entitled *There go the Irish* spoke out loud and clear for the homeland ...

Commenting on the wide and warm tributes paid to O'Casey's memory in his native city the Bulletin recalled the dramatist's statement: 'They'll get me in the end. They'll make me part of Ireland's literary glory, God help me!' And it answered this half-wish, half-protest, by paraphrasing Dylan Thomas with the remark: 'They'd be damn fools if they didn't.'

The Bulletin prefaced its O'Casey issue with the following quotation from the address given by President John F. Kennedy at Amherst College Convocation on 20th October 1963:

> The artist, however faithful to his personal vision of reality, becomes the last champion of the individual mind and sensibility against an intrusive society and an officious state. The great artist is thus a solitary figure. He has, as Frost said, a lover's quarrel with the world. In pursuing his perceptions of reality, he must often sail against the currents of his time. This is not a popular role ...

Sean O'Casey's role was not a popular one and he knew it. This was at the root of the controversial side of his character which as the *Irish Times* pointed out was as much a part of him as Dr. Johnson's outbursts of dialectical savagery. But the man behind the controversies was to those who knew him a warm and lovable human being who, despite all quarrels, thoroughly merited and received the affection of his countrymen.

For Sean O'Casey the long day's journey has ended but not necessarily into the night. 'Tell Sean' said the dying Bernard Shaw to Eileen O'Casey, 'I'll speak a good word for him.' But it is for those of us whom Sean O'Casey left behind him that the good word will be needed. He was what he was so absolutely that Shaw's kindly pleading will be gently brushed aside by the recording angel as wholly unnecessary.

October 1964